# Educational Alternatives for
# Students with Learning Disabilities

Susan A. Vogel
Editor

# Educational Alternatives for Students with Learning Disabilities

With 11 Illustrations

Springer-Verlag
New York Berlin Heidelberg London Paris
Tokyo Hong Kong Barcelona Budapest

Susan A. Vogel, Ph.D.
Department of Educational
 Psychology, Counseling, and
 Special Education
Northern Illinois University
DeKalb, IL 60115-2854
USA

Library of Congress Cataloging-in-Publication Data
Educational alternatives for students with learning disabilities/
 Susan A. Vogel.
      p.    cm.
   Includes bibliographical references and index.
   ISBN 0-387-97668-X
   1. Learning disabled children—Education—United States.
   2. Learning disabled children—United States—Language arts.
   3. Learning disabled children—United States—Language.   4. Language
disorders in children—United States.   I. Vogel, Susan Ann.
   LC4705.E38     1992
   371.9—dc20                                                91-24816

Printed on acid-free paper.

Camera-ready copy provided by the editor.
Printed and bound by Edwards Brothers, Inc., Ann Arbor, MI.
Printed in the United States of America.

9  8  7  6  5  4  3  2  1

ISBN 0-387-97668-X Springer-Verlag New York Berlin Heidelberg
ISBN 3-540-97668-X Springer-Verlag Berlin Heidelberg New York

# Dedication

To my sons, Evan and Henry, for the continuing joy that they provide; to all children and adults with learning disabilities for all they have taught me; and to their parents and teachers for all their devotion, concern, and nurturance.

# Preface

The field is being challenged as never before to validate educational practices that have been used with children with learning disabilities. The less-than-satisfactory progress that children with learning disabilities who receive special services make, the possibly stigmatizing effects of segregating students even if only for some part of the school day, and the scarcity of fiscal resources as well as efficacy studies have led some parents, policy planners, and decision makers to experiment with alternative service delivery models that themselves have not as yet been validated. These alternatives models have been referred to as the regular education initiative or the inclusion model for placing children with mild, moderate, and severe disabilities in regular classrooms.

This volume was written to address two purposes: (a) To provide teachers in preservice LD preparation programs with an overview of validated practices that have been proven effective for children with language learning disabilities, preschool-age through adolescence; (b) To provide regular education teachers preparing to enter the field or already in the classroom with knowledge about validated teaching strategies so that they can work more effectively in collaboration with an LD consultant.

The text is divided into three sections. The first section addresses oral language interventions. Chapter 1 focuses on language impairments and intervention strategies for preschoolers. Dr. Diane Paul-Brown presents a persuasive rationale for a classroom-based, individually designed language program. In this service-delivery model, the speech and language pathologist collaborates with the regular preschool educator and family to provide the child an individually designed specific language intervention program. General and specific suggestions are made to integrate the language goals and program into the child's daily activities in school and at home. Suggestions for teachers relate to the teacher's speaking style, e.g., loudness, rate, clarity, complexity, and amount of speech. Parents' strategies include parallel-talk and self-talk, two strategies found to be more effective than strong questioning or a directive style. Methods for evaluating the accomplishment of goals and modifying the individual plan are also provided.

In Chapter 2, Dr. Elisabeth Wiig addresses the language-learning needs of a neglected, if not ignored, segment of the language-learning disabled population, namely, adolescents. The higher level linguistic tasks that should be, but are not always, accomplished at this age involve a series of linguistic transitions in semantic, syntactic, and pragmatic development. Dr. Wiig describes the transitions leading to metalinguistic maturity, ways to assess an individual's progress toward achieving these transitions, and two language intervention approaches. She, like Dr. Paul-Brown, advises that these intervention strategies be implemented within the regular classroom.

Part II of the text addresses the traditional areas of reading, written language, and math intervention. Dr. Diana Brewster Clark provides in Chapter 3 an analysis of the reading process, an overview of the early stages of reading acquisition, the difficulties encountered by reading disabled children, and alternative validated instructional methods. Dr. Clark describes the major principles of effective reading instruction, namely, explicit, systematic, intensive, and interactive instruction. Programs that incorporate these principles are referred to as direct instruction. Also discussed are the whole language approach, phonological awareness training, and multisensory, synthetic, and analytic phonics approaches, as well as computer assisted instructional methods. A common criticism of programs for reading disabled children is that they neglect instruction in reading for meaning because of the child's significant difficulties at the decoding stage. This chapter includes strategies for developing comprehension skills and reading fluency as well as the pragmatics of using special instructional methods in the regular classroom.

In Chapter 4, Drs. Steve Graham and Karen Harris first review the literature on writing problems among the learning disabled including productivity, mechanics, spelling, handwriting, structure, organization, and vocabulary and syntactic complexity. A variety of strategy training programs is described. These are divided into three categories: strategies for planning, producing, and revising compositions. Step-by-step procedures are provided so that teachers can assist LD students in their classrooms to write effectively by using self-monitoring strategies. The strategy training was developed to address areas of difficulty among LD writers, namely limited text production, lack of knowledge, and limited ability to assess their own writing. For example, one of the revising strategies, SCAN, directs the child to: (a) *scan* each sentence to be sure it makes sense; (b) ask yourself is it *connected* to the central theme; (c) ask yourself can more detail be *added*; (d) *note* errors.

Dr. Joyce Steeves addresses in Chapter 5 the often-neglected area of mathematics intervention for junior high and high school students with learning disabilities. She places mathematical cognition within the context of the neurophysiology of learning and the specific functions of each side of the brain. She recommends that mathematical learning involves both hemispheres in an interactive, meaningful curriculum that utilizes language. Teaching techniques are described for use with the learning disabled that will benefit all learners including the use of calculators, computer assisted instruction, and metacognitive strategies.

Part III, On the Cutting Edge, is devoted to new methodologies, technology, less frequently addressed needs of the learning disabled, or segments of the LD population whose unique needs are only now being recognized. Dr. B. Keith Lenz provides an overview of the cognitive and metacognitive aspects of the

Strategies Intervention Model in Chapter 6. In the first section of this chapter, Dr. Lenz provides the definition of a strategy, and describes the unique aspects of strategy instruction and how to promote strategy acquisition. In part two, the four major dimensions of strategy acquisition are delineated including strategic content, design, usefulness, and instruction. In each of the four stages, specific steps are described that practitioners will find relevant.

In Chapter 7, Drs. Joseph K.Torgesen and Neal M. Horen address the difficulties that children with learning disabilities have in the acquisition of decoding skills. They focus specifically on the use of computers to provide novel exercises that can enhance young children's phonological awareness, word identification skills, and word reading fluency. The authors provide a comprehensive review of validated programs as well as those that are under development. This body of evidence will persuade even the reluctant novice that microcomputers can be used effectively by children with learning disabilities to improve in prereading skills and context-free word reading.

In Chapter 8, the social difficulties characteristic of children with learning disabilities are described in depth. In addition, Drs. Sharon Vaughn, Ruth McIntosh, and Nina Zaragoza describe three contrasting programs designed to enhance social skills and peer acceptance. These evaluated programs are described in sufficient detail so that practitioners can judge their appropriateness for present or future students. Nine specific pointers and an extensive list of activities to promote peer interaction are also provided.

In the last chapter, Dr. Ruth Spodak discusses a neglected segment of the population of children with learning disabilities, namely, the gifted learning disabled. She provides a thorough, reflective overview of the literature on the paradoxical existence of superior intelligence, creativity, talent, and achievement along with specific underachievement in reading, writing, spelling, or math. Problems of identification and aspects of intervention are discussed within the context of the regular classroom, the resource room, the self-contained class, the gifted class, and the LD gifted classroom. Instructional modifications that teachers can make in pacing, curriculum, mobility, environment, and resources for input of information within the context of the school day, after school, and within the home are suggested. As more and more states mandate programs for the gifted, special educators, regular teachers, LD teachers, curriculum specialists, and administration will find these clinically and empirically based recommendations helpful.

The intervention strategies described in this volume for children and adolescents with learning disabilities have the power to enhance the efforts of all concerned, not least important among them the affected individuals themselves. We hope that this overview of validated practices will contribute to teachers' ability to maximize their teaching effectiveness and assist the learning disabled in actualizing their potential.

Northern Illinois University                                        Susan A. Vogel
DeKalb, Illinois

# Acknowledgments

Without the contributors who invested their energies and insights willingly and generously, this volume would never have been published. In addition there are several other individuals who made a significant contribution to this book. First, Dr. Betty Levinson assisted in conceptualizing the issues and needs of professionals. These needs were first addressed in a national conference held in Washington, DC in January, 1989 under the auspices of the National Institute of Dyslexia Tri Services. This volume is an outgrowth and expansion of this conference. Second, Dr. Jane DeMouy served as the conference organizer and maintained close communication with the authors prior to and following the conference. Third, I am especially grateful to Ms. Deborah Holderness without whose microcomputer processing expertise this volume would never have been possible. Last, and most especially, heart felt thanks to the editorial staff of Springer-Verlag and, in particular, the editorial department, for their vote of confidence, support, high level of professionalism, friendship, wise counsel, and patience.

Susan A. Vogel
Editor

# Contents

## Part 1  Oral Language

## Part 2  Academic Skills Instruction

## Part 3  On the Cutting Edge

# Contributors

*Diana Brewster Clark*, Ed.D., Department of Special Education, Teachers College, Columbia University, New York, New York 10027, USA.

*Steve Graham*, Ph.D., Department of Special Education, University of Maryland, College Park, Maryland 20740, USA.

*Karen B. Harris*, Ph.D., Department of Special Education, University of Maryland, College Park, Maryland 20740, USA.

*Neal M. Horen*, M.A., Psychology Department, University of South Florida, Tampa, Florida 33620, USA.

*B. Keith Lenz*, Ph.D., Institute for Research in Learning Disabilities, University of Kansas, Lawrence, Kansas 66045, USA.

*Ruth McIntosh*, Ph.D., Department of Special Education, University of Miami, Coral Gables, Florida 33124, USA.

*Diane Paul-Brown*, Ph.D., Speech-Language Pathology Division, American-Speech-Language-Hearing Association, Rockville, Maryland 20842, USA.

*Ruth B. Spodak*, Ph.D., McLean School, Potomac, Maryland 20854, USA.

*Joyce Steeves*, Ed.D., Maryland Rehabilitation Center, Johns Hopkins University, Baltimore, Maryland 21218, USA.

*Joseph K. Torgesen*, Ph.D., Department of Psychology, University of Miami, Coral Gables, Florida 33124, USA.

*Sharon Vaughn*, Ph.D., Department of Teaching & Learning, School of Education & Allied Professions, University of Miami, Coral Gables, Florida 33124, USA.

*Elizabeth H. Wiig*, Ph.D., Professor Emeritus, Sargent College, Boston University, Boston, Massachusetts 02215, USA.

*Nina Zaragoza*, Ph.D., Department of Special Education, Michigan State University, East Lansing, Michigan 48824, USA.

# Introduction

It is with great pleasure that the contributing authors and I bring you this text. *Educational Alternatives for Students with Learning Disabilities* is in response to the pressing need to provide present and future teachers of the learning disabled whether in self-contained classrooms, in resource programs, or regular classrooms with practical knowledge regarding state-of-the-art interventions. Too few researchers have focused their attention on the effectiveness of teaching strategies employed to improve academic skills of the learning disabled, in spite of the fact that the hallmark characteristics of individuals with learning disabilities are deficits in reading, writing, and arithmetic (Berk, 1984).

In a review of research conducted in the area of learning disabilities (LD) between 1978 and 1987, Lessen, Dudzinski, Karsh, and Van Acker (1989) found that less than four percent of the articles published in eight of the major special education journals focused on academic interventions. Those that were identified, focused primarily on early reading skills of elementary-aged children in LD resource rooms. The interventions described were taught more than half the time on a one-to-one basis and only one-third examined the maintenance or generalization of the new skills.

This present text was designed to address many of the shortcomings reported in this survey and follows several of Lessen's et al. (1989) recommendations. First, the text addresses the needs of pre-school age children through adolescence, not just elementary-age children. (See chapters by Drs. Diane Paul-Brown, Elisabeth Wiig, and Keith Lenz.) Second, the neglected areas of oral language instruction, written expression, mathematics, and social skills intervention are included. Third, specific guidelines and recommendations for utilizing the described instructional practices are at the heart of each chapter, often with specific steps, materials, and/or procedures for teachers to use.

Chapter topics were selected because of their relevance in a wide range of settings: self-contained classrooms, resource rooms, and the mainstream. For example, in Chapter 6 Dr. Keith Lenz describes some of the instructional strategies particularly effective in content-area instruction with adolescents with learning disabilities that can be used with students individually or in small groups. Other chapters were included because of their timeliness (see Drs. Joseph Torgesen and Neal Horen's chapter on computer technology and computer assisted instructional software). Some were included because they address a sorely neglected segment of the population of students with learning disabilities, namely, Chapter 9 by Dr. Ruth Spodak on gifted LD individuals.

I believe these outstanding contributing authors have provided very useful information about validated practices, procedures, and/or recommendations that will be helpful to those who are preparing to be speech and language pathologists, LD specialists, and preschool through high school mainstream teachers. Moreover, it is hoped that classroom teachers who face new challenges because of the growing number of children with language impairments and/or specific learning disabilities in their classes will also find this volume helpful.

# References

Berk, R.A. (1984). *Screening and diagnosis of children with learning disabilities.* Springfield, IL: Charles C. Thomas.

Lessen, E.I., Karsh, K., & Van Acker, R. (1989). A survey of ten years of academic intervention research with learning disabled students: Implications for research and practice. *Learning Disabilities Focus, 4*(2), 106-122.

# Part 1
## Oral Language

# 1
# Preschool Language Intervention in the Classroom: Rationale and Organizational Structure

**Diane Paul-Brown**

## Preschool Language Impairment: Persistence, Prevalence, Impact

### Persistence

The preschool years mark a time of growth of understanding and production of oral language, as well as the development of metalinguistic skills, or an awareness of and ability to reflect on language (Clark, 1978, 1982). It is generally recognized that preschool language acquisition and aspects of metalinguistic skills are linked to later linguistic, reading, and academic achievement (e.g., Aram & Nation, 1980; King, Jones, & Lasky, 1982; Maxwell & Wallach, 1984). Language impairment in 3- to 6-year-old children may be the first indication of a persistent problem with oral and written language (e.g., Fornell & Hood, 1985; Lee & Shapero-Fine, 1984; Liberman, 1983; Stark, Bernstein, & Condino, 1984; Tallal, 1987; Vellutino, 1979). A language-impaired preschool child is likely to be called a learning disabled school-age child (Bashir, Kuban, Kleinman, & Scavuzzo, 1983).

One aspect of metalinguistic abilities, phonemic awareness, also is a recognized predictor of later reading achievement (e.g., Bradley & Bryant, 1983; Lundberg, Olofsson, & Wall, 1980). Phonemic awareness is a multifaceted skill that includes rhyming ability, alphabet recognition, sound symbol correspondence, sound segmentation, sound blending, and sound deletion (see Lewkowicz, 1980). These separate skills are highly intercorrelated and appear to represent a common cognitive construct (Stanovich, Cunningham, & Cramer, 1984). Children with limited phonemic awareness skills are more likely to have difficulty with later reading achievement than those children with demonstrated phonemic awareness (see Blachman, 1984, 1989; Catts, 1989, for review).

## Prevalence

Besides the persistence of a language impairment, the prevalence of a language problem in preschool children underscores the impact of this developmental disability. Over 60% of the preschool children identified as handicapped have been found to have a speech or language impairment as the primary handicapping condition (National Joint Committee on Learning Disabilities, 1987).

## Impact

In addition to having a strong effect on reading readiness, a language impairment can have a pervasive impact on other areas of a young child's growth, especially social development (see Bryan, 1986; Pearl, Donahue, & Bryan, 1986, for review). A language-impaired child, for example, may have difficulty in areas of language known to influence the development and maintenance of positive interpersonal relationships. These areas include the ability to adjust language to the social status and needs of a listener, the ability to recognize the nature and extent of a listener's background knowledge, and the ability to understand and use rules for engaging in cooperative, sustained conversation (e.g., Bryan, 1986). Problems in these language areas affect the perception of a conversational partner during communicative interactions. A child who does not make appropriate listener/situational adjustments in conversation may be viewed and responded to negatively.

In view of the persistence, prevalence, and strong impact of a language impairment in the preschool years, the necessity of early identification and intervention becomes apparent. Early intervention programs appear to be effective in improving communication skills of 3- to 6-year-old children with language impairment, particularly intervention programs that are highly structured, systematic, and specifically focused on target language goals (Snyder-McLean & McLean, 1987).

The purpose of this chapter will be to describe an organizational plan to conduct assessment and intervention for language-impaired preschool children. The rationale for a classroom-based intervention program will be discussed within this organizational framework.

# Organizational Plan for Language Intervention

An organizational plan can provide a clear direction for multiple facets of language intervention (see Guralnick, 1975). A general organizational plan, shown in Figure 1.1, includes components central to language intervention: (a) theoretical base; (b) service-delivery model; (c) principles of assessment and intervention; (d) assessment procedures; (e) intervention goals and strategies for the child, parent, and teacher; and (f) an evaluation plan. These components first will be described in general terms followed by a detailed outline of a specific language intervention plan.

## Theoretical Base

A sound, effective language intervention program may be generated from a firm theoretical base that describes the nature, purpose, and acquisition of language (Fey, 1986; McLean, 1989). The theory of language development determines the content, context, goals, procedures, and means to evaluate the outcome of language intervention. Without such a theoretical base, language goals would be selected on a haphazard, trial-and-error basis. The theoretical base allows individualization of language goals and provides a systematic process for independent judgments by speech and language professionals (McLean, 1989).

## Service-Delivery Model

From the theoretical base, a service-delivery model may be derived. This service-delivery model determines where, how, and when language intervention will be conducted. Options include the traditional service-delivery model best described as a "pullout" program where a speech-language pathologist works with children individually or in small groups in a separate therapy room. The frequency and time of service is typically determined on the basis of speech and language needs of the children, with consideration given to scheduling demands. Another model for service-delivery is a classroom-based approach where intervention efforts are conducted directly in the classroom setting. Certain theoretical frameworks may be more compatible with a particular service-delivery model.

## Principles of Assessment and Intervention

A well-developed theoretical base also can lead to certain principles that provide guidance for the context and content of language assessment and intervention. One principle, for example, may be that the setting for language assessment and intervention should be directly in the home or classroom. A set of principles enables a practitioner to operate in a clearly focused direction where the goals and sequence of language intervention are apparent. Decisions regarding assessment (e.g., what language behaviors to evaluate; where to conduct the evaluation) and intervention (e.g., what to do next; what to do if something goes wrong) can be predetermined on the basis of sound theoretical principles.

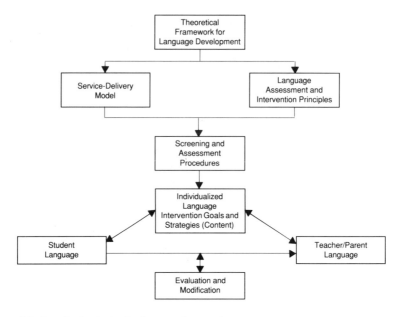

Figure 1.1. Organizational plan for language intervention.

## Assessment Procedures

Assessment procedures follow directly from these principles. Guidelines regarding the nature and scope of communicative behaviors to be evaluated lead to the selection of an appropriate assessment battery. For example, if a language principle is that language assessment and intervention should include a child's regular conversational partners, tests or observational measures can be administered that focus on a child's conversational interactions with peers, as well as with familiar and unfamiliar adults. The results of a comprehensive assessment can then be used to devise an individualized language intervention plan.

## Intervention Goals and Strategies

An individualized plan differentiates a general language arts curriculum from language intervention that is devised for a particular child based on documented language needs. In addition to the importance of individualized language intervention, the importance of establishing strategies for teaching particular skills must be stressed. Strategies highlight the generalities or patterns among language skills separate from the particular content. For example, regardless of the content or materials used, certain memory strategies can be taught to help a child remember information such as sentence patterns, vocabulary words, or conversational rules. Without general strategies, each new word would be viewed as an isolated entity, and the child would have no established means to learn new concepts. Individual goals and strategies may be devised for the language-impaired child, as well as for the teacher and the parent or anyone who interacts with the child on a regular basis. For example, one goal for a child who demonstrates difficulty following multistep directions may be to improve a child's ability to follow directions of increasing length and syntactic complexity. Teachers may present classroom directions one step at a time and systematically increase the use of multipart, complex directions as the child shows success in following more succinct directions. A child may be taught to repeat key words in directions as a strategy to aid recall.

## Evaluation

A means to evaluate the effectiveness of the language intervention program and make necessary modifications is the final component of the organizational plan. A major purpose of language assessment is to monitor change and to determine the effectiveness of language intervention (James, 1989). Measuring progress when alternative service-delivery models are used, such as a collaborative model or a classroom-based approach, may present a unique challenge to the clinician. Various procedures can be applied to evaluate progress that may be extended to different settings or interactive situations to correspond to a particular intervention model. Evaluation procedures may include (a) pre- and posttest comparisons; (b) periodic probes or checks of communicative behavior that correspond to individual goals selected for a child; (c) regular observations of teacher language, parent-child, and peer interactions; and (d) rating scales that assess language behavior or perceptions of language problems or progress at different intervals. Necessary modifications in intervention procedures can be made on a consistent basis as difficulties arise or if progress is not seen during the ongoing evaluation process.

This general organizational structure identifies the major components for consideration in planning language intervention: a theoretical plan; service-delivery model; assessment and intervention principles; assessment procedures, goals, and strategies for language intervention for students, parents, and teachers; and a plan for evaluation and modification. A specific organizational plan that corresponds to a particular theoretical perspective will be described and is detailed in Figure 1.2.

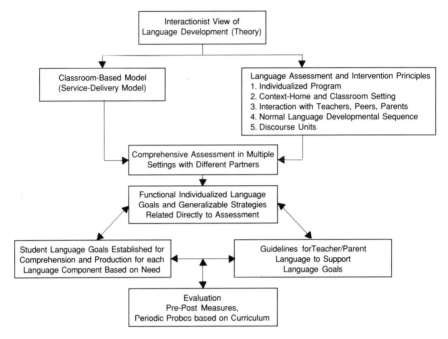

Figure 1.2. Organizational plan for language intervention within a specific theoretical framework.

# Specific Organizational Plan

## Theoretical Framework for Language Development

One leading theoretical framework proposed to explain the language acquisition process has been referred to as an interactionist view of language (see Fey, 1986). From this perspective, language is considered a separate developmental entity rather than only part of a broader cognitive developmental process. Cognitive and environmental influences are recognized as important influences in the language acquisition process. Central to the interactionist view is the complex interaction of three major language components: language content, form, and use (Bloom & Lahey, 1978).

## Service-Delivery Model

The interactionist theory of language acquisition stresses the importance of the use of language and the necessity of considering social or environmental influences on language development. A natural outcome of this framework is a service-delivery model that is conducted in a child's regular environment where language learning opportunities routinely occur. A classroom-based approach, rather than a more traditional pullout model, more directly addresses the language development needs of language-impaired children (see Miller, 1989; Ripich, 1987; Simon, 1987b).

## Rationale for Classroom-Based Approach

The rationale for a classroom-based model of language intervention can be drawn from information known about the nature of language and the acquisition process. The inefficiency of the traditional clinical model also provides a strong argument for such a model (see Miller, 1989; Simon, 1987a,c). Some of the major premises of a classroom-based intervention model, many of which have been identified by Simon (1987a, c), are outlined below.

### Interaction of Speaker/Listener/Content/Context

In recent years, the area of pragmatics, or the use of language in its social context (Bates, 1976), has acquired prominence in language acquisition and intervention research and in clinical practice. New language assessment and intervention approaches have been developed that acknowledge the importance of the development of the social component of language in addition to language structure (i.e., syntax) and meaning (i.e., semantics) (Marvin, 1987). Pragmatics focuses on the interaction of the speaker, the listener, the message content, and the context or setting in which the message occurs (Simon, 1987a). A classroom-based approach considers this four-way interaction. With this approach, the student is not the only focus of intervention efforts; attention is also directed to teacher-student interaction, peer interaction, and curricular content within a classroom. Language learning can occur throughout a child's day when language is taught in context.

### Communicative Demands of School Environment

The classroom setting imposes high expectations and demands on communication. A language-impaired child is at a disadvantage in the classroom where information must be readily understood and where clear expression is expected. The language-impaired child may have difficulty following the expected classroom routine. A wide range of communication skills are expected during classroom activities, including knowledge about the school routine (e.g., knowing when to ask and how to answer questions), knowledge about communicative routines (e.g., knowing how to initiate conversations, knowing how and when to modify language patterns for different listeners, greeting others appropriately), giving and following directions, and asking for clarification when a direction or information is unclear (Creaghead & Tattershall, 1985).

Beyond the preschool years, the curricular demands increase with concomitant demands for abstract and inferential thinking, comprehension and use of figurative language, and rapid recall of information (see Wiig & Semel, 1984). With these complex cognitive, linguistic, and social demands of the classroom, it follows that success could be optimized by teaching language in the context where many of a child's communication problems manifest themselves (see Nelson, 1989a).

**Inefficiency of Traditional Clinical Model**

The third reason for adopting a classroom-based model relates to the weaknesses of the traditional pullout model. With this model, students are typically taken out of their classroom and the speech-language pathologist works with them individually or in small groups. This approach is problematic, particularly beyond the preschool years, since students miss curriculum information when they are pulled from the classroom. Typically, the curriculum content is not a focus of the speech-language pathologist in this traditional role. Also, the information learned in the therapy room may not generalize easily to other settings, and the student may not use learned language skills on an independent basis. Finally, conversational interactions expected during classroom routines may be very different than those taught in a one-to-one setting (see Simon, 1987c).

**Collaborative Consultation for Speech-Language Pathologist**

An alternative role for the speech-language pathologist consistent with a classroom-based model has been referred to as collaborative consultation (see Damico, 1987). Collaborative consultation recognizes the importance of input from the teacher, parent, and student, as well as the speech-language pathologist. Such a model contrasts with an "expert" consultation approach where the speech-language pathologist acts in a more unitary role to provide information to the teacher. Collaborative consultation fosters more mutual problem solving among concerned professionals and with the students themselves. The advantage to such a team approach has been elucidated by Simon (1987a), "With everyone engaged in a team effort to improve classroom communication skills and learning strategies, a cohesive program can be designed as contrasted to each educator drilling on 'splinter skills'" (p. 98). A cohesive educational plan would be an important aim of a classroom-based model with the speech-language pathologist in a collaborative consultation role.

## Expanded Service Options

The speech-language pathologist may fill this collaborative consultation role in a number of different capacities: (a) as an *observer*, providing feedback on effective teaching strategies for particular children; (b) as a *model or aid*, providing help for individual children related, for example, to understanding concepts, following directions, or making classroom activity transitions; (c) as a *team teacher*, co-teaching a lesson, working with children in small groups, or monitoring children while they are engaged in classroom activities, with a focus on facilitating effective communicative interactions; (d) as a *specialist* who may work with children individually in a therapy room for short-term language intervention as needs arise, with assistance provided to ensure generalization to other settings; (e) as a *teacher trainer*, providing principles and a format for teachers to follow to conduct intervention within the classroom, with the speech-language pathologist available to modify specific procedures as needed; or (f) as a *parent trainer*, providing guidance to parents to facilitate language learning at home.

Serving in these different capacities, the speech-language pathologist's role following a classroom-based model actually provides greater service options than the more traditional clinical model. This expanded role provides greater assurance that communication skills taught will be applied directly to a child's regular communicative environment.

## Effectiveness More Apparent to Students Themselves

With a classroom-based model, a student's immediate communication needs are addressed directly on an ongoing basis. Students themselves may recognize the benefits of such a relevant, responsive approach to language intervention. For example, as children become more proficient in their conversational interactions, they may receive less negative feedback from their listeners, and they may feel less frustration. For school-age children, greater success on tests may provide direct feedback of the benefit of a classroom-based intervention model to students. Although the focus of such an intervention model should be on teaching strategies rather than teaching academic content directly (Nelson, 1989b), classroom vocabulary and curriculum content may be used as the material for implementing the strategies learned.

These premises for a classroom-based model highlight the point that language cannot be viewed as a separate, isolated subject. Rather, language is recognized as a complex, ongoing developmental process that encompasses all aspects of a child's day. Within the classroom or therapy room, oral and written language can be taught most appropriately in a functional way. In this regard, Dudley-Marling (1987) has argued that drilling of isolated language skills can only "...trivialize language and make meaningful language learning more difficult and, perhaps, exacerbate the learning difficulties of language-impaired students" (p. 87).

# Language Assessment and Intervention Principles

Five principles guiding language assessment and intervention procedures were selected to reflect salient aspects of an interactionist theory of language development (see Paul-Brown, 1988). The principles help determine the content and context of language assessment and intervention (see Figure 1.2). These five principles address the importance of individualization and identify the context, interactive partners, content, and particular discourse units for conducting language assessment and intervention.

## Individualization

A comprehensive diagnostic evaluation will help to identify individual goals and objectives. On the basis of the evaluation, individual needs, strengths, and weaknesses can be identified so that priorities can be established, based on the nature and severity of the present language problem (see Paul-Brown, 1988). Language inter-vention procedures can then be selected to relate directly to the initial evaluation. The fact that language intervention takes place in the classroom does not mean that children in class are viewed or treated as a single unit, since each child in a group does not function at the same level. Children may experience difficulties with different components of language. Consequently, as part of an intervention plan, semantic goals may be stressed more than goals pertaining to syntactic problems for one child. Another child may experience difficulties only with language use during conversational interactions (see Nelson, 1988). Rate of progression and specific content to be taught also may vary from individual to individual.

## Context: Home and Classroom Settings

This principle specifies the setting and timing of language assessment and intervention. A comprehensive diagnostic evaluation may include assessment of a child's language in multiple settings, rather than an assessment only in a clinical setting. The most appropriate context for language intervention may be the child's natural environment with language taught throughout the day in the home and classroom settings. As aptly described by Nelson (1989b, p. 453), "Perhaps the most important steps to be taken involve leading teachers to recognize that language is not something that can be relegated to an hour or half hour of the daily schedule, but is an integral part of all activities."

Teaching language in the child's natural environment still means that goals and activities can be as structured and systematic as they would be with a traditional model. In order to highlight a particular language skill, certain events may be created to optimize or increase chances for targeted language use (e.g., Hart & Rogers-Warren, 1978; Taenzer, Cermak, & Hanlon, 1981; Warren & Kaiser, 1986).

## Interaction with Teachers, Peers, Parents

Just as an interactive theory of language development recognizes the critical impact of the interactive partners in the construction of language, language assessment and intervention procedures can be expanded to include a child's regular interactive partners. Since communication is the primary purpose of language, language assessment and intervention could be conducted with a communicative exchange with multiple conversational partners, such as a child's peers, teachers, and parents.

## Normal Language Developmental Sequence

The metric for determining the existence of a language impairment and for selecting the sequence for teaching new language skills is typically based on information known about the normal developmental sequence (see Miller & Yoder, 1974). The normal sequence of development in the areas of phonology, syntax, semantics, and pragmatics may be considered when evaluating language skills and when designing language intervention programs. Developmental norms are more comprehensive for certain language components and for certain age levels. Specifically, relatively less developmental information is available in the area of pragmatics than other language areas. More ongoing modifications may be necessary for certain children when the sequence for a particular language skill is not well understood.

Reliance on the developmental sequence typically leads to teaching basic language components or recognized linguistic precursors before teaching more complex language skills. For example, in the area of semantics, the mastery of basic, concrete vocabulary can be expected prior to comprehension of words with multiple meanings or figurative language. Goals for vocabulary/concept development can reflect this sequence. Similarly, certain metalinguistic skills, such as phonemic segmentation, which may be precursors to reading and written language can be taught directly. This type of developmental teaching process may enhance the transition to the reading process (see Blachman, 1984, 1989; Catts, 1989, for review).

It is also important to consider levels of expertise when teaching new language skills. A child should not be expected to be a proficient or expert communicator before developing prerequisite skills or without achieving earlier levels of language competence. In this regard, Dreyfus and Dreyfus (1986) have identified five stages in the progression toward expert performance: beginner, advanced beginner, competent performer, proficiency, and expertise. When applied to language development, this model suggests that the level of expert communicator may not be a realistic goal for a language-impaired child, particularly at the beginning phases of language intervention. A more realistic approach to language intervention may be to allow sufficient time for repeated practice and rehearsal at different levels of expertise, which may lead to greater automaticity and proficiency of language skills.

## Discourse Units

Language assessment and intervention that corresponds to an interactionist perspective on language may be conducted within a meaningful unit of discourse (i.e., an extended sequence of related utterances for conversations or narratives). Teaching language in expanded discourse units is a more natural and realistic goal for language development than teaching words and utterances as separate units in a drill-like format (see Paul-Brown, 1988). Typically, conversations and narratives extend beyond a limited two-part sequence, with one speaker and one listener utterance.

These language assessment and intervention principles that have been described enable speech-language pathologists and teachers to create appropriate procedures, evaluate progress, and modify an approach as necessary according to a structured, organizational framework. Goals and activities need not be selected in a vacuum, but may be developed to correspond to a set of prescribed principles. Accordingly, teachers will know the steps to follow and will know how to proceed if modification is warranted.

# Speech and Language Assessment Procedures

A comprehensive language assessment battery is necessary to determine a complete profile of a child's skills. This information can then be used to identify strengths, weaknesses, and prioritize needs. Comparisons between a child's language and cognitive level can be made to determine whether a child's language abilities are commensurate with cognitive level of functioning. If a language impairment is identified, with language level below cognitive expectations, then assessment information can be used to devise individualized language intervention goals. Assessment procedures that follow directly from the service-delivery model and principles discussed, address the need for an in-depth assessment across language domains within different linguistic, situational, and listener contexts (see Figure 1.3).

A comprehensive assessment battery spans various linguistic domains including phonology, morphology, syntax, semantics, and pragmatics. A child's comprehension and production abilities can be evaluated within these domains.

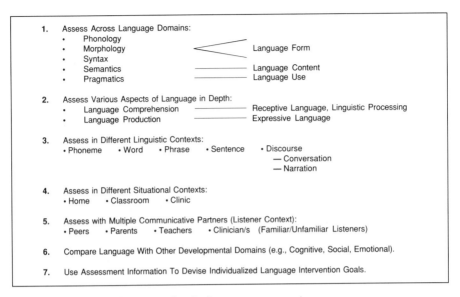

Figure 1.3. Guidelines for a comprehensive language assessment battery.

An assessment of a child's metalinguistic abilities, particularly phonemic awareness, may also be a part of the battery. The linguistic, situational, and listener context would be important variables to consider in the design of an assessment battery.

For a thorough evaluation of the linguistic context, assessment may include language samples within discourse units and not just single utterances. In this way, multiple functions of language can be observed, rather than simply responses to questions or responses obtained during picture-pointing tasks. Language used in different situational contexts also could be observed. Observations may be conducted in a child's classroom and home, rather than just in a clinic setting. Variations in language use with different listeners may be determined. Language differences, depending on whether talk was directed to adults vs. peers, teacher vs. parent, clinician vs. teacher, or familiar vs. unfamiliar partners, could be measured.

Where available, comparisons can be made with developmental norms. An in-depth diagnostic evaluation provides a comprehensive view of a child's language skills across linguistic domains within different linguistic, situational, and listener contexts. A child's complete language profile can be compared with other developmental information, such as a child's cognitive, emotional, and social levels. An interdisciplinary team could provide the most complete evaluation of a child's abilities. A range of formal and informal procedures will likely be included in any comprehensive language battery. Various reports have been published that describe and critique specific preschool language assessment

| MUTUAL INFLUENTIAL FACTORS | EMPHASIS IN INTERVENTION PROGRAM |
|---|---|
| 1. Link between early language problems and later problems with academic success and reading achievement | Teaching metalinguistic and narrative discourse skills as precursor to reading |
| 2. Importance of early identification and intervention | Starting language intervention as early as possible with at-risk or identified language impaired children to prevent or reduce severity of later language problems |
| 3. Impact of pragmatics, the use of language in context | Involving peers in language intervention as aid to communicative development |
| 4. Relation between peer interactions and communicative competence | Involving peers in language intervention as aid to communicative development |
| 5. Interaction between communicative and social competence | Incorporating language development activities throughout a child's day as means to improve social competence |

Figure 1.4. Factors influencing development of preschool classroom-based language intervention program

procedures (e.g., Spekman, 1983). One possible speech and language assessment battery for preschool children that corresponds to the assessment guidelines presented is shown in Table 1.1. This battery includes various language tests or informal procedures that can be used to assess comprehension and production within each language domain. Assessment procedures are specified for different linguistic, situational, and listener contexts.

## Individualized Language Intervention Goals and Strategies

From the information gained from the diagnostic evaluation, an individualized language intervention plan can be developed with specific goals for children and suggestions for interactive strategies for the teacher and parent. Specific plans for any intervention program for preschool children should consider the following five interrelated factors (see Figure 1.4).

**Table 1.1:** Sample Preschool Language Assessment Battery.

| LANGUAGE DOMAIN | LINGUISTIC LEVEL | RECEPTIVE OR EXPRESSIVE COMPONENT | ASSESSMENT PROCEDURE/INSTRUMENT |
|---|---|---|---|
| Phonology | Phoneme (Metalinguistic Skills) | Receptive/Expressive | Tasks to assess phonemic awareness and production:<br>■ alphabet recognition<br>■ alphabet sequence<br>■ position of phoneme in word<br>■ sound/letter correspondence<br>■ phonemic segmentation<br>■ syllable segmentation<br>■ accent (stress)<br>■ rhyming ability        (Paul-Brown, 1986)<br><br>Alternate Choices: (Analysis of the Language of Learning, Blodgett & Cooper, 1987; Test of Awareness of Language Segments, Sawyer, 1987) |
|  | Phoneme (Articulation, Phonological Process Analysis) | Expressive | Goldman-Fristoe Test of Articulation (Goldman & Fristoe, 1986)<br><br>Kahn-Lewis Phonological Analysis (Kahn & Lewis, 1986) (Optional) |
| Semantics | Single Word (Vocabulary) | Receptive | Peabody Picture Vocabulary Test-Revised (PPVT-R) (Dunn & Dunn, 1981) |
|  | Single Word (Concepts related to space, quantity, time) | Receptive | Boehm Test of Basic Concepts-Revised (Boehm, 1986) |

Table 1.1 continued

| LANGUAGE DOMAIN | LINGUISTIC LEVEL | RECEPTIVE OR EXPRESSIVE COMPONENT | ASSESSMENT PROCEDURE/INSTRUMENT |
|---|---|---|---|
| Morphology and Syntax | Single Word Phrase Sentence | Receptive | Test for Auditory Comprehension of Language-Revised (TACL-R) (Carrow-Woolfolk, 1985) |
| | Phrase (Memory) | Receptive | Token Test for Children (DiSimoni, 1978) |
| | Sentence | Receptive | Token Test for Children, Part 5 |
| | Phrase Sentence (Following Directions) | Receptive | J.F.K. Commands Test (Kennedy Institute for Handicapped Children, n.d.) |
| | Sentence (Memory) | Expressive (Imitation) | Binet Memory for Sentences (Terman & Merrill, 1986) |
| | Conversational Discourse | Expressive | Language Sample Analysis with Developmental Sentence Scoring (DSS) (Lee, 1974) |
| | Narrative Discourse | Expressive | Computation of Mean Length of Utterance (MLU) (Brown, 1983) Analysis with T-Unit Analysis (Roth & Spekman, 1989) |

Table 1.1 continued

| LANGUAGE DOMAIN | LINGUISTIC LEVEL | RECEPTIVE OR EXPRESSIVE COMPONENT | ASSESSMENT PROCEDURE/INSTRUMENT |
|---|---|---|---|
| Pragmatics | Conversational Discourse | Expressive | Language Sample in Multiple Contexts with Different Communicative Partners |
| | | | Analysis of Functions, Informativeness, Conversational Rules (see Roth & Spekman, 1984) |
| | Narrative Discourse | Expressive | Tasks to Assess Story Production, Story Recall, Structured Story (Roth & Paul-Brown, 1988) |
| General | Multilevel | Receptive/Expressive | Preschool Language Assessment Instrument (Blank, Rose, & Berlin, 1978) |
| | | | Preschool Language Scale-Revised (PLS-R) (Zimmerman, Steiner, & Pond, 1979) |

## Persistence of Language Problems

First, as previously discussed, a link between early language problems and later lack of reading and academic success has been established. Therefore, a preschool language intervention program should focus on developing the specific language skills that relate most closely to later reading achievement, if they are found to be deficit areas relative to expected norms. Phonemic awareness and narrative discourse would be two such related language skills. Instructional programs designed to teach phonemic awareness skills at the preschool level, such as rhyme recognition, sound and syllable segmentation, and sound blending, have been shown to facilitate reading acquisition (e.g., Bradley, 1988; Lundberg, 1988; Sawyer, 1988). Comprehension and production of narratives is also a skill that influences reading ability (see Westby, 1984). In fact, children who are read to at home and who come from homes where books are highly visible and frequently used are more successful at reading comprehension in the early school years than children from homes where reading was not stressed (Bennett, 1986; see Wallach & Miller, 1988, for discussion). Language-impaired and learning disabled students are known to have problems with recall and production of stories (e.g., Graybeal, 1981; Griffith, Ripich, & Dastoli, 1986; Roth & Spekman, 1986). Narrative discourse in the preschool years encompasses story recall and comprehension, recounting of personal events, and pretend or dramatic play enactment (Milosky, 1987). Certain instructional techniques, such as exposure to stories, training in prediction skills, and teaching of story grammar, have been used to facilitate narrative discourse skills (Page & Stewart, 1985; Westby, 1985). Common activities in preschools, such as pretend play, "show and tell," and story time, provide opportunities for oral narration (Milosky, 1987).

## Early Identification and Intervention

A second factor to be considered in planning intervention is the importance of early identification and intervention. This factor addresses the issue of when to start a language intervention program. Too often we hear of concerned parents who were advised that their child would outgrow a language problem. Referral to a speech-language pathologist is recommended for any concern related to delayed speech and/or language development. If a discrepancy is found between a child's cognitive and language level, an appropriate intervention program could be initiated. Likewise, an intervention program could be started early for children considered at-risk for language problems based on biological or genetic indicators or other factors, such as disease or trauma that may be associated with developmental delay (National Joint Committee on Learning Disabilities, 1987). Congressional laws have been enacted to ensure early identification and intervention for at-risk and handicapped children. The Education of the Handicapped Act Amendments of 1986 (Public Law 99-457) mandate services for handicapped infants and toddlers (birth to 2 years old) and encourages services for children at risk. Additional state support is provided for handicapped preschool children (3 to 5 years old). Such preschool programs were optional under the Education for All Handicapped Children Act of 1975 (Public Law 94-142). The amendments of PL 99-457 also specify requirements for services to be provided by qualified personnel, according to the highest state professional qualification standards.

## Impact of Pragmatics

The third factor underlying the development of preschool language intervention programs is related to the pragmatic language domain. Within the last fifteen years, the importance of pragmatics has been recognized and has influenced the content, setting, and participants of language intervention programs (see Snyder & Silverstein, 1988, for review). From a pragmatic perspective, a language intervention plan should incorporate goals, strategies, and activities that focus on major pragmatic components: (a) teaching multiple functions of language; (b) teaching children to supply sufficient background information to make language informative and to make appropriate adaptations in language style for different listeners; and (c) guiding children through conversational interactions by making rules of conversation explicit (see Roth & Spekman, 1984).

## Peer Interactions

The fourth factor related to preschool language intervention concerns the connection between peer relations and communicative success. Although most of the research on the communicative competence of preschool children has focused on interactions between children and adults, there have been studies that have addressed issues related to communicative interactions of peers (see Guralnick, 1981; Guralnick & Paul-Brown, 1989, for review). Studies have indicated that communicative interactions between peers are stylistically different from adult-child interactions and provide important developmental opportunities and challenges (Bates, 1975; Garvey, 1986; Guralnick, 1981). This research suggests a need to include peers as part of an intervention program as a means to provide a complete and varied range of communicative interactions.

## Social Competence

The final factor identified for consideration in language intervention focuses on the link between language and social competence. Children who have not mastered communication skills expected for their age are likely to experience social problems (see Bryan, 1986; Pearl et al., 1986, for review). Language-impaired children may appear competitive, rejecting, or less tactful because they misread nonverbal signals, misunderstand intonation cues, or are unaware of cues to social status. Language-impaired children may have less flexibility with language and fail to use polite forms when required by the situation (see Bryan & Bryan, 1978). Besides such problems with listener-situational adjustments, language-impaired children may not provide adequate information for a partner and their remarks may not be sufficiently explicit or cohesive. A listener is likely to be inattentive or frustrated (see Bryan, 1986). Finally, language-impaired children may not have effective conversational interactions due to difficulty initiating or maintaining a topic (e.g., Bryan, Donahue, & Pearl, 1981a; Bryan, Donahue, Pearl, & Sturm, 1981). They may interrupt others, make inappropriate comments, or engage in irrelevant talk. As a consequence, they are likely to be ignored or to be the targets of negative comments. Communicative competence thus directly affects interpersonal relationships. Therefore, language intervention programs must recognize that language is not an isolated domain, and language impairment strongly impinges on other facets of development. Language intervention may be implemented during any social involvement a child has throughout the day.

## Mutual Factors Influencing Language Intervention

Although discussed separately, these factors that influence the development of preschool intervention programs are strongly interrelated. Specifically, early identification and intervention of language problems (factor 2) may reduce the severity of later academic and reading difficulties (factor 1). Likewise, if language is taught in a natural social context (factor 3), a child may have more opportunities to practice frequent social skills with peers, which may lead to enhanced social competence (factor 5) and more successful peer relations (factor 4). These five factors complement the principles of language assessment and intervention discussed earlier in this chapter (i.e., individualization, normal developmental sequence, natural settings, multiple conversational partners, and meaningful discourse units).

A language intervention program was designed on the basis of these factors and principles (see Paul-Brown, 1988). Goals were devised on the basis of the five most frequent language problem areas identified for a group of children (4.2 to 6.9-year-olds) enrolled in a private developmental preschool/primary program (Paul-Brown, 1988):

1. Vocabulary and concept development
2. Comprehension of orally presented directions
3. Conversational skills
4. Narrative skills
5. Metalinguistic skills

Goals and specific strategies were adapted on an individual basis according to language needs as determined during initial assessment.

Language intervention procedures were implemented in the classroom with supplemental activities and suggestions provided for use in the home. The speech-language pathologist provided specific suggestions and feedback to teachers to enhance communication skills for each child. Individual language goals were posted in the classroom. Teachers capitalized on either ongoing interactions or structured situations to facilitate target language behaviors with appropriate models and prompts. Small-group activities were designed for each of the five language deficit areas and conducted twice daily by the speech-language pathologist. Individual language goals were targeted during small-group time.

Representative goals, strategies, and activities for language intervention are shown in Appendix A. Specific goals, strategies, and activities are presented for each of the five most frequent language problems identified. Some procedures may be more appropriate for children at certain levels of language development. For example, exposure to stories may be an appropriate procedure to enhance story narration skills for children at early and later levels of language development. However, teaching story grammar categories may be an appropriate procedure only for children at later language levels who have demonstrated higher metalinguistic processing abilities (see Wallach & Miller, 1988). All suggestions presented should be applied on an individualized basis and modified as necessary.

In addition to goals, strategies, and activities for children, general suggestions were provided to teachers related to their speaking style (Paul-Brown & Botuck, 1989). The suggestions were designed to enhance teacher-student communication (see Appendix B). Teacher training focused on modification of rate of speech, intonation, amount of speech, loudness level, clarity of speech, use of silence, word choice/vocabulary, and syntax (see Gruenewald & Pollak, 1984). Parents were taught general strategies to facilitate language development. For example, parents were encouraged to interact with their child in ways that are known to increase spontaneous language. Such facilitative interaction patterns include increasing parallel talk, such as following the child's lead during play and commenting on a child's ongoing activities or using self-talk to describe a parent's own actions. These examples of facilitative strategies contrast with asking a lot of questions or using a strong directive style during adult-child interactions. Questions and directives tend to decrease spontaneous talk (Hubbell, 1977). The importance of reading and discussing books to enhance language development was also stressed (Snow, Midkiff-Borunda, Small, & Proctor, 1984).

## Evaluation and Modification

A critical component of language intervention is evaluation. The evaluation component completes the organizational plan depicted in Figure 1.2, but evaluation should not be considered the final step in language intervention. Rather, evaluation should be an ongoing process during intervention so that appropriate modifications can be made in the program as needed. In addition to pre- and post-measures obtained at the beginning and end of a school year, periodic probes or checks using observation scales or behavior checklists can be conducted based on the individual language goals and the procedures or curriculum devised to address each child's needs. A child's style of interaction with parents, teachers, and peers also can be assessed on an ongoing basis. Questions can be addressed to determine whether target language behaviors have changed during different linguistic, situational, and listener interactions. Teachers', parents', and students' perceptions of the effectiveness of a classroom-based model of language intervention also can be assessed. Comparisons can be made between perceived effectiveness and measured change. Ongoing assessment can help determine the effectiveness of particular intervention procedures. A classroom observation may reveal that a child rarely answers a teacher's questions with more than a single-word response. If appropriate responding to questions was a targeted language area, the teacher could be asked to increase use of open-ended questions that require comparison, analysis, or synthesis on the part of the child, rather than asking only yes-no questions (see Bloom, Engelhart, Furst, Hill, & Krathwohl, 1956). Modifications can be made in the content or context of the intervention program and changes can be made in teacher, parent, or child language.

## Conclusion

The impact of a language impairment in the preschool years on communicative competence in these early years as well as on reading readiness and later academic achievement cannot be overly emphasized. A young language-impaired child also is likely to experience social difficulties with peers and adults. Speech and language disorders also can lead to mild to moderate emotional problems (e.g., Cantwell & Baker, 1980). Certainly a problem of this potential magnitude necessitates a well-planned and carefully implemented intervention program. The organizational structure presented in this chapter provides the framework to devise a language intervention program that would be responsive to the needs of language-impaired preschool children.

# Acknowledgment

The author extends thanks to Ann Kathleen Jordan for her excellent editorial assistance.

# References

Aram, D., & Nation, J. (1980). Preschool language disorders and subsequent language and academic difficulties. *Journal of Communication Disorders, 13,* 159-170.

Bashir, A. S., Kuban, K. C., Kleinman, S. N., & Scavuzzo, A. (1983). Issues in language disorders: Considerations of cause, maintenance, and change. In J. Miller, D.E. Yoder, & R. Schiefelbusch (Eds.), *Contemporary issues in language intervention* (pp. 92-106). ASHA Reports 12. Rockville, MD: American Speech-Language-Hearing Association.

Bates, E. (1975). Peer relations and the acquisition of language. In M. Lewis & L.A. Rosenblum (Eds.), *The origins of behavior: Vol. 4. Friendships and peer relations* (pp. 259-292). New York: John Wiley & Sons.

Bates, E. (1976). *Language and context: Studies in the acquisition of pragmatics.* New York: Academic Press.

Bennett, W.J. (1986). *What works: Research about teaching and learning.* Washington, DC: U.S. Department of Education.

Blachman, B.A. (1984). Language analysis skills and early reading acquisition. In G.P. Wallach & K.G. Butler (Eds.), *Language learning disabilities in school-age children* (pp. 271-297). Baltimore: Williams & Wilkins.

Blachman, B.A. (1989). Phonological awareness and word recognition: Assessment and intervention. In A.G. Kamhi & H.W. Catts (Eds.), *Reading disabilities: A developmental language perspective* (pp. 133-158). Boston: College-Hill Press.

Blank, M., Rose, S., & Berlin, L. (1978). *Preschool language assessment instrument–The language of learning in practice.* Moline, IL: Lingui-Systems.

Blodgett, E.G., & Cooper, E.G. (1987). *Analysis of the language of learning.* Moline, IL: Lingui-Systems.

Bloom, B.S., Engelhart, M.D., Furst, E.J., Hill, W.H., & Krathwohl, D.R. (Eds.) (1956). *Taxonomy of educational objectives: The classification of educational goals. Handbook I: Cognitive domain.* New York: David McKay.

Bloom, L., & Lahey, M. (1978). *Language development and language disorders.* New York: John Wiley & Sons.

Boehm, A.E. (1986). *Boehm Test of Basic Concepts–Revised.* New York: Psychological Corporation.

Bradley, L. (1988). Rhyme recognition and reading and spelling in young children. In R.L. Masland & N.W. Masland (Eds.), *Preschool prevention of reading failure* (pp. 143-162). Parkton, MD: York Press.

Bradley, L., & Bryant, P. (1983). Categorizing sounds and learning to read: A causal connection. *Nature, 301*, 419-421.

Brown, R. (1983). *A first language: The early stages.* Cambridge, MA: Harvard University Press.

Bryan, T. (1986). A review of studies on learning disabled children's communicative competence. In R.L. Schiefelbusch (Ed.), *Language competence: Assessment and intervention* (pp. 227-259). San Diego: College-Hill Press.

Bryan, T., & Bryan, J. (1978). *Understanding learning disabilities* (2nd ed.). Sherman Oaks, CA: Alfred Publishing.

Bryan, T., Donahue, M., & Pearl, R. (1981a). Learning disabled children's peer interactions during a small group problem solving task. *Learning Disability Quarterly, 4*, 13-22.

Bryan, T., Donahue, M., & Pearl, R. (1981b). Studies of learning disabled children's pragmatic competence. *Topics in Learning and Learning Disabilities, 1*, 29-39.

Bryan, T., Donahue, M., Pearl, R., & Sturm, C. (1981). Learning disabled children's conversational skills: The TV talk show. *Learning Disability Quarterly, 4*, 250-259.

Cantwell, D.P., & Baker, L. (1980). Academic failures in children with communication disorders. *Journal of Child Psychiatry, 19*, 579-591.

Carrow-Woolfolk, E. (1985). *Test for Auditory Comprehension of Language: Revised edition.* Allen, TX: Teaching Resources.

Catts, H.W. (1989). Phonological processing deficits and reading disabilities. In A.G. Kamhi & H.W. Catts (Eds.), *Reading disabilities: A developmental language perspective* (pp. 101-132). Boston: College-Hill.

Chapman, E. (1981). Explaining children's communicative intents. In J. Miller (Ed.), *Assessing language production in children: Experimental procedures* (pp. 111-136). Baltimore: University Park Press.

Clark, E. (1978). Awareness of language: Some evidence from what children say and do. In A. Sinclair, R.J. Jarvella, & W.J.M. Levelt (Eds.), *The child's conception of language* (pp. 17-43). New York: Springer-Verlag.

Clark, E.V. (1982). Language change during language acquisition. In M.E. Lamb & A.L. Brown (Eds.), *Advances in developmental psychology* (Vol. 2, pp. 171-195). Hillsdale, NJ: Lawrence Erlbaum.

Creaghead, N.A., & Tattershall, S.S. (1985). Observation and assessment of classroom pragmatic skills. In C.S. Simon (Ed.), *Communication skills and classroom success: Assessment of language-learning disabled students* (pp. 105-131). San Diego: College-Hill Press.

Damico, J.S. (1987). Addressing language concerns in the schools: The SLP as consultant. *Journal of Childhood Communication Disorders, 11*, 17-40.

DiSimoni, F. (1978). *The Token Test for Children.* Hingham, MA: Teaching Resources.

Dreyfus, H., & Dreyfus, S.E. (1986). *Mind over machine.* New York: Macmillan.

Dudley-Marling, C. (1987). The role of SLP's in literacy learning. *Journal of Childhood Communication Disorders, 11*, 81-90.

Dunn, L.M., & Dunn, L.M. (1981). *Peabody Picture Vocabulary Test–Revised.* Circle Pines, MN: American Guidance Service.

Fey, M.E. (1986). *Language intervention with young children.* San Diego: College-Hill Press.

Fornell, E.R., & Hood, J. (1985). A longitudinal study of two groups of children with early reading problems. *Annals of Dyslexia, 35*, 97-116.

Garvey, C. (1986). Peer relations and the growth of communication. In E.C. Mueller & C.R. Cooper (Eds.), *Process and outcome in peer relationships* (pp. 329-345). Orlando, FL: Academic Press.

Goldman, R., & Fristoe, M. (1986). *Goldman-Fristoe Test of Articulation.* Circle Pines, MN: American Guidance Service.

Graybeal, C.M. (1981). Memory for stories in language-impaired children. *Applied Psycholinguistics, 2*, 269-283.

Grice, H. (1975). Logic and conversation. In P. Cole & J. Morgan (Eds.), *Syntax and semantics* (Vol. 3, pp. 41-58). New York: Academic Press.

Griffith, P., Ripich, D., & Dastoli, S. (1986). Store structure, cohesion and propositions in story recalls by learning-disabled and non-disabled children. *Journal of Psycholinguistic Research, 15*, 539-555.

Gruenewald, L.J., & Pollak, S.A. (1984). *Language interaction in teaching and learning.* Baltimore: University Park Press.

Guralnick, M.J. (1975). Early classroom based intervention and the role of organizational structure. *Exceptional Children, 42*, 25-31.

Guralnick, M.J. (1981). Peer influences on the development of communicative competence. In P. Strain (Ed.), *The utilization of classroom peers as behavior change agents* (pp. 631-687). New York: Plenum Press.

Guralnick, M.J., & Paul-Brown, D. (1989). Peer-related communicative competence of preschool children: Developmental and adaptive characteristics. *Journal of Speech and Hearing Research, 32*, 930-943.

Hart, B., & Rogers-Warren, A. (1978). A milieu approach to teaching language. In R. Schiefelbusch (Ed.), *Language intervention strategies* (pp. 193-235). Baltimore: University Park Press.

Hubbell, R.D. (1977). On facilitating spontaneous talking in young children. *Journal of Speech and Hearing Disorders, 42*, 216-231.

James, S. (1989). Assessing children with language disorders. In D.K. Bernstein & E. Tiegerman (Eds.), *Language and communication disorders in children* (2nd ed., pp. 157-207). Columbus, OH: Merrill.

*J.F. Kennedy Commands Test.* (no date). Unpublished manuscript. Baltimore: Kennedy Institute for Handicapped Children.

Khan, L.M.L., & Lewis, N.P. (1986). *Khan-Lewis phonological analysis.* Circle Pines, MN: American Guidance Service.

King, R.R., Jones, C., & Lasky, E. (1982). In retrospect: A fifteen-year follow-up report on speech-language disordered children. *Language, Speech, and Hearing Services in Schools, 13*, 24-32.

Lee, A.D., & Shapero-Fine, J. (1984). When a language problem is primary: Secondary school strategies. In G.P. Wallach & K.G. Butler (Eds.), *Language learning disabilities in school-age children* (pp. 338-359). Baltimore: Williams & Wilkins.

Lee, L.L. (1974). *Developmental sentence analysis.* Evanston, IL: Northwestern University Press.

Lewkowicz, N.K. (1980). Phonemic awareness training: What to teach and how to teach it. *Journal of Educational Psychology, 72,* 686-700.

Liberman, I. (1983). A language oriented view of reading and its disabilities. In H.R. Myklebust (Ed.), *Progress in learning disabilities* (Vol. 5, pp. 81-102). New York: Grune & Stratton.

Lundberg, I. (1988). Preschool prevention of reading failure: Does training in phonological awareness work? In R.L. Masland & M.W. Masland (Eds.), *Preschool prevention of reading failure* (pp. 163-176). Parkton, MD: York Press.

Lundberg, I., Olofsson, A., & Wall, S. (1980). Reading and spelling skills in the first school years predicted from phonemic awareness skills in kindergarten. *Scandinavian Journal of Psychology, 11,* 1-15.

Marvin, C.A. (1987). Consultation services: Changing roles for SLP's. *Journal of Childhood Communication Disorders, 11,* 1-15.

Maxwell, S.E., & Wallach, G.P. (1984). The language-learning disabilities connection: Symptoms of early language disability change over time. In G.P. Wallach & K.G. Butler (Eds.), *Language learning disabilities in school-age children* (pp. 15-33). Baltimore: Williams & Wilkins.

McLean, J. (1989). A language-communication intervention model. In D.K. Bernstein & E. Tiegerman (Eds.), *Language and communication disorders* (2nd ed., pp. 208-228). Columbus, OH: Merrill.

Miller, J., & Yoder, D. (1974). An ontogenetic language teaching strategy for retarded children. In R. Schiefelbusch & L. Lloyd (Eds.), *Language perspectives: Acquisition, retardation, and intervention* (pp. 505-527). Baltimore: University Park Press.

Miller, L. (1989). Classroom-based language intervention. *Language, Speech, and Hearing Services in Schools, 20,* 153-169.

Milosky, L.M. (1987). Narratives in the classroom. *Seminars in Speech and Language, 8,* 329-343.

National Joint Committee on Learning Disabilities. (1987). Learning disabilities and the preschool child. *Asha, 29,* 35-38.

Nelson, N.W. (1988). *Planning individualized speech and language intervention programs: Objectives for infants, children, and adolescents.* Tucson, AZ: Communication Skill Builders.

Nelson, N. W. (1989a). Curriculum-based language assessment and intervention. *Language, Speech, and Hearing Services in Schools, 20,* 170-184.

Nelson, N. W. (1989b). Language intervention in school settings. In D.K. Bernstein & E. Tiegerman (Eds.), *Language and communication disorders in children* (2nd ed., pp. 417-468). Columbus, OH: Merrill.

Page, J.L., & Stewart, S.R. (1985). Story grammar skills in school-age children. *Topics in Language Disorders*, *5*, 16-30.

Paul-Brown, D. (1986). *Phonemic Awareness Test*. Unpublished manuscript.

Paul-Brown, D. (1988). A classroom-based model of language intervention for preschool language-impaired children: Principles and procedures. *Annals of Dyslexia*, *38*, 193-207.

Paul-Brown, D., & Botuck, D.A. (1989, March). *Teacher language: Enhancing the instructional environment of learning disabled students*. Paper presented at the annual conference of the New York Branch of the Orton Dyslexia Society, New York.

Pearl, R., Donahue, M., & Bryan, T. (1986). Social relationships of learning-disabled children. In J.K. Torgeson & B.Y.L. Wong (Eds.), *Psychological and educational perspectives on learning disabilities* (pp. 193-224). Orlando, FL: Academic Press.

Public Law 94-142. (1977, August). Implementation of Part B of the Education of the Handicapped Act. *Federal Register*.

Public Law 99-457. (1986, October). Education of Handicapped Amendments of 1986. *Federal Register*.

Ripich, D. N. (Ed.). (1987). Classroom remediation for language-impaired children [Special issue]. *Seminars in Speech and Language*, *8*.

Roth, F.P., & Paul-Brown, D. (1988). *The nature of story narration abilities in young language-impaired children*. Unpublished manuscript.

Roth, F. P., & Spekman, N.J. (1984). Assessing the pragmatic abilities of children: Part 1. Organizational framework and assessment parameters. *Journal of Speech and Hearing Disorders*, *49*, 2-11.

Roth, F.P., & Spekman, N.J. (1986). Narrative discourse: Spontaneously generated stories of learning-disabled and normally achieving students. *Journal of Speech and Hearing Disorders*, *51*, 8-23.

Roth, F.P., & Spekman, N.J. (1989). The oral syntactic proficiency of learning disabled students: A spontaneous speech sampling analysis. *Journal of Speech and Hearing Research*, *32*, 67-77.

Sawyer, D.J. (1987). *Test of Awareness of Language Segments*. Rockville, MD: Aspen.

Sawyer, D.J. (1988). Studies of the effects of teaching auditory segmenting skills within the reading program. In R.L. Masland & M.W. Masland (Eds.), *Preschool prevention of reading failure* (pp. 121-142). Parkton, MD: York Press.

Simon, C.S. (1987a). *Classroom communication screening procedure for early adolescents: A handbook for assessment and intervention*. Tempe, AZ: Communi-cog.

Simon, C.S. (Ed.). (1987b). Making the collaborative consultation model work: The speech-language pathologist as consultant and teacher in mainstream education [Special issue]. *Journal of Childhood Communication Disorders*, *11*(1).

Simon, C.S. (1987c). Out of the broom closet and into the classroom: The emerging SLP. *Journal of Childhood Communication Disorders, 11*, 41-66.

Snow, C., Midkiff-Borunda, S., Small, A., & Proctor, A. (1984). Therapy as social interaction: Analyzing the contexts for language remediation. *Topics in Language Disorders, 4*, 72-85.

Snyder, L.S., & Silverstein, J. (1988). Pragmatics and child language disorders. In R.L. Schiefelbusch & L.L. Lloyd (Eds.), *Language perspectives: Acquisition, retardation, and intervention* (2nd ed., pp. 189-222). Austin, TX: Pro-Ed.

Snyder-McLean, L., & McLean, J.E. (1987). Effectiveness of early intervention for children with language and communication disorders. In M.J. Guralnick & F.C. Bennett (Eds.), *The effectiveness of early intervention for at-risk and handicapped children*. New York: Academic Press.

Spekman, N.J. (1983). Preschool language assessment. In C. Dunst (Ed.), *Infant and preschool assessment: Reliability, validity, and utility*. Baltimore: University Park Press.

Stanovich, K.E., Cunningham, A.E., & Cramer, B.B. (1984). Assessing phonological awareness in kindergarten children: Issues of task comparability. *Journal of Experimental Child Psychology, 38*, 175-190.

Stark, R.E., Bernstein, L.E., & Condino, R. (1984). Four-year follow-up study of language-impaired children. *Annals of Dyslexia, 34*, 29-48.

Taenzer, S.F., Cermak, C., & Hanlon, R.C. (1981). Outside the therapy room: A naturalistic approach to language intervention. In J.M. Panagos (Ed.), *Language intervention with the learning disabled, 1*(2), 41-46.

Tallal, P. (1987). Developmental language disorders. In *Learning disabilities: A report to the U.S. Congress*. Washington, DC: Interagency Committee on Learning Disabilities.

Terman, L.M., & Merrill, M.A. (1973). *Stanford-Binet Intelligence Scale-Revised*. Boston: Houghton Mifflin.

Vellutino, F. (1979). *Dyslexia: Theory and research*. Cambridge, MA: MIT Press.

Wallach, G.P., & Miller, L. (1988). *Language intervention and academic success*. Boston: College-Hill Press.

Warren, S.F., & Kaiser, A.P. (1986). Incidental language teaching: A critical review. *Journal of Speech and Hearing Disorders, 51*, 29-299.

Westby, C.E. (1984). Development of narrative language abilities. In G.P. Wallach & K.G. Butler (Eds.), *Language learning disabilities in school-age children* (pp. 103-127). Baltimore: Williams & Wilkins.

Westby, C.E. (1985). Learning to talk–talking to learn: Oral-literate language differences. In C.S. Simon (Ed.), *Communication skills and classroom success: Therapy methodologies for language-learning disabled students* (pp. 181-213). San Diego: College-Hill Press.

Wiig, E.H., & Semel, E.M. (1984). *Language assessment and intervention for the learning disabled* (2nd ed.). Columbus, OH: Charles E. Merrill.

Zimmerman, I.K., Steiner, V.G., & Pond, R.E. (1979). *Preschool Language Scale: Revised edition*. Columbus, OH: Charles E. Merrill.

# Appendix A: Preschool Language Intervention Goals/Strategies/Activities

I.   **VOCABULARY AND CONCEPT DEVELOPMENT**

A.   Increase use of precise, diverse expressive vocabulary with the following teaching strategies:

   1.   Require use of specificity and precision in word choice.

   - Limit child's use of "this," "that," "there."
   - Use referential communication tasks to increase child's use of specific vocabulary (e.g., A child can describe a picture hidden from the view of a peer. The peer then attempts to create the same picture based on the oral description).

   2.   Teach observation of facial cues so a child knows when to clarify a word.

   Encourage a child to change a misunderstood word by:

   - using a related word.
   - pronouncing the misunderstood word more clearly.
   - choosing a more specific, or precise word.

   3.   Teach the use of word-finding strategies such as:

   - recalling function.
   - using related words.
   - using word in carrier phrase.
   - making word associations.
   - recalling word categories.
   - chunking related information.

   4.   Increase variety and specificity of vocabulary by teaching a child to:

   - classify and categorize objects and pictures.

- name words in different categories (e.g., organization of types of clothing by season).
- discuss related words by function, similarity (synonyms), difference (antonyms).
- use comparatives and superlatives appropriately.
- ask for clarification or provide clarification when a referent is not clear (e.g., giving precise directions during referential communication tasks; recognizing when more specific information is needed and asking for it).

B.  Increase appropriate use of time-related concepts. A child should:

- discuss events by talking about what comes "before," "next," "after," or what happened "yesterday," "today."
- categorize objects and activities according to times of day–"morning," "afternoon," "evening."
- put pictures in sequence and talk about "first," "second," "third," "last."

C.  Increase a child's ability to recognize and express emotions related to a child's inner state and perceptions of another child's feelings. A teacher should:

- talk about consequences of words and actions (e.g., when you say __, that child feels ___); talk about things to say that won't hurt another person's feelings.
- express feelings when events occur that make a child feel particular emotions like anger (e.g., "Don't take my toy; that makes me feel angry").
- discuss different types of emotions and what each part of the face and body looks like (e.g., When you're happy, your eyes ____, your mouth looks like ____, your body looks like ____, you feel ___).
- discuss different emotions in different situations (e.g., Happiest moment? Saddest moment? When did you feel surprise? Anger?).

## II.  COMPREHENSION OF ORALLY PRESENTED DIRECTIONS

Increase ability to follow multipart commands to aid in following directions in the classroom using the following teaching strategies:

A.  Gain child's attention.

B.  Systematically increase length and complexity of command for child to follow:

- one object, one action.
  Example: "Touch the book."
- one action, two objects.
  Example: "Touch the ball and the book."
- two objects, two actions.
  Example: "Kick the ball and open the book."
- three objects, three actions.
  Example: "Throw the ball, open the book, and clap your hands."

C.  Vary the use of related with unrelated commands.

Example: "Push car" vs. "Push book."

D.  Vary the use of naturally sequential with nonsequential directions.

Example:     "Stand up, walk to the board, and pick up the chalk" vs. "Pick up the chalk, open the book, and sit down."

E.  Teach strategies to aid in recall.

- visual imagery
- verbal rehearsal
- key words

**General Procedures:**

Encourage the use of recall strategies to enable children to follow directions during ongoing classroom activities.

Encourage children to retell information presented by peers during "Sharing time" when children talk about themselves (e.g., trips, family, pets).

Have children give and follow directions to each other as a means to solve a maze or puzzle.

III. **CONVERSATIONAL SKILLS**

Increase use of appropriate conversational conventions in different situations during interactions with peers and adults.

A.  Communicative Functions (intentions)

Increase use of language to convey different communicative intentions (i.e., use language for different purposes):

1.  Social greetings
    Example: "Hi. How are you?"
2.  Giving information
    Example: "This is a big ball."
3.  Getting information
    Example: "What's this?"
4.  Describing an ongoing event
    Example: "Billy is running."
5.  Getting a listener to do, believe, or feel something
    Example: "Touch this turtle."
6.  Expressing one's own intentions, beliefs, or feelings
    Example: "I don't like that."
7.  Indicating readiness for further communication
    Example: "And what's this?"
8.  Solving problems
    Example: "This goes here and that goes there."
9.  Entertaining
    Example: "I'm gonna tell you a joke."
    Increase comprehension and use of language of humor.
    (Communicative intents based on Chapman, 1981)

**General Procedures**:

Encourage use of diverse communicative intentions during ongoing classroom activities. Provide appropriate models and varying opportunities for talk. Set up role-play situations to provide opportunities to practice a variety of communicative functions.

Conversational interactions may be structured to encourage use of utterances for different purposes. Opportunities should also be provided to teach different ways that utterances may be used depending on the listener and situation (e.g., "Get over here now" vs. "Please come here").

B.  Seeking and Providing Information

Increase appropriate responses to questions by providing sufficient related information. Ask appropriate questions to obtain information.

1.  Response to questions

- Discuss type of response expected for different types of "Wh" questions: "Who," "What," "When," "Where"; then provide relevant responses to different types of questions.
- Give specific responses to questions (e.g., use referential communication tasks or "barrier" games, where another child asks for specific information to create matching pictures; a barrier placed between the children prevents direct observation).

2.  Asking questions

- Recognize unknown information and ask relevant questions (e.g., follow directions given by a peer hidden by a barrier).

**General Procedures:**

Encourage child to provide follow-up responses to give more elaborate, detailed information in response to a question. Encourage child to organize or limit talk when response is tangential or disorganized.

Give time and remind peers to give others time to formulate answers or to initiate information.

C.  Conversational Conventions

1.  Turn-taking

During structured activities when a teacher is leading a group, a child should:

- raise his/her hand to talk.
- not talk when someone else is talking.
- give other children a chance to talk.

During unstructured activities with peers or adults, a child should:

- not talk when someone else is talking.
- alternate talking time with the conversational partner.

2.  Topic establishment and maintenance

Increase child's ability to follow four conversational rules (Grice, 1975):

a)  *Be informative*

A child should:

- provide background information when necessary (e.g., if a child mentions someone's name during conversation, the child should tell who the person is, if the conversational partner does not know ["Ian and I went to the park–Ian's my brother."]).
- provide only as much information as is needed–not more, not less; a child should learn not to say too much or too little.
- initiate conversations in order to share information with peers and adults about past events and present activities.

b)  *Be truthful*

A child should:

- talk about what he/she knows (e.g., children should raise their hands to answer a question when they know the answer); if a child does not know an answer, he/she should learn to say, "I don't know," rather than staring and giving no response or giving inaccurate information.

c)  *Be relevant*

A child should:

- answer questions directly when asked by a peer or adult.
- be responsive and give answers that are relevant to the ongoing topic.
- use topic-changing signals (e.g., say, "Now I'd like to talk about...").

d)  *Be clear*

A child should:

- be brief and orderly when talking.
- provide information in an appropriate sequence.
- talk at an appropriate rate (e.g., not too fast) to help speech intelligibility.

3.  Gaze and proximity

    Increase a child's ability to look directly at a peer or adult when talking (i.e., establish appropriate eye contact). A child should learn to stand or sit close enough to a conversational partner to make each person feel comfortable and learn not to get too close or stand too far away.

4.  Interruptions

    Increase a child's ability to wait to talk when someone else is talking or interrupt in a polite way (e.g., say, "Excuse me," or touch a teacher gently).

5.  Repair or clarification strategies

    Increase a child's ability to ask an adult or a peer for clarification (e.g., "Huh?" "What did you say?") when a message is not understood. A child should also learn to repeat a message more clearly when he/she is not understood.

**General Procedures:**

Encourage use of appropriate conversational conventions during ongoing classroom activities. Language expectations differ for different classroom activities (e.g., teacher-directed circle time and presentation vs. child-directed free-play). Provide appropriate models as necessary when conversational difficulties occur.

Have conversational time ("talk time") to encourage discussion of past, present, and future events. Have particular themes or script notions (e.g., going to a restaurant, going to the zoo, getting ready for bed). An activity board or table may be center of talk. "Show and tell" time may be used to encourage recall and description.

Provide reminders to stay on topic (e.g., "We're talking about _____ now") and to signal topic shifts appropriately.

D.  Peer Interactions

    Develop skills to improve and increase appropriate peer interactions. A child will demonstrate an ability to:

    ■   initiate conversational interactions with peers.

- tell a peer to do something and use adaptive strategies if the companion does not comply.
- tell a companion directly when not pleased with a companion's behavior rather than telling the teacher.
- respond appropriately to questions posed by a peer.
- use utterances appropriately to include a peer in a play situation (e.g., "Come play with me") or exclude a peer in a polite way (e.g., "Let's play later").
- make prosocial statements when another child is hurt (e.g., "I'm sorry").

**General Procedures**:

Set up situations to encourage a child to initiate an interaction with peers. Suggested activities include: passing out items at snack or lunch time and asking peers what items they need; having a child tell a story to another child; having a child describe an art project to another child; setting up tutorial situations where a child teaches a peer how to play with a particular toy; set up peer dyads and give instructions like, "Tell _____ how to _____," "Try to get _____ to say _____."

Model appropriate interaction for a child ("Tell Bill, 'Please take turns.'")

Set up role-play situations to highlight critical incidents.

Examples:

- Child wants another child's toy.
- Child wants to use the occupied swings.
- Child wants peer to stop an inappropriate behavior.

Children should role-play such events and respond to prompts such as "What would you say?" "What could you do next?" Set up problem-solving situations.

- Teach children to help each other accomplish a specific task.

## IV. NARRATIVE SKILLS

To improve narrative discourse ability, increase recall of stories, ability to generate stories, and ability to explain personal events.

A. Exposure to stories

- Listen to well-formed stories.

- Answer questions to reconstruct stories.
- Order sequential pictures to create stories.

B.  Prediction skills

- Identify cause-effect relationships.
- Discuss connections critical to stories.
- Discuss related experiential activities.
- Sort scrambled stories.
- Complete a partially presented story.
- Tell own story.

C.  Story-grammar strategy

- Identify story-grammar components and relationships.
- Sort and sequence story elements.
- Use self-questioning techniques to monitor completeness and organization of story (strategies based on Page & Stewart, 1985).

D.  Recall of daily events in sequence

- Follow pictures presented in sequence and retell events of day.
- Arrange pictures of daily events in sequence.
- Respond to questions of daily events given organizational framework, "The first thing you did... ."
- Produce school-day story book.

E.  Recall of past events in sequence

- Draw pictures and tell about past events (e.g., vacation, weekend plans, field trips, holidays).
- Act out past events (e.g., charades).

F.  Sequential task

- Arrange pictures in order and follow actual steps to create a product (e.g., baking a potato, making fruit salad, making trail mix, cooking soup, baking cookies, making popcorn, making a sandwich, planting a seed).
- Arrange pictures and talk about daily events in sequence (e.g., brushing teeth, getting dressed, going to bed).

V.  **METALINGUISTIC SKILLS** (Phonemic Awareness)

To increase phonemic awareness skills, a child should:

- listen to books read by an adult on a regular basis.
- recognize and produce words that rhyme.
- recognize and produce sounds that correspond to letters.
- use manipulatives to segment words into syllables.
- use manipulatives to segment words into phonemes.
- identify position of sound in word.
- blend sounds into words after listening to words presented as syllable or sound segments.

# Appendix B: General Suggestions to Enhance Teacher-Student Communication: Speaking Mode

A.  **Rate of Speech**: The rate of the teacher's speech may interfere with a student's comprehension of the task if the rate is too fast or too slow.

### SUGGESTIONS:

1.  Variety of rate is important to maintain a student's attention.
2.  If a teacher's rate is fast, it may be necessary to rephrase more often.
3.  Use a slower rate of speech to present new information.
4.  Have pauses between major segments of information.

B.  **Intonation**: Variations in pitch and stress may change meaning. "Go over this. Go *over* it;" "I *told* you not to do that." "You said I could." "No, I told you *not* to do that."

### SUGGESTIONS:

1.  Vary intonation appropriately to make meaning clear.
2.  Make student aware of the reason for utilizing different vocal tone; listening for intonation is important because changes in intonation change meaning (e.g., "I said it that way to get your attention," or "I said it that way because I want you to know I'm serious," or "I said that jokingly").

C.  **Amount**: An excessive amount of talk by teachers may prompt students to stop listening.

### SUGGESTIONS:

1.  Limit the amount and length of information presented.
2.  Provide opportunities for students to use language.
3.  Limit use of irrelevant information.
4.  Consider balance in teacher/student talk ratio.

5. Have a student paraphrase your explanations.
6. Have a student paraphrase *another child's* explanation.

D.   **Loudness**: Loudness level should vary for maximum effectiveness.

1. Speaking softly may be a strategy to gain attention in a noisy room; however, speaking softly for long periods of time may lead to inattentiveness by the student.
2. Speaking in too loud a voice may adversely affect the intelligibility of your speech, especially for students who have auditory figure-ground problems (e.g., unable to distinguish your voice from other sounds in the room).
3. Overstimulation may result from loud voices or distracting room noises; try to keep room noise to a minimum. For the same reason, it would be ineffective to call to a student or give instructions from a distance.
4. Being firm does not necessarily mean being loud.

E.   **Clarity of Speech**: Articulation, rate, word choice, and utterance length may affect clarity of speech.

**SUGGESTIONS**:

1. Speak more slowly or precisely to improve clarity, but don't overarticulate.
2. Repeat an utterance more clearly if misunderstanding occurs, e.g., shorten, rephrase, elaborate, break down into steps, pause between utterances, etc.

F.   **Silence**: Silence may be used effectively to aid understanding by giving students time to think and process the information presented.

**SUGGESTIONS**:

1. Allow pauses or periods of silence to give students an opportunity to formulate responses.
2. Try to use silence as a way to get students' attention.
3. Allow pauses between utterances to let processing "catch up," to let students ponder, or to emphasize a major point.

G.   **Word Choice/Vocabulary**: A teacher's choice of words will influence a student's comprehension level. If a limited vocabulary is used with relatively common words, the opportunity for a student's mastery of new words is limited. On the other hand, extensive use of new words may adversely affect comprehension.

**SUGGESTIONS:**

1. Use new, less familiar words in your sentences to help a student's vocabulary growth. Also use some words that are more difficult or abstract. Use the word in more than one sentence and make meaning clear. Provide contextual cues to make new word meanings clear. Pair new word with a familiar word (e.g., "a lot of/an abundance of").
2. It is important to continue to juxtapose the new word and the meaning to bond the two. (In a book, definitions are given only once, but you can refer back for the meaning. Teachers need to be referring back to the meaning constantly because a student's short-term memory may be deficient.)
3. Try to refrain from using too many new words back to back.
4. Be specific in word choice. Limit use of words like "thing."
5. Limit use of fillers like "you know," "so."

H.   **Syntax:**  A teacher's use of appropriate syntax may make it easier for students to understand explanations.

**SUGGESTIONS:**

1. Use a mixture of simple and complex sentences appropriate for the language level of the student.
2. Provide extended time for processing when complex sentences are used. Alternate simple and complex sentences to aid comprehension.
3. Give more opportunities for review and use more checks of comprehension when complex sentences are presented.
4. Modifying syntax does not mean "talking down" to students. Rather, it means using relevant language that students can understand and providing models for advancement of their language.
5. Passive constructions (e.g., "The club was formed by all the interested students") and embedded (e.g., "Before going to the back of the room, get the chalk"; "The book that the first-period teacher was reading is the one I want you to get") are syntactically and conceptually more complex than active, simple sentences. (Based in part on Gruenewald & Pollak, 1984.)

# 2
# Linguistic Transitions in Children and Adolescents with Language Learning Disabilities: Characteristics and Training

Elisabeth H. Wiig

## Language Competence and Metalinguistic Ability

Adult competence in language is hard to describe. Yet everyone knows when it is present in an adult and when it is missing. Children with normal language development reach a level of language competence close to that of adults between the ages of 11 and 13 years. We recognize immediately that some of the acquired language competence is lost when an adult suffers a left-hemisphere stroke with resulting aphasia. We recognize that language competence is reduced after traumatic head injury. We also recognize that some individuals with developmental and cognitive handicaps never attain what we consider adult competence in language. Let us therefore take a closer look at the abilities that are involved.

Most important among the linguistic attainments that indicate language competence and metalinguistic maturity is the ability to view "language as object" (Menyuk, 1983), in other words, to be able to use language as a tool that is distinct and separate from one's person. This distancing allows the language user to analyze words, phrases, sentences, and intents. It also allows the language user to superimpose strategic thinking onto internalized linguistic repertoires to maximize efficiency in communication.

There are other attainments that are important. They are more closely tied to the linguistic domains of semantics, syntax, and pragmatics. In the area of semantics, the transition to language competence and metalinguistic ability is characterized by increasing knowledge of vocabulary and concepts, awareness of the multiple meanings and uses of words, knowledge of the semantic relations among words and of the possible combinations of words for expressing thoughts and ideas (Owens, 1988; Wiig & Secord, 1991).

In the area of pragmatics, and subsumed under this in the area of syntax, there is improved sociolinguistic awareness and knowledge that is reflected in code switching and perspective taking in speaker-listener interactions. Interfacing with the linguistic attainments is an increasing ability to relate spoken information to one's own past experiences and internalized knowledge and to make inferences.

If the transition from linguistic skill-based communication to strategic language use (metalinguistic behavior) is delayed or does not take place, the negative impact on learning and living can be drastic. Recent investigations indicate that the majority of students in the age range from 8 to 12 years with diagnosed learning disabilities, perhaps as many as 90%, exhibit language disorders (Gibbs & Cooper, 1989). At the same time, only a small proportion, perhaps as low as 6%, of these children receive the services of a speech-language pathologist. With these discouraging data as a background, we shall now take a look at the interfaces between language, academic achievement, and the demands of the traditional curriculum.

## Language and Curriculum

Halliday (1978) comments on the interaction between language and academic achievement as follows:

> Suppose that [language] functions that are relatively stressed [or acquired] by one group are positive with respect to school. They are favored and extended in the educational process, while those that are relatively stressed [or acquired] by another group are largely irrelevant or even negative in the educational context. We have, then, a plausible interpretation of the role of language in educational failure. (p. 106)

As suggested earlier, the stage is set for the majority of the students with diagnosed learning disabilities to experience educational failure. The normal developmental pattern raises expectations that children will progress through major stages in the approach to problem solving (cognition) and communication (linguistics) (Flavell, 1963; Inhelder & Piaget, 1964; Menyuk, 1983; Piaget, 1952, 1968, 1970). At the same time, grade related changes in the curriculum require a shift towards language competence and metalinguistic ability to respond to the increasing demands for cognitive, linguistic, social, and emotional maturity.

## Progressions in the Curriculum

The changes in the curriculum can be summarized as follows (Wiig & Semel, 1984). The preschool curriculum focuses on language development and social-emotional growth. Auditory, visual, visual-spatial, and motor skills are taught in a sensorimotor approach with concrete, manipulative, and three-dimensional materials.

The early grades (K-2) emphasize preoperational cognitive attainments. Basic academic skills for reading, writing, spelling, and arithmetic are taught. Teaching materials are primarily one-dimensional. The curriculum content is more abstract with symbolic representations. It is at this level that students with language-learning disabilities tend to experience their first academic failures.

During the middle years (grades 3-4), basic skills are reviewed, but no longer taught. Content areas such as social studies and science are emphasized. Students are expected to use symbolic and linguistic skills to abstract, analyze, and synthesize information. This requires concrete operational cognitive skills and emerging metalinguistic abilities. At this level, the achievement gap in language-based curriculum areas widens for students with language-learning disabilities.

In the upper elementary years (grades 5-6), students are expected to recall information taught earlier and to display fluency and flexibility in using basic academic skills and language. In junior high and high school the demand for formal operational cognitive operations and metalinguistic abilities is increased further. Students are expected to listen to lectures, take notes, and reorganize information cognitively and linguistically. Many of the curriculum requirements for language use are outside the range of performance for many students with language-learning disabilities. The record of academic underachievement therefore broadens.

## Linguistic Transitions

The essence of the linguistic transitions which take place during the school years appears to be a move from relying on linguistic skills and repertoires to applying strategies to the existing linguistic repertoires for communication (Haslett, 1987; Wiig, 1988, 1990; Wiig & Secord, 1988). Stated differently, the transition reflects the difference between functional use of language (linguistic ability) and ability to think and talk about language as an object or entity and to use it in problem solving (metalinguistic ability). To better understand these statements, the terms *skill*, *repertoire*, and *strategy* will be defined (Wiig, 1988, 1990).

A *skill*, as used here, can be defined as a linguistic response, developed and elicited in a one-to-one relationship to a specific stimulus or task. It is often learned in a repetitive or rote fashion, which may or may not include opportunities for generalization. Among early linguistic skills are labeling objects, actions, and attributes.

A *repertoire*, as used here, is a class or set of related linguistic skills, used in response to a set of related stimuli or tasks, according to a rule system. The phonological conditioning rules for noun plurals, noun possessives, and past tense are examples of linguistic repertoires. Variations in sentence structure, which can be used to express the same intent (e.g., telling, asking, commanding), are also examples.

A *strategy*, as used here, can be considered a set of alternative linguistic responses or response options to stimuli or tasks (Restle, 1962; Swanson, 1989). Strategies are inferred over a series of trials in a process. The process involves (a) pattern recognition, (b) hypothesis formulation and testing, (c) formulation of response options or plans of action, (d) selection of the best course of action, and (e) evaluation of the effectiveness relative to the outcome.

An example of strategic communication would be an interaction with an objective such as asking someone for a date. To be effective, the speaker may need to plan for the interaction. He or she may need to revise during the interaction and should evaluate the efficiency on the basis of the outcome.

## Metalinguistic Development

Evidence of the emergence of metalinguistic abilities appears in the late preschool and early elementary grades with the emergence of role taking while communicating intentions (Wiig & Secord, 1988). Some metalinguistic abilities show the greatest development during the middle childhood years and are linked with cognitive changes that reflect the emergence of concrete operational thought (Hakes, 1980). This seems to be the case for aspects of metalinguistic ability required to segment words into phonological (phonemes) and meaning units (morphemes) and seeing relationships between spoken and written words.

Yet, other aspects of metalinguistic ability appear to change most drastically during the period from 8 or 9 to 11 or 13 years, the period associated with late concrete operational and early formal operational thought. Among them are the ability to interpret ambiguities in sentences, figurative language, jokes, and sarcasm, and to plan for spoken or written language production. There seem to be similarities in the pattern of the linguistic transitions across these dimensions of language and communication. Prerequisite linguistic skills and repertoires appear to be acquired at ages 6 to 7 years. Recognition of the need to apply a strategy appears at about ages 8 to 9 years, but communication is not yet strategic or metalinguistically mature. Spontaneous use of strategies for interpretation and communication appears in place at about ages 11 to 13 years (Allen & Brown, 1977; Alvy, 1973; Anglin, 1977; Asch & Nerlove, 1960; Delia & Clark, 1977; Mathinos, 1988; Nippold, Cuyler, & Braunbeck-Price, 1988; Wiig, 1989, 1990; Wiig, Gilbert, & Christian, 1978; Wiig & Secord, 1988; Winner, Rosenstiel, & Gardner, 1976). We shall now take a more detailed look at the early approaches used by children to acquire a vocabulary, sentence structure rules, and pragmatic rules and repertoires.

## Semantic Strategies

The child's early acquisition of words and meanings is guided by operating principles and approaches (Crais, 1990; Wiig & Secord, 1991). The overriding principle used for creating meaning for early words is that in the language there is only one form for expressing a given meaning. A second principle is that if one meaning has already been assigned to a word, a second meaning cannot be attached to the same word. A third principle is to look for differences among word meanings rather than for similarities. A fourth, somewhat later, principle is that if the meanings of two words are different and yet related in some way, then it should be assumed that the words are complementary terms (ungradable contrasts), as in the case of the words "boy-girl."

These operating principles or tactics serve the child well in acquiring a large vocabulary rapidly. However, the exclusive use of these principles has to be broken before the child can acquire multiple-meaning words and synonymy, prerequisites for figurative language and metalinguistic maturation. To complete the transitions in the semantic domain, the learner must modify or add to the early principles. One addition is to incorporate the principle that there may be two word forms for expressing a given meaning (synonymy). A second is that if one meaning has been attached to a word, a second meaning that relates to a distinctly different referential context may be attached to the same word (multiple-meaning words).

A more complex operational principle must be added to account for the transition to figurative language ability. The acquisition of strategies for interpreting metaphoric expressions presupposes a process of moving from literal, referential interpretations of words and phrases to abstract, psychological interpretations. In this process, meaning is transferred by analogy or other means. The process is obvious in the acquisition of metaphors (Billow, 1975, 1977; Gardner, Kircher, Winner, & Perkins, 1975; Nippold, Leonard, & Kail, 1984; Pollio & Pollio, 1979; Winner, Rosenstiel, & Gardner, 1976).

In the process of developing preferences for metaphoric endings, ages 3 to 4 constitute a predevelopmental stage in the acquisition of preferences for metaphoric endings in which choices are inappropriate. At age 7, literal endings are generally preferred over metaphoric endings. At age 12, conventional and appropriate metaphoric endings are selected and they are often embellished. At age 19, metaphoric endings are preferred and conventional endings are elaborated upon, indicating metaphoric maturity (Gardner, Kircher, Winner, & Perkins, 1975).

## Deficits in Semantic Development

Recent research has substantiated that children and adolescents with learning disabilities may be delayed in the acquisition of the semantic repertoires and strategies that constitute metalinguistic ability. Delays have been observed in the acquisition of strategies for interpreting sentences with lexical ambiguities (Wiig & Secord, 1986a, 1988) and metaphoric expressions (Nippold & Fey, 1983; Wiig & Secord 1986a, 1988). Delays have also been observed for making inferences on the basis of linguistic information (Wiig & Secord, 1988). The delays can be observed already in learning disabled (LD) children in the early elementary grades. This is because the prerequisite semantic repertoires are significantly delayed in their emergence. In relation to the operational principles for constructing word knowledge, the child with a language-learning disability seems to adhere to early approaches or tactics by assigning one meaning to each word and one word to each referent beyond the expected age or developmental level. Furthermore, they seem to construct word meanings by considering differences in meaning more than similarities in meaning. The resulting delays are in the acquisition of semantic networks and semantic relations among words (e. g., directional opposition, complementarities, antonyms, converseness, orthogonal opposition, hyponymy, collectives, synonymy, semantic sets). There are also delays in the acquisition of multiple meanings for words and sentences and in figurative language development.

Interpretations of metaphoric expressions by preadolescents and adolescents with language-learning disabilities are often literal or partial and metaphors are confused as in saying that "She cast a spell over him" means "She turned him into a toad." When asked to match metaphoric expressions for their common meaning and intent, they are trapped by form and/or content and select expressions that are similar either in wordings or in structure (Wiig & Secord, 1986a).

## Syntax and Pragmatics

The young child also acquires knowledge of the structure of the native language in an active construction process. The process is activated by mental strategies for segmenting sentences into their smallest constituents. One of the earliest approaches or strategies for segmenting sentences may be that whenever a function word (e.g., determiner, preposition, conjunction, pronoun, quantifier) is encountered, a new constituent larger than one word is begun (Clark & Clark, 1977; Kimball, 1973). This approach is later modified and expanded to account for subordination and relativization by stating that the unit after the conjunction or relative pronoun is a new clause.

A corollary to this early operational principle is that the first constituent, generally marked by a determiner, functions as the noun phrase. The second constituent functions as the verb phrase. If there is a second noun phrase it is a direct object.

A second operational principle is to look for content words that are appropriate for the type of constituent identified by the beginning of the constituent. During development, this principle is modified and expanded to account for, among others, identification of complements and subordinate and coordinate conjunctions. The third operational principle is to use affixes to help decide if a content word is a noun, verb, adjective, or adverb. There are four additional operational principles that shall not be covered here. With the three early operational principles the child can construct the six basic sentence structures in English. Using adaptations and expansions of the early principles, the child can progress to higher level transformations and syntactic maturity.

The acquisition of strategies for interpersonal communication can be viewed as a process of acquiring script (underlying schemata) and moving from a self-oriented to an other-oriented perspective. These changes take place in an attempt to produce recognizable scripts and achieve a shared speaker-listener orientation (perspective) for effectiveness. Politeness dimensions and shared perspective are achieved by changing semantic and syntactic features such as forms of pronouns and verb phrases (e.g., use of modals or remote verb tense). These adaptations are also called code switching or social-register changes.

The developmental progression in social-register changing and perspective taking can be delineated in five major stages. The example that will be used to illustrate the sequence is for requests for action (e. g., asking for help to carry something). At Stage 1 (age 6), a child's requests reflect a self-centered approach and show little evidence of stylistic adaptation, regardless of who the listener is. At Stage 2 (around age 7), the perception of the listener as a controlling variable and of listener characteristic emerges, but the linguistic style is not yet fully adapted to the listener. At Stage 3 (around age 8), a growing orientation towards others may result in insecurity and failure to communicate effectively. This stage leads to a transition (Stage 4) in which adaptations to listener characteristics, needs, or perspectives are in evidence, but are not yet mature. At Stage 5 (around age 12), perspective taking is in evidence and the communication style is adapted effectively by changing social register or code switching. At this age, syntactic maturity is also expected.

Loban (1976) summarizes the features of less efficient communicators. They are:

- Lack of fluency (i.e., rapid and consistent ability to find words to express semantic intent).
- Lack of coherence (i.e., ability to plan and organize the content of a message before it is communicated).
- Lack of effectiveness and control (i.e., ability to master conventional grammar and use a variety of structural patterns and to express higher level concepts or ideas by using conditional statements).

Among less efficient communicators, these features of incom-petence persisted over the period of 13 years of Loban's study. These cardinal features also describe the communicative behaviors of students with learning disabilities and language disorders(language-learning disabilities).

There are numerous accounts of the nature of syntactic and pragmatic delays associated with language-learning disabilities (Donahue, Pearl, & Bryan, 1982; Mathinos, 1988; Ripich & Spinelli, 1985; Simon, 1985; Wallach & Butler, 1984; Wiig & Semel, 1976, 1980, 1984). The characteristics have been summarized aptly by Simon (1979). She provides a listing of features of incompetence in relation to the form, function, and style of communication. We shall consider only a few examples that relate to strategy acquisition and metalinguistic maturation.

To explore ability to plan and organize a message before it is communicated (coherence), Wiig & Secord (1986b, 1988) used a task of recreating spoken intents (speech acts). Children and adolescents with language-learning disabilities were asked to recreate what a child, adolescent, or adult could have said in a pictured context with given word choices. Children, ages 4 to 9, were given only two word choices for each illustrated context. Preadolescents and adolescents, ages 9 to 18, were given three words, one of which forced a complex sentence (e.g., if, because, before, after, although). The younger LLD children violated basic semantic-syntactic rules in their productions. Further-more, they were often unable to do the role-taking required for the task. Their age peers with normal language development were well able to role play. This suggests significant differences in the emergence of metalinguistic prerequisites in the two groups. The older students with language-learning disabilities violated either syntactic features (e.g., "either" must occur before "or" in the structure) or semantic implications associated with the words (e.g., "but" signifies that the two propositions being conjoined must express a contrast) (Wiig & Secord, 1986b). These findings again point to delays in syntactic-pragmatic and metalinguistic abilities.

Studies of discourse, narrative, descriptive communication, and ability to express complex intentions among students with language-learning disabilities support the presence of pragmatic deficits. Children and adolescents with language-learning disabilities seem to experience the greatest problems at the level of cohesion, related to the surface structure, both in narrative and discourse production (Donahue, 1985). When LLD students engage in discourse with their classmates, the willingness of classmates to listen seems to be influenced more negatively by production factors such as dysfluencies and false starts rather than by the level of complexity of the narrative. Within a broader perspective, teenagers with language-learning disabilities have been observed to be deficient in the social-cognitive and linguistic strategies required to carry out persuasive appeals (Donahue, 1985).

## Behavioral Observations

There are also behavioral features in the linguistic performances of preadolescents and adolescents with language-learning disabilities that point to delays in the acquisition of linguistic competence and strategic language use.

First, the responses are often immediate and little time is taken for reflecting before responding. This pattern suggests impulsivity in responding. Second, the responses may be significantly delayed (30 seconds or more). This pattern suggests that processing, problem solving, and/or planning processes are inefficient or ineffective.

Other behavioral observations reflect problems at specific levels of processing linguistic stimuli and problem solving with linguistic input. First, targeting of the significant features in the linguistic stimuli or communicative context is often in error or inefficient. The wrong words or phrases are often considered to be significant in multiple-meaning sentences, jokes, sarcastic remarks, or figurative expressions. This leads to erroneous or partial conclusions and responses. In a similar vein, the wrong variables or factors are often considered to be significant in interpersonal communication. As an example, if an adult authority figure wears informal clothing, the peer register rather than the authority register may be used for communication, often leading to rejection by the listener.

Second, there is a tendency to generate only one hypothesis or alternative in response to a linguistic stimulus or communicative context. This tendency is inadequate in situations where there are several response options or alternatives, as is the case in interpersonal communication (pragmatics). The tendency leads to a single course of action, not always the most efficient or appropriate one. Third, hypotheses and responses are not always evaluated. As a result, responses are not revised or repaired when they are incorrect or if the situation or the listener's feedback calls for it. Within the framework of the structure of intellect model (Guilford, 1967) the lack of alternative hypotheses, action plans, or responses suggest deficiencies in fluency, flexibility, originality, and elaboration (divergent production). Within the framework of information processing and hypothesis theory (Bruner, Olver, & Greenfield, 1966; Estes, 1970; Hagen, 1972; Neisser, 1967), the same behaviors suggest inadequacies in cognitive-linguistic strategy acquisition.

In everyday interactions inadequacies in cognitive-linguistic strategy acquisition and use can have negative consequences. Language-learning disabled students are often perceived by others, both in interactions for learning and socialization, to be:

- Inflexible or rigid in their interpretations of and approaches to communication.
- Stubborn and hard to sway by persuasive arguments and proofs.
- Social "klutzes," because they respond inappropriately to multiple meanings, jokes, sarcasm, figurative usage.
- Insensitive to other people's feelings, because they fail to take their perspective or to show perspective-taking in language and communication.
- Concrete and unable to catch implications and to make the right inferences in verbal interactions.
- Defensive in their communication posture, suggesting behavior problems or abnormal affective reactions.

- Unable to express their real feelings and reactions, resulting in secondary emotional problems that may compound the linguistic and social inadequacies. (Wiig & Secord, 1987)

# Models for Language Intervention

## Assessment

Language intervention to support the linguistic transitions to metalinguistic maturity and strategic language use cannot be planned unless language assessment is designed to establish the existing point in the linguistic transition. The procedures selected for assessment must be sensitive to the cognitive-linguistic shifts associated with the middle school years and adolescence. Procedures must be selected that emphasize evaluation of flexibility, divergent production, planning and organization, and strategic language use.

Tests for probing divergent production and cognitive-linguistic flexibility and strategy use must require: (a) problem solving, (b) planning and organization for production, and/or (c) alternative interpretations, inferences, solutions, or responses to the same stimulus. There are standardized tests that explore aspects of cognitive flexibility and divergent production. They are, however, limited in number and are not always standardized for age levels beyond preadolescence (age 12). The *Test of Problem Solving* (TOPS) (Zachman et al., 1984) is an example. It requires that a situation be viewed from different perspectives to generate verbal accounts of causes, inferences, and outcomes.

The *Test of Language Competence-Expanded* (TLC-E) (Wiig & Secord, 1988) provides a second example. TLC-E covers the age range from 4 to 18 years in two levels. This test has been described to be a situational, strategic measure of emerging and developing metalinguistic ability. It features tasks that evaluate divergent production and planning for production and assess use of cognitive-linguistic strategies. TLC-E contains four major subtests at two levels of difficulty. They are (a) Ambiguous Sentences, (b) Listening Comprehension: Making Inferences, (c) Oral Expressions: Recreating Speech Acts/Sentences, and (d) Figurative/Metaphoric Expressions. The Upper Level also contains a supplemental paired-associate word recall task, Remembering Word Pairs, designed to assess the acquisition of memory strategies. The Test of Language Competence: Upper Level has been used in several investigations (Santos, 1987; Wiig, Alexander, & Secord, 1987; Wiig & Secord, 1986a, 1986b, 1988).

The combined findings indicate that the TLC results, in combination with error pattern analyses and behavioral observations, can differentiate deficits and patterns in linguistic strategy acquisition. In addition, it can differentiate (a) "good" from "poor" readers, (b) patients with traumatic closed head injury who have reached a high level of recovery of cognitive functioning from patients at lower levels of recovery, (c) identify error patterns that provide suggestions for the locus and level of semantic, syntactic, pragmatic problems, and (d) suggest a focus and objectives for language intervention.

## Acquisition of Strategic Language Use

Before specific models for language intervention are introduced, it may be helpful to take a closer look at how expertise or strategic functioning is acquired. Expertise, regardless of the area, seems to be acquired in identifiable stages in a universal process (Dreyfus & Dreyfus, 1986). The process contains five levels the learner must pass through to arrive at the level of expertise. The five levels can be summarized as follows:

At Level 1, the level of the Novice or Beginner, the learner acquires and applies a small set of rules to context-free features. Rules are applied in a system deprived of situational knowledge and in a trial-and-error fashion. As a result, the learner performs in a disjointed and unpredictable pattern. Learning the rules for moving  chess pieces and using the rules without referring to the game context as a whole is a good example for this level.

At Level 2, the level of the Advanced Beginner, the learner recognizes features and patterns in a situation. This recognition occurs after several learning trials or teaching examples. It is based on similarities between aspects of a new situation and already experienced prototypical instances. A practical example exists in learning chess or Chinese checkers. The advanced beginner recognizes a good opening move or next move based on past experiences with similar patterns. However, she or he may not know how to follow through on the basis of pattern recognition. This is because each pattern is dealt with independently of others or of a whole (gestalt) and does not yet form a part of a larger schema or plan.

At Level 3, the level of the Competent Performer, the learner  organizes his or her behavior by selecting goals, plans, and perspectives. These determine what facts to consider and what rules to apply.  As an example, the competent player of Chinese checkers formulates a game plan before making the opening move. The initial game plan is then revised as the game progresses. The competent player uses strategies, but must go through a conscious planning and monitoring process. The performance is, therefore, slow and somewhat inflexible.

At Level 4, the level of Proficiency, the appropriate goals, plans, perspectives, and strategies are selected automatically, based on previous experiences. A context is understood intuitively and holistically. Nonetheless, the decisions involved in selecting a plan of action may still require conscious analysis and decision making. In other words, the learner can be described as a strategist. We can observe examples of proficient performance in advanced-level bridge and tennis tournaments. Decisions about actions seem to be made rapidly and effortlessly and without conscious effort. When the game gets very complex, however, the players may revert to slower and more deliberate decision-making process and performance.

At Level 5, the level of Expertise, any situation or problem is understood intuitively. The expert has a vast store of decisions, actions, and strategies he/she has found to be efficient in the past. Expert performance is therefore characterized by speed, fluency and flexibility, features that are subsumed under divergent production.

Relative to the model of acquisition of expertise, many adolescents and young adults with language-learning disabilities have not gone beyond Level 2, Advanced Beginner, or Level 3, Competent Performer, in the progression towards expertise as communicators. Their communicative behaviors may not be organized according to the communication goals, the underlying plans or schemata, or the appropriate perspectives. The objective for language intervention becomes to facilitate the progression towards expertise from the current level of functioning of the person with a language-learning disabilities.

## Training Models

Traditional practices in language intervention are not fully tuned to the processes and stages involved in developing expertise. Language intervention often focuses almost exclusively on the acquisition of syntactic and semantic skills and repertoires. Much less attention is given to linguistic strategy acquisition (Silliman, 1987; Simon, 1985; Wallach, 1990; Wiig, 1988). In special education there have been significant changes in the direction of teaching tactics (i.e., specific strategic approaches to problem-solving tasks) or heuristics (i.e., steps in a problem-solving process) (DeBono, 1976; Feuerstein, 1981; Meichenbaum, 1977; Swanson, 1989).

We can assume that linguistic strategies are acquired in a process with steps and that the steps are related to the thinking processes involved. We can also assume that differences in acquiring strategies for mathematics and strategies for communication should depend on the rule system and the content to which the strategies are to be applied.

## The Macro-Level Model

Wiig has developed and applied two models for training strategic language use (Wiig, 1985, 1988). The first is a macro-level model. It applies to overall planning of intervention. The model has been termed the Levels of Competence Model. It features four levels, described below. An overview of parallels between this model and the model of expertise (Dreyfus & Dreyfus, 1986) is featured in Table 2.1.

*Basic Training.* Concepts, rules, or schemata that are prerequisites for higher level (strategic) communication or performance are trained. As an example, consider that the curriculum is dealing with means of transportation and requires labeling and identification in response to where, when, why, and how questions. In that case, basic training would be designed to expand the student's knowledge of means of transportation (e.g., speed, miles per gallon, capacity), develop classification schemes, and verbalize likenesses and differences among classes, subclasses, and members of classes within the class.

*Extension to Pragmatic Uses.* Knowledge of basic concepts, rules, or schemata that was expanded in basic training is extended to everyday use. In relation to means of transportation, students might be given statements or questions from everyday life. After hearing an expression, they would be asked to respond to questions. As a concrete example, the students may be introduced to a rumor such as "Sue told me the Smith family wants to buy a bigger car." The student may be asked to give reasons why the Smiths might want a bigger car. They may be asked what kind of car the family might want. In other words, they would be asked to come up with hypotheses about causes and effects, and to make inferences based on world knowledge.

*Extension Across Variables, Across Participants, Settings, and Media.* At this level, the students are asked to generalize the already acquired knowledge to new situations, listeners, and media for communication. As an example, students may carry out an assignment that identifies where to buy or lease different means of transportation They may be asked to (a) use schedules for buses, trains, and planes to plan trips; (b) do comparative shopping for cars in magazines, newspapers, and journals; and (c) study and report on how transportation has changed since 1700 and project how it may change in the future. They may be asked to telephone for information and to write reports. This level of training is not unlike what would be carried out in the classroom in response to the curriculum. However, the emphasis here is on language and communication, not on memorization and recall of facts.

*Self-Directed Study.* At this level, students may select their own assignments. To complete the example, they may explore and prepare a report on means of transportation that were not part of basic and extended training. They may conduct and report interviews with commuters or transportation managers or personnel. They may explore means of transportation in an unfamiliar country and culture. The level of complexity will, of course, depend upon the students' ages and cognitive/social maturity. At this level, the objective is for the students to guide the learning process and to use the strategies that have been taught to prepare and present verbal or written reports.

## The Micro-Level Model

The second language intervention model is a micro-level model (Wiig, 1988). The model is concerned with the trainer-learner interactions at any point during basic and extended training. The micro-level model is very similar to the executive strategy training model introduced by Ellis, Deshler, and Schumaker

**Table 2.1.** Overview of stages to expertise (Dreyfus & Dreyfus, 1986) and stages in the Levels of Competence model (Wiig, 1988). Copyright © 1991 by E.H. Wiig. Used by permission.

|  | LEVELS OF COMPETENCE |
|---|---|
| **BEGINNER:**<br>Learns and applies a finite set of rules to context-free features. | **BASIC TRAINING:**<br>To develop awareness of significant features and patterns. |
| **ADVANCED BEGINNER:**<br>Recognizes patterns based on similarity to prototypical cases. | **EXTENSION TO PRAGMATIC USES:**<br>To extend knowledge of patterns to real-life uses. |
| **COMPETENT PERFORMER:**<br>Organizes behavior by selecting, goals, plans, and perspectives to guide rule selection. | **EXTENSION TO OTHER CONTEXTS:**<br>To generalize knowledge to complex tasks with several controlling variables. |
| **PROFICIENT PERFORMER:**<br>Selects goals, plans, and perspectives holistically and automatically. | **SELF-DIRECTED TRAINING:**<br>To foster independent use of knowledge to establish competence. |
| **EXPERT:**<br>Understands intuitively and uses strategies automatically. | |

(1989). According to both models, the student must go through a series of steps in a problem-solving process to acquire strategies. The two models are summarized for comparison in Table 2.2.

The Process Model for Strategy Development delineates the steps in the process as follows (Wiig, 1989).

*Targeting Features.* The first step is to assist the student to target significant, or potentially significant, features of the linguistic, or nonlinguistic, stimulus and the surrounding context. This is an active identification process that must be driven by the student and guided by the trainer. As an example, the student may have to decide which words are significant in a figurative expressions (e.g., "Don't go at it *head over heels*"). In a second example, the student may have to decide which words or phrases are significant in relation to the context in which an expression was used, as in the sarcastic remark, "You are *perfect*," said to a person who answered a question incorrectly.

**Table 2.2.** Overview comparison of the Executive Strategy Model (Ellis, Deshler, & Schumaker, 1989 and the Process Model for Strategy Development (Wiig, 1985, 1988). Copyright © 1991 by E.H. Wiig.  Used by permission.

| EXECUTIVE STRATEGY | PROCESS MODEL FOR STRATEGY |
|---|---|
| STEP 1.<br><br>Focusing on the problem situation. | STEP 1.<br><br>Identify potentially significant features of stimuli and tasks. |
| STEP 2.<br><br>Identifying and analyzing critical features. | STEP 2.<br><br>Perceive patterns in targeted features of stimuli and contexts. |
| STEP 3.<br><br>Generating a series of problem-solving steps. | STEP 3.<br><br>Formulate and test hypotheses about perceived patterns. |
| STEP 4.<br><br>Monitoring the effectiveness of the self-generated strategy and making necessary modifications. | STEP 4.<br><br>Select and execute responses with a potentially high level of probability.<br><br>STEP 5.<br><br>Self-monitor and evaluate the efficacy of responses and repair and revise as needed. |

*Recognizing Patterns.* The second step in the process is for the student to see a pattern in the features of the linguistic stimulus and its supportive context that have been targeted. As an example, there is a related pattern in metaphoric expressions with words that refer to body parts. The expressions are usually part-whole (metonymy) metaphors and the qualities or functions of the body part stand for the whole as in the indirect request, "I could use *a strong arm* now," said while trying to move a piano. Recognizing this pattern allows the student to interpret expressions such as, "Do you have to *elbow* your way through the world?" and "She gave him the *cold shoulder.*"

*Forming and Testing Hypotheses.* As the third step, the perceived pattern should lead the student to form and test one or more hypotheses about the meaning or intent of the linguistic stimulus. In the case of figurative expressions with an orientational perspective and variations of the word up-down, the hypotheses might take forms such as "It probably is about someone's health; money; status; or maybe love." In general, preadolescents become increasingly able to formulate and test several hypotheses simultaneously. This seems to be the tendency in children who have reached the formal operational cognitive stage.

Young children tend to form and test a single hypothesis, sometimes on the basis of scant evidence. In all events, the trick is to teach the student with language-learning disabilities not to lock himself or herself into a choice too early and to keep the discarded hypotheses in mind, if the one selected does not pan out.

*Selecting a Plan of Action.* As the fourth step, the student must select and commit to a plan of action. This involves accepting one of the hypotheses, preferably the one with the best fit or highest prob-ability of being correct or effective. It also involves getting ready to act on the selected plan. The trick for the student, at this level, is to cast all doubts aside and trust in the ability to revise or repair, if something goes wrong. Since an assessment of probability is involved and since revising messages may be difficult, this can be a hard step for LLD students. It is, however, a step that can be supported with positive reinforcement and with modeling.

*Acting.* The fifth step in the process requires the student to carry out  the selected plan of action. At this point, the learner is committed. The selected plan of action should be followed to its natural conclusion or to the point when the need to revise is recognized. At this level, evaluation of the response or plan of action must take place. This evaluation requires judgment of a current response against either a communication goal, a standard, a previous model, or an externally imposed criterion or model. In real life, the need to evaluate and revise is often recognized when the listener does not understand, when a question for information or elaboration is asked, or when subtle facial or body language reactions are negative. In the teaching process, the student should be supported in arriving at his/her own evaluation. This can be supported by giving additional cues, prompts, or directives to focus attention on missed features or cues.

*Evaluating and Revising.* The last step requires revision or repair of the action plan or response, if it is judged to be inadequate. This is achieved by returning the student's attention to a lower level in the problem-solving process. Often, all the previous steps may have been performed accurately, but the student may not have several options available for responding. As a result, the student may fall back on immature semantic-syntactic choices. As an example, a preadolescent or adolescent with a language-learning disability may recognize that a request for action should be polite. Yet, he/she may resort to an imperative followed by a "please" to make up for the directness (e.g., "Give me that book. Please.").

The process model for strategic language use implies that the roles of the educator and student may not follow traditional norms. In this process, the student is the active partner and the educator is the quiet partner. The educator provides structure to the input to allow the student to perceive patterns or schemata in the linguistic and contextual stimuli, whether semantic, syntactic, or pragmatic, and guides the student in the problem-solving process. The student's responses should be left open for his/her own evaluation. The student should also be asked to come up with several hypotheses and response options. The student should feel comfortable about making errors and willing to revise and repair responses. Since the student's role is active, training is often superior when carried out in groups. The group format allows for vicarious learning, distributes responses, diminishes the impact of failure, and increases the probability of success.

Lastly, it should be clear that pattern recognition depends on knowledge of the underlying plan or structure (schema) in linguistic stimuli. In figurative language, the structure of metaphors model (Lakoff & Johnson, 1980) provides a point of departure for identifying patterns. For discourse and narratives, speech act theory, turn unit models, and narrative structure may provide the underlying patterns or schema (Austin, 1962; Lahey, 1988; Scollon & Scollon, 1981; Searle, 1969; Stubbs, 1983).

The process model can be used in any setting. It can be used to reach objectives as diverse as acquiring constraint-seeking question strategies (e.g., Is it an animal?) or acquiring scripts for negotiating exchanges. The process is akin to the Aristotelian question procedure and can be internalized in a few trials. It is also easy to teach others to use this procedure, especially in face-to-face or videotaped demonstrations. Students with language-learning disabilities are readily engaged in the problem-solving process, because it is not threatening and reinforces divergent thinking and production.

In summary, this chapter introduced models for training and developing metalinguistic strategies for communication. These models were compared with models for developing expertise and with the executive strategy model. Metalinguistic strategy training, to be successful, requires opportunities for application and repeated practice and generalization that are relevant to academic or real-life endeavors (Goodman, 1986). Furthermore, there must be positive consequences or payoffs as a result of increasing competence. For these reasons, metalinguistic strategy training should be part of classroom-based procedures and interventions. These interventions can be facilitated by consultation from the speech-language pathologist or through collaboration among professionals (e.g., teacher, learning disabilities specialist, speech-language pathologist) (Freedman & Wiig, 1991; Secord & Wiig, 1991).

# References

Allen, R.R., & Brown, K.L. (1977). *Developing communication competence in children*. Skokie, IL: National Textbook.

Alvy, K.T. (1973). The development of listener adapted communications in grade-school children from different social backgrounds. *Genetic Psychology Monographs, 87*, 33-104.

Anglin, J. (1977). *Word, object and conceptual development*. New York: Norton.

Asch, S.E., & Nerlove, H. (1960). The development of double function terms in children. In B. Kaplan & S. Wapner (Eds.), *Perspectives in psychological theory*. New York: International Universities Press.

Austin, J.L. (1962). *How to do things with words*. London: Oxford University Press.

Billow, R.M. (1975). A cognitive developmental study of metaphor comprehension. *Developmental Psychology, 11*, 415-423.

Billow, R.M. (1977). Metaphor: A review of the psychological literature. *Psychological Bulletin, 84*, 81-92.

Bruner, J.S., Olver, R.R., & Greenfield, P.M. (1966). *Studies in cognitive growth.* New York: Wiley.

Clark, H.H., & Clark, E.V. (1977). *Psychology and language: An introduction to psycholinguistics.* New York: Harcourt Brace Jovanovich.

Crais, E.R. (1990). Word knowledge to world knowledge. *Topics in Language Disorders, 10*, 45-62.

DeBono, E. (1976). *Teaching thinking.* Hammondsworth, England: Penguin.

Delia, J., & Clark, R.A. (1977). Cognitive complexity, social perception, and the development of listener-adapted communication in six-, eight-, ten-, and twelve-year-old boys. *Communication Monographs, 4*, 326-345.

Donahue, M. (1985). Communicative style in learning disabled children: Some implications for classroom discourse. In D.N. Ripich & F.M. Spinelli (Eds.), *School discourse problems* (pp. 97-124). San Diego: College Hill.

Donahue, M., Pearl, R., & Bryan, T. (1982). Learning disabled children's syntactic proficiency on a communicative task. *Journal of Speech and Hearing Disorders, 47*, 397-403.

Dreyfus, H., & Dreyfus, S.E. (1986). *Mind over machine.* New York: Macmillan.

Ellis, E.S., Deshler, D.D., & Schumaker, J.B. (1989). Teaching adolescents with learning disabilities to generate and use task-specific strategies. *Journal of Learning Disabilities, 22*, 108-119.

Estes, W.K. (1970). *Learning theory and development.* New York: Academic Press.

Feuerstein, R. (1981). *Instrumental enrichment.* New York: Academic Press.

Flavell, J.H. (1963). *The developmental psychology of Jean Piaget.* New York: Van Nostrand Reinhold.

Freedman, E., & Wiig, E.H. (1991). *Strategies for vocabulary: Developing words and concepts across the curriculum.* Allen, TX: DLM.

Gardner, H., Kircher, M., Winner, E., & Perkins, D. (1975). Children's metaphoric productions and preferences. *Journal of Child Language, 2*, 125-141.

Gibbs, D.P., & Cooper, E.B. (1989). Prevalence of communication disorders in students with learning disabilities. *Journal of Learning Disabilities, 22*, 60-63.

Goodman, K. (1986). *What's whole in whole language?* Portsmouth, NH: Heinemann.

Guilford, J.P. (1967). *The nature of human intelligence.* New York: McGraw-Hill.

Hagen, J.W. (1972). Strategies for remembering. In S. Farnham Diggory (Ed.), *Information processing in children.* New York: Academic Press.

Hakes, D.T. (1980). *The development of metalinguistic abilities in children.* Berlin: Springer Verlag.

Halliday, M.A.K. (1978). *Language as social semiotic*. Baltimore: University Park Press.

Haslett, B. (1987). *Communication: Strategic action in context*. Hillsdale, NJ: Erlbaum.

Inhelder, B., & Piaget, J. (1964). *The early growth of logic in the child*. New York: Norton.

Kimball, J.P. (1973). Seven principles of surface structure parsing in natural language. *Cognition, 2*, 15-47.

Lahey, M. (1988). *Language development and language disorders* (2nd ed.). New York: John Wiley.

Lakoff, G., & Johnson, M. (1980). *Metaphors we live by*. Chicago: University of Chicago Press.

Loban, W. (1976). *Language development: Kindergarten-grade 12*. Urbana, IL: National Council of Teachers of English.

Mathinos, D.A. (1988). Communicative competence of children with learning disabilities. *Journal of Learning Disabilities, 21*, 437-443.

Meichenbaum, D. (1977). *Cognitive behavior modification: An integrative approach*. New York: Plenum.

Menyuk, P. (1983). Language development and reading. In T.M. Gallagher & C.A. Prutting (Eds.), *Pragmatic assessment and intervention issues in language*. San Diego: College-Hill Press.

Neisser, U. (1967). *Cognitive psychology*. New York: Appleton Century Crofts.

Nippold, M.A., Cuyler, J.S., & Braunbeck-Price, R. (1988). Explanation of ambiguous advertisements: A developmental study with children and adolescents. *Journal of Speech and Hearing Research, 31*, 466-474.

Nippold, M.A., & Fey, S.H. (1983). Metaphoric understanding in preadolescents having a history of language acquisition difficulty. *Language, Speech, & Hearing Services in Schools, 14*, 171-180.

Nippold, M.A., Leonard, L.B., & Kail, R. (1984). Syntactic and conceptual factors in children's understanding of metaphors. *Journal of Speech and Hearing Research, 27*, 197-205.

Owens, R.E. (1988). *Language development: An introduction* (2nd ed.). Columbus, OH: Merrill Publishing.

Piaget, J. (1952). *The language and thought of the child*. London: Kegan Paul.

Piaget, J. (1968). *Six psychological studies*. New York: Random House.

Piaget, J. (1970). Piaget's theory. In H.P. Mussen (Ed.), *Carmichael's manual of child psychology* (Vol. 1, 3rd ed.). New York: Wiley.

Pollio, M.R., & Pollio, H.R. (1979). A test of metaphoric comprehension: Preliminary data. *Journal of Child Language, 6*, 111-120.

Restle, F. (1962). The selection strategies in cue learning. *Psychological Review, 69*, 329-343.

Ripich, D.N., & Spinelli, F.M. (1985). *School discourse problems*. San Diego: College-Hill Press.

Santos, O. (1987). *Linguistic competence and reading achievement*. Doctoral dissertation, Boston University School of Education.

Scollon, R., & Scollon, B.K. (1981). *Narrative, literacy and face in interethnic communication*. Norwood, NJ: Ablex.

Searle, J. (1969). *Speech acts*. Cambridge: Harvard University Press.

Secord, W., & Wiig, E.H. (Eds.). (1990). *Best practices in school speech/language pathology* (Vol. 1). *Collaborative programming in the schools: Concepts, models, and procedures*. San Antonio, TX: The Psychological Corporation.

Silliman, E.R. (1987). Individual differences in classroom performance of language-impaired children. *Seminars in Speech and Language, 8*, 357-375.

Simon, C.S. (1979). *Communicative competence: A functional- pragmatic approach to language therapy*. Tucson: Communication Skill Builders.

Simon, C.S. (1985). *Communication skills and classroom success*. San Diego: College-Hill Press.

Stubbs, M. (1983). *Discourse analysis: The sociolinguistic analysis of natural language*. Chicago: University of Chicago Press.

Swanson, H.L. (1989). Strategy instruction: Overview of principles and procedures for effective use. *Learning Disabilities Quarterly, 12*, 3-15.

Wallach, G. (1990). Magic buries Celtics: Looking for broader interpretations of language learning and literacy. *Topics in Language Disorders, 10*, 63-80.

Wallach, G., & Butler, K.G. (1984). *Language disabilities in school age children*. Baltimore: Williams & Wilkins.

Wiig, E.H. (1985). *Words, expressions, and contexts: A figurative language training program*. San Antonio: Psychological Corporation.

Wiig, E.H. (1988). *Steps to language competence: Developing metalinguistic strategies*. San Antonio: Psychological Corporation.

Wiig, E.H. (1990). Linguistic transitions and learning disabilities: A strategic learning perspective. *Learning Disability Quarterly, 13*, 128-140.

Wiig, E.H., Alexander, E.W., & Secord, W. (1987). Linguistic competence and level of cognitive functioning in adults with traumatic closed head injury. In H.A. Whitaker (Ed.), *Neuropsychological studies of non-focal brain damage: Dementia and trauma*. New York: Springer-Verlag.

Wiig, E.H., Gilbert, M.F., & Christian, S.H. (1978). Developmental sequences in the perception and interpretation of lexical and syntactic ambiguities. *Perceptual and Motor Skills, 46*, 959-969.

Wiig, E.H., & Secord, W. (1986a). *Strategies for interpreting metaphors in LLD and non-LLD adolescents*. Paper presented at the Annual Convention of the American Speech-Language-Hearing Association, Detroit.

Wiig, E.H., & Secord, W. (1986b). *Strategies for recreating propositions by LLD and non-LLD adolescents*. Paper presented at the Annual Convention of the American Speech-Language-Hearing Association, Detroit.

Wiig, E.H., & Secord, W. (1987). Linguistic competence in early adolescents with learning disabilities: Assessing and developing strategies for learning and socialization. In M.D. Levine & E.R. McAnarney (Eds.), *Early adolescent transitions*. Lexington, MA: D.C. Heath.

Wiig, E.H., & Secord, W. (1988). *Test of language competence-Expanded.* San Antonio: Psychological Corporation.

Wiig, E.H., & Secord, W. (1991). *Test of word knowledge.* San Antonio: The Psychological Corporation.

Wiig, E.H., & Semel, E.M. (1976). *Language disabilities in children and adolescents.* Columbus, OH: Charles E. Merrill.

Wiig, E.H., & Semel, E.M. (1980). *Language assessment and intervention for the learning disabled.* Columbus, OH: Charles E. Merrill.

Wiig, E.H., & Semel, E.M. (1984). *Language assessment and intervention for the learning disabled* (2nd ed.). Columbus, OH: Charles E. Merrill.

Winner, E., Rosenstiel, A.K., & Gardner, H. (1976). The development of metaphoric understanding. *Developmental Psychology, 12,* 289-297.

Zachman, L., Jorgensen, C., Huisingh, R., & Barrett, M. (1984). *Test of problem solving.* Moline, IL: LinguiSystems.

# Part 2
## Academic Skills Instruction

# 3
# Beginning Reading Instruction for Reading Disabled and At-Risk Students

Diana Brewster Clark

Among school-classified learning disabled students, reading problems are so prevalent that the terms *learning disabled* and *reading disabled* have come to be used synonymously, despite the fact that the former term is meant to connote a broader range of learning deficits (e.g., math, handwriting, or attentional problems). Moreover, the diagnosis of a learning disability is usually the direct result of a student's failure to respond to the school's reading curriculum. Whether the problems underlying this failure represent actual deficits or normal variation within a broad range of human verbal processing ability is an issue beyond the realm of this chapter. The chapter focuses instead on teaching beginning reading skills to children for whom traditional basal reading instruction has not worked, as well as to young children for whom it will not work. For the sake of consistency, the former group of children will be referred to as reading disabled and the latter as being at risk for reading disability.

This chapter provides a brief analysis of the reading process and an overview of the early stages of reading acquisition. It discusses where in the acquisition process reading disabled children falter and outlines general instructional requirements for these children. It then describes specific teaching methods that have proven effective with these children. Lastly, it discusses issues related to the implementation of appropriate reading instruction for reading disabled and at-risk students.

## The Reading Process: What Is Involved?

Although the primary purpose of reading—getting meaning from print—appears simple and straightforward, reading is an extremely complex skill, the nature of which is still not fully understood. In the last two decades, however, extensive research has led to important new perspectives on the psychological processes involved in proficient reading. Examining these perspectives, or theoretical models, helps to explain where and why learning disabled children tend to falter in the reading process. For example, reading has been depicted as an information processing system involving several or more subsystems that process specific areas of information in the text. A number of information processing models of reading have been developed; some are better supported by the research than others. It is important to realize that these models are only theoretical constructs; the field of reading education is not without considerable controversy.

One area of controversy concerns the extent to which proficient reading is guided by the printed information in the text or by what the reader brings to the text, in terms of experience, knowledge, and purpose for reading. Both positions have been represented by serial processing models of reading. Print-based models depict reading as a bottom-up procedure, moving from the smallest units of textual information, individual letters, to ever-larger chunks of information; meaning is attached only after words have been identified (LaBerge & Samuels, 1974). Meaning-based models describe reading as a top-down procedure driven by the reader's intention for reading a given text. According to staunch proponents of this position, good readers do not read every word in the text but select out only the amount of information needed to meet these predictions and rely heavily on context to guess at less readily identified words (Goodman, 1967; Smith, 1978). Goodman, a leading advocate of this theory, described proficient reading as a "psycholinguistic guessing game." However, research does not support this view. Extensive studies of readers' eye movements indicate that when reading for meaning, good readers fixate their vision on almost all words in the text and tend to process all letters (Just & Carpenter, 1980, 1987).

Serial processing models of reading have more lately given way to interactive models that emphasize the interdependence of the component processes of the reading system. Adams's interactive model contains four processing subsystems, or sources of knowledge, that enable the reader to comprehend written text: an orthographic processor, which perceives letters and letter sequences in words; a phonological processor, which matches written letters with their equivalent speech sounds; a meaning processor, which attaches meaning to words; and a context processor, which controls the interpretation of the text (Adams, 1990). In proficient reading, all of these processing subsystems work together, making connections within and among themselves.

Reading is first a visual act; it begins with the orthographic processor perceiving the print on the page. Through teaching and practice, proficient readers come to recognize and interpret automatically not just individual letters but also conventional letter sequences (blends, digraphs, diphthongs, spelling patterns, syllables, etc.). Adams believes that these learned interletter associations are essential for fluent reading and that they "are responsible for the easy, holistic manner in which we respond to familiar words" (p. 24). She also maintains that failure to establish interletter associations in memory underlies the letter-order confusion evidenced by so many poor readers.

The major role of the context processor, according to Adams, is to choose the intended meanings for the words in the printed text; in other words, to cope with semantic ambiguities. Although context for good readers may speed the processing of orthographic information, it never replaces it and only has effect after a word has been visually identified.

Adams's model acknowledges the important role that phonological processing plays in reading. In an alphabetic writing system such as ours, letters and letter clusters (the orthography) in and of themselves do not represent ideas but instead correspond to speech sounds that carry meaning only when blended together. In contrast to the belief that fluent readers access meaning directly from print, there is increasing evidence that even when reading highly familiar words, they automatically combine phonological translation, or recoding, with visual recognition; the two systems, orthographic and phonological, serve as checks against and backups for each other (Liberman, 1984; Pennington et al., 1987; Perfetti, Bell, & Delaney, 1988). Furthermore, because the greater amount of meaning in a text is usually carried by the least frequent, less familiar words, automatic phonological decoding is one of the hallmarks of the skillful reader (Adams, 1990).

Unfortunately, Adams's model of reading provides only a minimal role for the meaning processor, which is held primarily responsible for learning and processing word meanings and smaller semantic units within words. Conspicuously absent is reference to the role that the reader's background knowledge, or broader knowledge of the world, plays in the comprehension of text. Such knowledge has been shown to influence strongly the reader's interpretation of text (Eckwall & Shanker, 1983). Another shortcoming of Adams's model is the limited attention it pays to syntactical processing, which can be described as knowledge of sentence patterns (Rumelhart, 1977). On the other hand, the model makes a valuable contribution to the field of reading education by emphasizing the importance of the learner's establishing strong interletter associations in memory and forming automatic connections between these letter units and their phonological and semantic counterparts. Fast, automatic word decoding frees up cognitive resources for comprehending the message in the text (LaBerge & Samuels, 1974). Because automaticity usually develops through reading practice, reading disabled children, who tend to eschew reading as a laborious task, are doubly jeopardized (Adams, 1990; Stanovich, 1986).

# Learning to Read

Unlike speaking, reading is not an innate skill. Rather than occurring naturally in the course of a child development, reading must be taught. Although this is true for all literate cultures, regardless of the writing system, our alphabetic writing system presents particular challenges to the beginning reader who must learn to decipher its phonetic code. The advantage of the code is its extraordinary efficiency; with only 26 letters an almost infinite number of words can be reproduced. However, there are several trade-offs. One, as previously mentioned, is that the letters, or graphemes, correspond to "units of speech rather than units of meaning" (Perfetti, 1984), and therefore an intermediary translation step must take place in order to extract meaning from print. Another trade-off for the alphabet's efficiency is the unequal ratio of its letters to the sounds in our language; each vowel letter corresponds to more than a few sounds (e.g., "cat", "cake", "call", "card") (Perfetti, 1984), and the pronunciation of many consonants varies with their positions and neighboring letters in words (e.g., "get," "gym"; "sit," "his"; "city," "country"). Additionally, the phonemes that correspond to the graphemes, particularly the consonants, are not discrete units but are coarticulated as we speak. For example, it is impossible to pronounce the consonant *p* without producing a schwa sound ("puh"). This characteristic makes it hard for teachers to demonstrate letter sounds in isolation, as well as for students to identify them in the context of words.

Another challenge for the beginning reader is that understanding the alphabetic principle requires a level of linguistic knowledge that does not come all at once but develops from awareness of larger to smaller units of speech: first words in sentences, then syllables in words, then phonemes in syllables. Studies in which children were asked to tap out the number of sounds in spoken words found that whereas most five-year-olds could divide words by syllables, only a small percentage could do so by phonemes, and only 70% of six-year-olds could segment by phonemes (Liberman, Shankweiler, Liberman, Fowler, & Fischer, 1977). Furthermore, those six-year-olds who could not segment by phonemes proved to be among the poorest readers in second grade. Such research indicates that educators cannot take phonological awareness for granted among schoolchildren and in addition demonstrates a strong relationship between phonological awareness and learning to read. The relationship seems to be both causal and reciprocal. Predictive studies, like that of Liberman et al. (1977) and training studies that have shown beneficial effects of phonological awareness instruction on learning to read support a causal relationship (Bradley & Bryant, 1985). At the same time, there is considerable evidence that the experience of learning to read makes the learner more conscious of the phonological aspects of written language (Ehri, 1985; Morais, Cary, Algeria, & Bertelson, 1979).

Chall (1983a) has described learning to read in terms of developmental stages. In the *prereading stage*, from birth to approximately age six children acquire language and gain knowledge about the world, both of which are crucial scaffolding for building reading skills. Before formal reading instruction begins, children may be expected to have developed readiness concepts such as understanding the purpose of reading, being aware of print and its relationship to pictures and to spoken language, using context--pictures and memory for story content--to guess at words in print. They may also be able to recognize, to name, or even to write letters of the alphabet; some can read words in popular signs or familiar books. At the same time, children's linguistic awareness should expand to include the ability to rhyme words, to match initial sounds in words (alliterate), and to segment units of speech (sentences into words and words into syllables, if not syllables into phonemes).

For most children, the *decoding stage* covers first and second grades. Mastering the alphabetic principle and learning the alphabetic code (the letter-sound correspondences) is the primary achievement of this period. If their readiness skills are intact, children increasingly attend to the graphemic elements in words, rather than reading them as wholes, and begin to analyze them in terms of grapheme-phoneme relationships. As they progress through this stage, their knowledge of sound-symbol associations should extend beyond individual letters to larger conventional letter sequences (Adams, 1990). However, if their readiness skills are underdeveloped and they are unable to apply an analytical approach, they will continue to view words holistically, as in the previous stage, and to rely on visual memory or on contextual cues such as pictures or memory for stories. During the decoding stage, children should also be acquiring a repertoire of high-frequency words that they can recognize on sight, many of which are not phonetically decodable.

The next stage, which for normally achieving students begins towards the end of second grade and lasts through third, involves securing knowledge learned in the previous stage and *gaining fluency*. Phonic skills continue to develop, enabling them to decode larger multisyllable words, but the major accomplishment of this stage is the coordination of all four information processors identified by Adams (1990) and the integration of orthographic, phonological, semantic, and contextual information. Students are able to process larger chunks of graphic information at a time, to recognize automatically a greater number of words, and, given extensive practice with reading materials having familiar content, to expand their decoding strategies to include taking advantage of the "redundancies of the language and the redundancies of the stories" (Chall, 1983a). Children who do not master the earlier decoding stage cannot move successfully through this stage but remain, as Chall expressed it, "glued to print," struggling to decode letter by letter.

# Where Learning Disabled Students Falter

Many children subsequently classified as learning disabled, are not referred for diagnostic testing until late second or third grade when their halting reading style stands in blatant contrast to their classmates growing fluency. However, their reading difficulty really begins at the decoding stage when they should be learning the letter-sound correspondences of the alphabetic code. And research suggests the source of this difficulty can be traced to an even earlier point in development, to the prereading stage, when they should be acquiring phonological awareness (Liberman et al., 1977). Unlike normally developing readers, those who become classified as learning disabled seem not to discover naturally that words can be broken down into phonological units. Without this knowledge they are unable to grasp the alphabetic principle. Although they tend to try to compensate for their phonological deficits by memorizing whole words, their repertoire of easily recognized words falls further and further behind that of the good readers in their class. This is so in part because of their lack of adequate practice in reading, as Adams (1990) pointed out, but also, it may be presumed, because they have not established stable grapheme-phoneme relationships to cue and support their visual memory. They are left with the frustrating alternative of guesswork. Because so much of their attention is taken up with decoding, there is little left for comprehending the message in the text. Thus, learning disabled students tend to remain "glued to print" and unable to move on to higher levels of reading proficiency.

# Instructional Needs of Reading Disabled Children

Although there is no established standard for how reading is taught in this country, most schools adopt basal reading programs, and the majority of these programs emphasize a meaning-based, whole-word approach. Phonics instruction, when included in these programs, is seldom systematically applied (Chall, 1983b). Students are usually expected to learn letter-sound correspondences with a minimum of explicit teaching, through exposure to whole words in the text and by analogy (becoming aware of the sounds in the words taught and of the similarities in letter patterns between words having the same sound). Given their phonological weaknesses, it is not surprising that students at risk for learning disabilities classification make little reading progress in basal reading programs. On the other hand, with appropriate teaching, most of these at-risk students will learn to read.

One of the major principles of effective teaching for reading disabled and at-risk students is that it be explicit, systematic, and intensive and that it involve a maximum amount of student-teacher interaction (Haring & Bateman, 1977). This approach, generally referred to as *direct instruction*, involves a number of teaching techniques that help to support and reinforce learning for these students. Most of these techniques or instructional principles are incorporated in the reading programs to be described in this chapter.

*Allocation of instructional time* is an important aspect of direct instruction, since disabled readers need more time to learn than normally achieving students and generally do best with the greatest amount of one-on-one instruction (Haring & Bateman, 1977). To compensate for a larger student-to-teacher ratio, several programs incorporate unison oral response. Some programs use teacher scripts to help teachers manage instructional time. In addition, *careful pacing of instruction* avoids overloading students with too much information to be processed at one time (Bryant et al., 1980)

To counteract distractibility and potential lack of motivation, direct instruction usually includes techniques for *gaining and maintaining pupil attention*, such as arranging seating to maximize teacher-student eye contact, using hand signals to direct group response, even manipulating puppets to demonstrate concepts. *Teacher modeling* of required behaviors or skills is another important element of effective reading programs for at-risk students. *Prompting techniques* have been incorporated to decrease student error, as, for example, using pictures to cue memory for letter sounds, and having students trace or copy letter models having arrows that demonstrate directionality of letter formations. As proficiency develops, prompts are gradually faded.

*Teaching to mastery* is critical for effecting durable gains in reading acquisition with learning disabled students (Rosenshine, 1983). Most adaptive programs establish criteria for skills mastery at various points in the curriculum that students must meet before moving on to more advanced skills. Mastery involves *gaining automaticity* at basic decoding skills, as well as developing a substantial sight word vocabulary, and requires *extensive practice.*

*Academic feedback* is another essential component of direct instruction. Students should be informed as soon as possible whether or not their responses are appropriate in order to correct and not reinforce errors (Rosenshine & Stevens, 1984). Feedback need not necessarily be provided directly by the teacher; in some programs, students are led under teacher guidance to discover for themselves if their answers are right (Cox, 1984; Lindamood & Lindamood, 1975).

*Monitoring and evaluating student performance* is extremely important for ensuring successful teaching. Studies have shown significantly greater gains for students whose progress was closely followed (Zigmond & Miller, 1986). Monitoring helps teachers determine whether and where the curriculum needs adjusting. Furthermore, informing students of their progress can increase their motivation.

## Print Readiness Instruction

Like all prereaders, children at risk for learning disabilities benefit from readiness experiences and activities that expose them to stories, to books, and to print, thus helping to develop their fund of background knowledge, their awareness of print and the left-to-right directionality of print, their concept of what a word is, both in speech and in print, and their understanding that printed words consist of letters. Preschool and kindergarten classrooms should be "print-rich" (Adams, 1990), filled with printed labels or captions on visual displays and activity charts with students' printed names appearing in many places. Language experience activities, where children dictate stories to teachers, help them to realize that print is "talk written down" and to begin to note relationships between sounds and symbols in printed language (Adams, 1990). Whole language materials, such as "big books" which teachers share with a whole class at a time, can be particularly effective during the readiness stage of reading acquisition (Stahl & Miller, 1989).

During this period, children should also be learning to name the letters of the alphabet. Although several reading programs for reading disabled students teach letter sounds before names, the rationale being that letter-sound knowledge is essential for reading and that teaching letter names in the early stages of their learning to read will only confuse them, Adams (1990) makes a convincing case for teaching letter names first and early. One reason is that it is the conventional approach; a second is that the names, unlike the sounds, provide consistent labels for each letter to be used during instruction; a third is that labels are important for teaching concepts. Additionally, the more naturalistic and more effective progression is to teach the letter names by rote, most likely through the Alphabet Song, before teaching recognition of letter shapes: "By thoroughly learning the names first, the child has a solid mnemonic peg to which the percept of the letter can be connected as it is built.  By thoroughly teaching the names first, the teacher can methodically exploit them toward developing the child's sense of the functionally equivalent and distinctive differences between characters." (p. 359)

## Phonological Awareness Training

More than normally developing readers, children at risk for reading disabilities need training in phonological awareness. Indeed, evidence of weakness in this domain can be one of the earliest indicators of potential reading problems. Practitioners should be admonished, however, that qualifying and quantifying this weakness during the prereading stage is not yet a precise art (Stanovich, Cunningham, & Cramer, 1984). Many tasks have been devised to measure phonological awareness: recognition of rhyme; sound-to-sound matching; word-to-word matching; isolation of a beginning, medial, or final sound in a word; phonemic segmentation, or sounding out words by individual phonemes; counting the phonemes in a word; blending individual sounds to make words, deleting phonemes in words; specifying which phoneme has been deleted; and substituting phonemes (Lewkowicz, 1980). Some, such as rhyming, have proven too easy to be discriminatory and others, such as "strip initial consonant" have proven too difficult (Stanovich, Cunningham, & Cramer, 1984). Both the *Lindamood Auditory Conceptualization Test* (Lindamood & Lindamood, 1979), in which students are asked to manipulate colored blocks to represent the sounds they hear in spoken words, and the *Test of Auditory Analysis Skills* (Rosner, 1975), which uses a deletion task to assess auditory segmentation ability, have been normed for children in kindergarten, but they must be individually administered and therefore may not be practical for classroom use.

Thus at the kindergarten or beginning first-grade level the question arises as to which children should be eligible for specific instruction in phonological awareness. One answer is to provide this instruction to all children in the class, and, at the very least, rhyming and alliteration activities should be part of the regular class curriculum. Bradley and Bryant (1985) in England conducted a study with normally achieving six-year-olds that showed significant advantages in reading acquisition for those who had been trained to categorize words according to sound, as compared to a control group of students taught to categorize words by concept (animals, furniture, etc.). The training requires students to select out words (represented by pictures) that differ in sound from the other three or four words in a set and involves both rhyme (finding the word with a differing end sound, e.g., bun, *hut*, gun, sun; finding the word with a differing middle sound, e.g., *hug*, pig, dig, wig) and alliteration (finding the word that begins with a different sound (bun, bus, *rug*, bud). Two groups were given sound categorization training; one group worked only with pictures, the other, in the second year of training, was given plastic letters with which to form the words in the pictures. It is important to note that the latter group did significantly better at the end of two years on both reading and spelling tests than the former group.

The Lindamood program, *Auditory Discrimination in Depth* (Lindamood & Lindamood, 1975), which can be used with whole classes as well as individuals, is the most structured and intensive program in phonological awareness training. In this program, students are taught to identify and classify speech sounds that have been given labels on the basis of how the mouth is formed when the sound is made; for example, /p/ is a "lip popper." They learn to track sounds in nonsense words using colored blocks, each color representing a different sound. Letters are introduced only after students become efficient at encoding nonsense words (syllables) in this manner.

Blachman (1987) incorporated the *Elkonin method* (Elkonin, 1963) in developing a reading program for first graders performing at the bottom third of the class. In this method, words are represented by simple line drawings, each having a series of squares underneath that correspond to the number of phonemes in the word. As students slowly pronounce a word, they move a counter into the square corresponding to the phoneme being pronounced.

The *ABD (analysis, blending, decoding) reading program* (Williams, 1980) was also designed for group administration. It begins with auditory syllable analysis, followed by phoneme analysis using an adaptation of the Elkonin method. Then the phonemes, represented by wooden squares, are blended into bigrams and trigrams, and the child learns to identify the phoneme sounds within these words. Later, letter names are introduced on squares and the child manipulates the squares to make different words.

All of the programs described have been successful in enhancing phonological awareness and in addition, have demonstrated transfer effects to reading tasks (Blachman, 1987; Bradley & Bryant, 1985; Howard, 1986; Williams, 1980). Thus the value of phonological awareness training has been established. It seems clear from Bradley and Bryant's research that including letters in the training leads to significantly greater effects on reading acquisition, but to prevent overloading the student, letters should be introduced only as proficiency is gained (Williams, 1980).

## Teaching Phonics Skills

Phonics instruction is critical for students with, or at risk for, reading disability since their major difficulty lies with the phonological aspects of written language. There are essentially two approaches to teaching phonics. One approach, most often referred to as *synthetic phonics instruction*, teaches the individual letter-sound correspondences first in isolation, and only after they are so learned introduces them in syllables and words. Letter-sound correspondences are introduced in systematic progression, although the sequence varies somewhat among programs. The other approach, known as *analytic phonics instruction*, introduces whole words first and encourages students to infer the letter-sound correspondences as they appear in those words. Words are selected on the basis of their phonemic patterns, rather than for their frequency in children's vocabularies as are the words in basal readers. *Multisensory phonics* instruction, which will also be discussed in this chapter, is a variation of synthetic phonics instruction, which incorporates multisensory teaching techniques.

*Synthetic Phonics Instruction.* A good example of a synthetic phonics approach to decoding instruction is *DISTAR's Reading Mastery* program (Engelmann & Bruner, 1983) It was designed for use in classroom settings with students considered to be at risk for reading failure, and as its name implies (the acronym, DISTAR, stands for Direct Instructional System of Teaching Arithmetic and Reading), the program adheres strictly to the principles and techniques of direct instruction. The reading curriculum is composed of six levels, extending from preschool through grade six. Only the first two levels, Reading Mastery I and II which cover preschool through second grade, are discussed here.

Reading Mastery I teaches letter sounds, emphasizing the oral pronunciation of these sounds; letter names are not introduced until Reading Mastery II. Each letter sound is introduced by the teacher saying it aloud and the students imitating in unison the teacher's pronunciation. Students are then shown the corresponding letter in written form. Line diagrams with arrows pointing from left to right are provided to help pronunciation and to demonstrate the difference between continuous sounds and stop sounds. For continuous sounds (e.g., /s/, /m/, certain digraphs, and all vowels), students are instructed to move their finger slowly along the line as they pronounce the sound (e.g., *aaa*); for stop sounds, they are asked to trace the line quickly and say the sound fast.

Letter sounds are introduced slowly with a great deal of review. Students learn to write the corresponding letters from the first lesson. Reading begins when six sounds have been taught. Each new sound is presented in a word that is used throughout the program as a mnemonic cue for the letter sound. To assist sound blending, each word is introduced with a line diagram; children are instructed to sound out a word first, moving their finger slowly along the line as they pronounce each phoneme, and then to say the word fast. Even high- frequency sight words that are not phonetically spelled, such as *was* and *said*, are taught in this manner, rather than as whole words, to emphasize those parts that are phonetically predictable. All words studied become part of the student's reading vocabularies and are incorporated first in simple sentences and later in stories.

DISTAR is unique among phonics programs in that all lessons follow scripts that tell the teacher exactly what to say and do, including how to anticipate and correct errors. Because instruction is designed for group administration, teachers use hand signals to direct the type and timing of unison responding. Another distinguishing feature of DISTAR is its modified orthography, which is used in the early stages of the program but phased out by the middle of Reading Mastery II. The modification is intended to compensate for the larger number of sounds relative to corresponding letters in the English alphabet, to help children read words that do not follow phonic rules, and to stress differences between visually similar letters. For example, silent letters are printed smaller, long vowel sounds are accented with heavy macrons above the corresponding letters, and consonant blends are printed as joined letters.

DISTAR differs in several other ways from most other synthetic phonic programs. It introduces comprehension activities from the very first lesson. Rather than being totally integrated with reading instruction, spelling instruction in DISTAR is a separate and optional curriculum, albeit strongly recommended and designed to follow the sequence of the reading curriculum. Neither handwriting nor written expression are emphasized in DISTAR, although students are taught manuscript letter formations as part of the reading curriculum.

DISTAR has proven successful with socioeconomically deprived children for whom it was originally designed (Meyer, Gersten, & Gutkin, 1983), but there is limited research on its use with learning disabled students. However, one study that involved primary-grade learning disabled students found that those receiving DISTAR instruction evidenced greater achievement on reading tests than those receiving another form of phonics instruction (Stein & Goldman, 1980). Despite DISTAR's popularity in several communities with both parents and teachers, there have been complaints that teachers are too restricted by the scripts (Meyer, Gersten, & Gutkin, 1983) and further, that some children have difficulty making the transition from the modified to traditional orthography (Bartlett, 1979).

*Analytic Phonics Instruction.* The *Merrill Linguistic Readers* (Fries, Wilson, & Rudolph, 1966) represent an analytic phonics approach to early reading instruction. The program teaches letter sounds within the context of whole words rather than as isolated units by focusing on word endings having invariable spelling patterns (e.g., cat, sat, mat) and applying the principle of "minimal contrasts"; children are taught to attend to the word endings and to note the varying initial consonants. This method is sometimes referred to as the "word family" method or alternatively, a phonics linguistic approach.

Since there is a high degree of consistency of spelling patterns among the words introduced, children are able to read continuous text early on in this program (e.g., The fat cat sat on a mat.). The program, developed for use in first-grade classrooms, comprises six readers and six corresponding workbooks. All new "Words in Pattern" and any high-frequency words not belonging to that pattern are presented at the beginning of the chapter in which they appear, as well as being introduced by the teacher on the chalkboard. In the early books, only words having the same spelling pattern appear together; at more advanced levels, increasing numbers of different spelling patterns are presented in the same text. Because of the strongly controlled vocabulary, text content is necessarily bland and semantic interest level low, affording little opportunity for comprehension development.

In addition to the Merrill, the *SRA Basic Reading Program* (Rasmussen & Goldberg, 1976), the *Stern Structural Reading Series* (Stern & Gould, 1965), and the *Glass Analysis for Decoding Only* method (Glass & Glass, 1976) are among the most popular of the more than ten analytic phonics programs available. As yet there is no substantial research on the effectiveness of these programs with reading disabled students. Because they avoid sounding out individual letters, they may help children who lack blending skills. On the other hand, because they do not provide explicit instruction in letter-sound correspondences, for children at risk for reading disabilities these programs are best applied after the letter sounds have been taught.

*Multisensory Phonics Instruction.* The term *multisensory* refers to the simultaneous engagement of two or more sensory modalities in the learning process (visual, auditory, kinesthetic, and tactile). The use of multisensory teaching techniques is based on the premise that kinesthetic involvement reinforces learning of grapheme-phoneme correspondences through strengthening visual-auditory associations (Orton, 1966). It has been posited that these procedures encourage students to attend to details in letters and words (Gates, 1927) and help them retrieve words from long-term memory.

The prototype of multisensory phonics instruction is the *Orton-Gillingham approach* (Gillingham & Stillman, 1960). This method was designed for one-to-one remedial instruction, and all teaching is direct and systematic. Letters and phonograms (digraphs and diphthongs) are treated as discrete elements and introduced in a prescribed sequence, on individual cards. The letter name is taught first; the teachers says the name, and the child repeats it. When the name is learned, the letter sound is taught in the same way. *Auditory-to-auditory* association is then established as the teacher says the letter sound and asks for the letter name. To establish *visual-kinesthetic* association, the teacher writes the letter, describing its formation and orientation; the student traces the letter, then copies it, then writes it from memory, and lastly writes it with eyes closed. For *auditory-kinesthetic* reinforcement, the teacher gives the letter sound and asks the student to write the corresponding letter. When writing, the student always says the letter name, not the sound. Each letter or phonogram is given a *key word* (e.g., u-umbrella). In subsequent drill exercises, the student states the key word along with the letter name and sound.

The difference between vowels and consonants is emphasized by drawing attention to open or closed mouth positions in pronunciation and reinforced by using different colored cards for vowels and consonants. Reading only begins when two vowels and eight consonants have been learned. The teacher lays out letter cards to form consonant-vowel-consonant (CVC) words (e.g., b-a-t); the student pronounces each phoneme in succession and repeats them with increasing speed until able to pronounce the word. To avoid the schwa sound when pronouncing consonants in isolation, the student is encouraged to pronounce the first two letters together (e.g., ba-t). The student traces, copies, and then writes the words from memory. *Spelling* in the Orton-Gillingham approach, as well as in all other multisensory phonics programs, is taught concommitantly with reading.

Text reading does not begin until the student can read easily all CVC words and words of four letters with consonant digraphs that she has studied. The instructor's manual contains stories containing these words. All nonphonetic sight words that the student has not yet encountered are underlined and told to the student before reading. First the student reads silently, asking for help if needed. When reading orally, the student is urged to read with inflection, although no attention is paid to word meaning or comprehension.

*Syllabication* starts with students reading words with syllables separated, followed by their rearranging scrambled syllables to make real words. Students are taught to place stress marks on accented syllables. Knowledge of syllable patterns is linked to spelling rules and used to decode unfamiliar multisyllable words.

A number of reading programs have adapted Orton-Gillingham–based-multisensory instruction to school settings. The *Slingerland program* (Slingerland, 1971) is designed for whole classes of children at risk for reading disability. *Project Read* (Greene & Enfield, 1985) is used with groups of children within regular classrooms. *Alphabetic Phonics* (Cox, 1984) was originally developed to teach small groups, as well as individual students, outside the regular classroom; a recent adaptation of this program has been developed for whole classroom use (Vickery, Reynolds, & Cochran, 1987). In these programs, the role of multisensory instruction has been expanded. Kinesthetic activities include having children write letters and words in the air, using their whole arm, while saying each letter name aloud as they write it, and having them spell words by placing individual letters in pocket charts (see Clark, 1988 for a fuller description of these programs).

Research has documented the success of these multisensory phonics programs with disabled readers, as well as with students considered to be at risk for reading failure (Enfield & Greene, 1983; Frankiewicz, 1985; Kline & Kline, 1975; McCulloch, 1985; Roy, 1986; Wolf, 1985), although there is as yet no empirical evidence that substantiates the use of multisensory techniques per se. Most of these programs require extensive teacher training (see Clark, 1988).

## Developing Whole Word Recognition

Besides learning phonic skills in order to decode unfamiliar words, disabled readers must develop a repertoire of words they can read on sight. Proficient reading is strongly dependent upon fast accurate word recognition (Stanovich, Cunningham, & Feeman, 1984).

Most of the reading programs emphasizing phonics instruction teach words that do not follow phonics generalizations as "sight words," to be studied and memorized as wholes (only DISTAR encourages first sounding them out). In the Orton-Gillingham-based programs these words are usually taught with multisensory spelling exercises—tracing, copying, skywriting, while saying the individual letter names—and with flash-card drills.

Teaching to mastery is an important component of effective whole word instruction (Bryant, Payne, & Gettinger, 1982). In the early stages, words to be learned are presented in small groups of only four or five, and practice includes distinguishing the words from others similar in appearance. When students have learned to readily and consistently identify the words in isolation, they are given practice reading them in context—first phrases, then sentences, and finally paragraphs.

Children at risk for reading disability, who tend to become "glued to print," need to practice reading even phonetically spelled words quickly and accurately. Recognition practice with these conventionally spelled words should also help to establish in memory interletter associations (predictable letter sequences) that are essential for fast word identification (Adams, 1990). In the Orton-Gillingham approach, for example, all words introduced are filed on cards in a word bank for later drill in recognition. Monitoring and recording both rate and accuracy during flash card drill may help to motivate students, as well as to inform teachers of their progress.

*Computer assisted instruction (CAI)* has proven effective in increasing disabled readers' word recognition skills. In one study, learning disabled students given practice on a computer made significant gains in both speed and accuracy in reading a list of one syllable, phonetically regular words (Jones, Torgesen, & Sexton, 1987), and the effects of this practice generalized to reading unpracticed words containing the same medial vowels though differing in initial and final consonants. In another study, practice with two- and three-syllable words using a multiple-choice format generalized to oral reading of these words in print (Torgesen, Waters, Cohen, & Torgesen, 1988).

Though still at a formative stage, CAI seems to be a promising medium for word recognition instruction with at-risk students. It affords extensive one-to-one practice in classroom settings with a minimal amount of teacher supervisory time and with protection from possible embarrassment in front of classmates (Boettcher, 1983). It provides immediate response feedback so that errors can be promptly corrected. It can be designed to monitor both speed and accuracy of responses and to pace instruction according to mastery requirements. By incorporating game formats, CAI can alleviate the boredom of traditional drill exercises.

## Developing Reading Fluency

Reading disabled students are apt to read connected text in a halting manner, which tends to detract from their comprehension of the text. Thus, methods have been developed to promote their reading fluency. In the Slingerland program, for example, students practice reading words and phrases from a chalkboard before encountering them in stories that they read aloud in round-robin format.

One of the more commonly used approaches to fluency practice is *repeated reading*, where the student reads short meaningful passages several times until a satisfactory level of mastery has been reached. Although both dimensions of mastery are measured, speed is emphasized over accuracy. Techniques for implementing this approach include: *audio support*, having a student read silently while listening to a tape recording of the passage; having the student *read for one minute* and count the words read in that time and then record them on a graph; and *paired reading*, having students read alternately in pairs, keeping word-count records for each other (Samuels, 1986).

Another variation on the repeated reading approach is *imitative reading*, where first the teacher reads a passage aloud with the student following along silently and then the student reads the passage aloud imitating the teacher's intonation and phrasing (Henk, Helfeldt, & Platt, 1986). In the *neurological impress* method, the teacher and student read a passage aloud together, while the teacher controls the pace with her voice and finger. CAI programs have also been developed for repeated reading practice with reading disabled students and applied with some success (Rashotte & Torgesen, 1985).

*Cloze exercises*, which encourage students to take advantage of context as they read, bringing the context processor into play, as Adams (1990) might express it, are another approach to fluency development. These entail deleting every fifth word or so and having students read the text, hesitating as little as possible, using the context to guess at the missing words. However, care must be taken in making the deletions in order to ensure reasonable guesses.

## Developing Comprehension Skills

Most of the reading programs developed for students with or at risk for reading disabilities focus almost exclusively on building decoding skills, at least in the early stages of reading acquisition; minimal attention is directed toward reading for meaning. Although decoding difficulties are their major weakness, these students need comprehension instruction as much, if not more, than normally developing readers. Unfortunately, the highly controlled vocabulary in most of the instructional texts designed for these students affords a generally low semantic interest level. However, comprehension instruction should not and need not wait until they are able to read high-interest materials.

Some of the remedial or intervention programs do provide comprehension instruction at beginning levels. In DISTAR, for example, prereaders practice interpreting pictures and ordering events in sequence. When they begin to read stories, the teacher asks comprehension questions during the reading and, after summarizing the story, asks students to predict what will happen next. In the Slingerland program, a *phrase reading method* is used in small group round-robin reading, wherein the teacher directs students' comprehension of text by applying *wh* questions to their oral reading (e.g., Teacher: "Where does the story take place?" "Find the phrase that tells where the story takes place." Student: "At the beach."). Project Read introduces a program in reading comprehension and vocabulary development once students have mastered basic decoding skills, usually at the end of first grade, though the major emphasis on comprehension instruction really begins in fourth grade. The program distinguishes two levels of text analysis and presents a sequence of comprehension skills within each level. The literal level includes such skills as identifying the subject of the text, defining unfamiliar words, noting punctuation and its purpose, and determining whether the text content is fiction, nonfiction, or procedural (telling how to do something). The interpretive level includes identifying and sequencing the information in the text, finding supporting details, making inferences, and drawing conclusions.

Teachers need to provide reading comprehension instruction in those programs where it is lacking or inadequate. Supplementary instruction can begin with comprehension activities centered on stories read aloud by the teachers. Language experience activities, where children dictate their own stories, and whole language materials, such as "big books" with predictable stories which students read together under the teacher's direction also provide the opportunity to develop comprehension skills. For suggestions on constructing reading comprehension lessons see Maria (1990).

## Implementation Issues

Planning an appropriate reading curriculum for students with or at risk for reading disabilities involves a great many factors, and these factors will vary from case to case. Questions to consider in this regard include: a) At what point in the student's education is special or alternative instruction provided? b) Who will be working with the student? c) How many students need special instruction? d) What is the severity of the student's reading difficulty? e) What is the school's philosophy of reading education? f) What reading program is used in the regular classroom? g) What educational placements are available for special instruction?

## At What Point Is the Student Provided Alternative Instruction?

The answer to this question will be strongly influenced by the school's philosophy of reading education, the instructional options the school can provide, and the severity of the student's reading or readiness deficits. A school that acknowledges the challenges of the alphabetic principle and the fact that some children require explicit instruction in phonological awareness and decoding may adopt a "stitch in time" philosophy by introducing this instruction early in the children's school career and providing it for groups of students rather than selected individuals. On the other hand, a school espousing either a basal reader or a whole language approach might wait until the student has experienced failure in the classroom reading program before providing instructional support. Many of the reading programs discussed in this chapter are designed specifically for group or whole class administration beginning with the first grade (e.g., DISTAR, the Slingerland program, Project Read) and some for kindergarten use (e.g., Auditory Discrimination in Depth). The decision as to which students will receive alternative instruction may be based on a formal screening process (e.g., the Slingerland program) or by informally distinguishing those children performing at the lower third or so of the class (e.g., Project Read).

## Who Will Be Working With the Student?

The professional providing special instruction may be the regular classroom teacher, an assistant teacher in the regular classroom, a specialist (e.g., resource room or remedial reading) teacher, or a private tutor. Additional training may be required to prepare this person in the alternative approach.

## How Many Students Need Alternative Instruction?

A large elementary school may have sufficient numbers of young students at risk for reading failure to justify a self-contained classroom providing DISTAR or multisensory phonics instruction. On the other hand, a small school may have as few as one child per class needing special instruction, in which case the instruction might be provided in a resource room. Often there are enough students to form small groups to be taught within the regular classroom or in a resource room.

## What Is the Severity of the Student's Reading Difficulty?

The severity of the reading difficulty dictates the type of special instruction the student requires, as well as the choice of instructional setting for the student.

Group instruction, for example, is inefficient when there is too much disparity in reading ability among students. On the other hand, if the student in question is able to keep up with classmates in subjects other than reading, the student should remain in the regular classroom and receive special reading instruction either within the classroom from a second teacher or in a resource room during the classroom reading period. Sometimes minimal adjustments of the classroom reading program combined with supplemental instructional activities can sufficiently accommodate students with mild deficits.

## What Is the School's Philosophy of Reading Education?

The school administration's position on how reading should be taught will no doubt affect its willingness and ability to accommodate the needs of students requiring alternative or supplementary instruction. If the school supports a phonics approach, students at risk for reading failure will be more likely to receive appropriate early reading instruction. If the administration recognizes that children differ in their ability to learn, it will be more willing to support alternative instruction for students requiring it. Even advocates of a whole language approach acknowledge that some children need more intensive instruction than this approach generally provides and, as such, recommend a supplementary program, *Reading Recovery* (Clay, 1985) for these children. This program provides one-to-one 30-minute teaching sessions daily on a short-term basis to low-achieving first graders and follows whole language principles (Pinnell, Fried, & Estice, 1990). Instruction is highly eclectic and determined by individual need as assessed by a Reading Recovery specialist teacher. Letter-sound correspondences are taught if necessary, but only in the context of words, rarely if ever in isolation.

## What Reading Program Is Used in the Regular Classroom?

Often the classroom reading program can be applied to the needs of reading disabled students. For example, predictable books used in the whole language approach are excellent for practicing whole word recognition and promoting fluency. Basal readers can also be adapted for this purpose by providing adequate prereading practice with unfamiliar words and phrases that appear in a text, as in the Slingerland program. The most important requirement, regardless of whether or not classroom reading program is used, is that disabled readers are given ample practice in reading connected text, as well as sufficient opportunity to exercise comprehension skills.

# What Educational Placements Are Available for Special Instruction?

In addition to the factors already considered, the choice of educational setting will depend to a great extent upon the school's resources: the size of the teacher-student ratio, the number of specialist teachers, the amount of classroom space, the money available for teacher training, etc. The possible placement options are discussed below.

*Resource room.* This placement affords individualized instruction and the greatest amount of flexibility in planning an alternative curriculum. Several of the programs described or mentioned in this chapter were expressly designed for *one-to-one instruction* (e.g., Orton-Gillingham, the Glass Analysis method); most of the others can be adapted for this purpose.

*Small group instruction* can also take place in the resource room, if there are adequate numbers of students whose academic schedules, as well as educational needs, concur. Many of the programs described can be used with small groups in a resource room (e.g., the Slingerland program, Alphabetic Phonics, Auditory Discrimination in Depth, Project Read, The Merrill Linguistic Readers). However, if students are removed from the regular classroom for special instruction, it is essential that the reading specialist and the classroom teacher work together to coordinate the resource room curriculum with the classroom curriculum (Allington & Broikou, 1988).

*Self-contained classroom.* When there are enough students with similar instructional needs, a whole classroom setting is workable and usually cost-effective, although it may require additional teacher training. One drawback to this approach is that children may be included who do not require special instruction; another is that instruction may not be adequately individualized. DISTAR and the Slingerland program were both designed for whole class instruction with students at risk for reading failure. Alphabetic Phonics or Project Read can be used in self-contained classrooms where smaller classes or a second classroom teacher are financially feasible.

*Within the regular classroom.* Special instruction can be administered within the regular classroom to individual students or to small groups of students. Project Read was specifically designed for this purpose. The significant advantages of this arrangement are that it avoids the stigma of removal from the mainstream and allows for better coordination between the regular and alternative curricula. The specialist can come into the classroom during reading periods to work with students having reading problems or to help the classroom teacher adjust the curriculum for them. CAI and peer tutoring are additional ways to individualize instruction within the regular classroom.

# Summary and Conclusion

This chapter focused on providing appropriate or alternative reading instruction for children with, or at risk for, reading disabilities. It addressed the instructional requirements that most of these children need to prevent reading failure, described many of the teaching methods found to be effective with disabled and at-risk learners, as well as reading programs designed specifically for them, and finally, discussed the implementation of these instructional approaches in schools.

Unfortunately, space constraints limit the focus of this chapter to children in the early elementary grades and prevent consideration of instructional intervention for disabled readers beyond the acquisition of basic reading skills. It needs to be said that spelling instruction and writing instruction are also essential components of effective language arts curricula for these students. Furthermore, for many of these students, alternative approaches to language arts instruction will need to be applied well beyond the elementary grades.

# References

Adams, M.J. (1990). *Beginning to read: Thinking and learning about print.* Cambridge, MA: The MIT Press.

Allington, R.L., & Broikou, K.A. (1988). Development of shared knowledge: A new role for classroom and special teachers. *The Reading Teacher, 41,* 806-811.

Bartlett, E.J. (1979). Curriculum, concepts of literacy, and social class. In L.B. Resnick & P.A. Weaver (Eds.), *Theory and practice of early reading* (Vol. 2, pp. 227-242). Hillsdale, NJ: Lawrence Erlbaum Associates.

Blachman, B.A. (1987). An alternative classroom reading program for learning disabled and other low-achieving children. In *Intimacy with language* (pp. 49-55). Baltimore: The Orton Dyslexia Society.

Boettcher, J.V. (1983). Computer-based education: Classroom application and benefits for the learning disabled. *Annals of Dyslexia, 33,* 203-219.

Bradley, L., & Bryant, P.E. (1985). *Rhyme and reason in reading and spelling.* Ann Arbor, MI: University of Michigan Press.

Bryant, N.D. et al. (1980). The effects of some instructional variables on the learning of handicapped and nonhandicapped populations: A review. *Integrative reviews of research* (Vol. 1, pp. 1-70). New York: Teachers College, Institute for the Study of Learning Disabilities.

Bryant, N.D., Payne, H.R., & Gettinger, M. (1982). Applying the mastery learning model to sight word instruction for disabled readers. *Journal of Experimental Education, 50,* 116-121.

Chall, J.S. (1983a). *Stages of reading development.* New York: McGraw-Hill.

Chall, J.S. (1983b). *Learning to read: The great debate.* New York: McGraw-Hill.

Clark, D.B. (1988). *Dyslexia: Theory and practice of remedial instruction.* Parkton, MD: York Press.

Clay, M.M. (1985). *The early detection of reading difficulties: A diagnostic survey with recovery procedures.* Auckland, New Zealand: Heinemann.

Cox, A.R. (1984). *Structures and techniques.* Cambridge, MA: Educators Publishing Service.

Eckwall, E.E., & Shanker, J.L. (1983). *Diagnosis and remediation of the disabled reader.* Boston: Allyn and Bacon.

Ehri, L. (1979, March). *Learning to read and spell.* Paper presented at the Annual Meeting of American Educational Research Association, Chicago.

Ehri, L. (1985, March). *Learning to read and spell.* Presented at the annual meeting of the American Educational Research Association, Chicago.

Elkonin, D.B. (1963). The psychology of mastering the elements of reading. In B. Simon & J. Simon (Eds.), *Educational psychology in the U.S.S.R.* (pp. 165-179). London: Routledge & Kegan Paul.

Enfield, M.L., & Greene, V.E. (1983). *An evaluation of the results of standardized testing of elementary Project Read and SLD students based on district wide tests administered in October, 1983.* Bloomington, MN: Bloomington Public Schools.

Engelmann, S., & Bruner, E.C. (1983). *Reading mastery I and II: DISTAR reading.* Chicago, IL: Science Research Associates.

Frankiewicz, R.G. (1985). *An evaluation of the impact of Alphabetic Phonics Program offered in the one-to-one mode.* Houston: Neuhaus Foundation.

Fries, C. C., Wilson, R. G., & Rudolph, M. D. (1966). *Merrill linguistic readers.* Columbus, OH: Charles E. Merrill.

Gates, A.L. (1927). *The improvement of reading: A program of diagnostic and remedial methods.* New York: Macmillan.

Gillingham, A., & Stillman, B. (1960). *Remedial training for children with specific disability in reading, writing, and penmanship.* Cambridge, MA: Educators Publishing Service.

Glass, G.G., & Glass, E.W. (1976). *Glass analysis for decoding only: Teachers guide.* Garden City, NY: Easier to Learn.

Goodman, K. (1967). Reading: A psycholinguistic guessing game. *Journal of the Reading Specialist, 6,* 126-135.

Greene, V.E., & Enfield, M.L. (1985). *Project Read reading guide.* Bloomington, MN: Bloomington Public Schools.

Haring, N.G., & Bateman, B. (1977). *Teaching the learning disabled child.* Englewood Cliffs, NJ: Prentice-Hall.

Henk, W.A., Helfeldt, J.P., & Platt, J.M. (1986). Developing reading fluency in learning disabled students. *Teaching Exceptional Children, 12,* 202-206.

Howard, M. (1986). *Effects of pre-reading in auditory conceptualization on subsequent reading achievement.* Unpublished doctoral dissertation, Brigham Young University.

Jones, K.M., Torgesen, J.K., & Sexton, M.A. (1987). Using computer guided practice to increase decoding fluency in learning disabled children: A study using the Hint and Hunt I program. *Journal of Learning Disabilities, 20*(2), 122-128.

Just, M.A., & Carpenter, P.A. (1980). Theory of reading: From eye fixations to comprehension. *Psychological Review, 87,* 3329-3354

Just, M.A., & Carpenter, P.A. (1987). *The psychology of reading and language comprehension.* Boston: Allyn and Bacon.

Kline, C., & Kline, C. (1975). Follow-up study of 216 dyslexic children. *The Bulletin of The Orton Society, 25,* 127-144.

LaBerge, D., & Samuels, S.J. (1974). Toward a theory of automatic information processing in reading. *Cognitive Psychology, 6,* 293-323.

Lewkowicz, N.K. (1980). Phonemic awareness training: What to teach and how to teach it. *Journal of Educational Psychology, 72,* 686-700.

Liberman, I.Y. (1984). A language-directed view of reading disabilities. *Thalamus, 4,* 1-41.

Liberman, I.Y., Shankweiler, D., Liberman, A.M., Fowler, C., & Fischer, F.W. (1977). Phonetic segmentation and recoding in the beginning reader. In A.S. Rober & D.L. Scarborough (Eds.), *Toward a psychology of reading* (pp. 207-225). Hillsdale, NJ: Lawrence Erlbaum.

Lindamood, C.H., & Lindamood, P.C. (1975). *The A.D.D. program, Auditory discrimination in depth: Books 1 and 2.* Hingham, MA: Teaching Resources.

Lindamood, C.H., & Lindamood, P.C. (1979). *The LAC test: Lindamood auditory conceptualization test.* Allen, TX: DLM Teaching Resources.

Maria, K. (1990). *Reading comprehension instruction: Issues and strategies.* Parkton, MD: York Press.

McCulloch, C. (1985). *The Slingerland approach: Is it effective in a specific language disability classroom?* Unpublished master's thesis, Seattle Pacific University, Seattle, WA.

Meyer, L.A., Gersten, R.M., & Gutkin, J. (1983). Direct Instruction: A Project Follow-Through success story in an inner-city school. *Elementary School Journal, 84,* 241-252.

Morais, J., Cary, L., Algeria, J., & Bertelson, P. (1979). Does awareness of speech as a sequence of phonemes arise spontaneously? *Cognition, 7,* 323-331.

Orton, J. (1966). The Orton-Gillingham approach. In J. Money (Ed.), *The disabled reader* (pp. 119-146). Baltimore: The Johns Hopkins University Press.

Pennington, B.F., Lefly, D.L., Van Orden, G.C., Bookman, M.O., & Smith, S.D. (1987). Is phonology bypassed in normal or dyslexic development? *Annals of Dyslexia, 37,* 62-89.

Perfetti, C.A. (1984). Reading acquisition and beyond: Reading includes cognition. *American Journal of Education, 93,* 40-60.

Perfetti, C.A., Bell, L.C., & Delaney, S.M. (1988). Automatic (prelexical) phonetic activation in silent word reading: Evidence from backward masking. *Journal of Memory and Language, 27,* 1-22.

Pinnell, G.S., Fried, M.D., & Estice, R.M. (1990). Reading recovery: Learning how to make a difference. *The Reading Teacher, 43*(4), 283-295.

Rashotte, C.A., & Torgesen, J.K. (1985). Repeated reading and reading fluency in learning disabled children. *Reading Research Quarterly, 20,* 180-188.

Rasmussen, D.E., & Goldberg, L. (1976). *SRA basic reading.* Chicago, IL: Science Research Associates.

Rosenshine, B. (1983). Teaching functions in instructional programs. *Elementary School Journal, 83,* 335-340.

Rosenshine, B., & Stevens, R. (1984). Classroom instruction in reading. In P. D. Pearson (Ed.), *Handbook of reading research* (pp. 745-798). New York: Longman.

Rosner, J. (1975). *Helping children overcome learning disabilities.* New York: Walker & Co.

Roy, B.J. (1986, January). *A cooperative teacher education and language retraining program for dyslexics in West Texas.* Paper presented at the Action in Research V Conference. Lubbock, TX.

Rumelhart, D.E. (1977). Toward an interactive model of reading. In S. Dornic (Ed.), *Attention and performance VI* (pp. 45-67). Hillsdale, NJ: Erlbaum Associates.

Samuels, S.J. (1986). Automaticity and repeated readings. In J. Osborn, P. T. Wilson, & R. C. Anderson (Eds.) *Reading education: Foundations for a literate America* (pp. 215-230). Lexington, MA: D.C. Heath.

Slingerland, B.H. (1971). *A multi-sensory approach to language arts for specific language disability children: A guide for primary teachers, Books 1-3.* Cambridge, MA: Educators Publishing Service.

Smith, F. (1978). *Understanding reading: A psycholinguistic analysis of reading and learning to read.* New York: Holt, Rinehart, and Winston.

Stahl, S.A., & Miller, P.D. (1989). Whole language and language experience approaches for beginning reading: A quantitative research synthesis. *Review of Educational Research, 59,* 87-116.

Stanovich, K.E. (1986). Matthew effects in reading: Some consequences of individual differences in the acquisition of literacy. *Reading Research Quarterly, 21,* 360-407.

Stanovich, K.E., Cunningham, A.E., & Cramer, B.B. (1984). Assessing phonological awareness in kindergarten children: Issues of task comparability. *Journal of Experimental Child Psychology, 38,* 1-90.

Stanovich, K.E., Cunningham, A.E., & Feeman, D.J. (1984). Intelligence, cognitive skills, and early reading progress. *Reading Research Quarterly, 29,* 278-303.

Stein, C., & Goldman, J. (1980). Beginning reading instruction for children with minimal brain dysfunction. *Journal of Learning Disabilities, 13,* 52-55.

Stern, C., & Gould, T. (1965). *Children discover reading.* New York: Random House.

Torgesen, J.K., Waters, M.D., Cohen, A.L., & Torgesen, J. (1988). Improving sight-word recognition skills in LD children: An evaluation of three computer program variations. *Learning Disability Quarterly, 11*(2), 125-133.

Vickery, K.S., Reynolds, V.A., & Cochran, S.W. (1987). Multisensory teaching for reading, spelling, and handwriting, Orton-Gillingham based, in a public school setting. *Annals of Dyslexia, 37,* 189-202.

Williams, J.P. (1980). Teaching decoding with an emphasis on phoneme analysis and phoneme blending. *Journal of Experimental Psychology, 72,* 1-15.

Wolf, B.J. (1985). *The effect of Slingerland instruction on the reading and language of second grade children.* Unpublished doctoral dissertation, Seattle Pacific University, Seattle, WA.

Zigmond, N., & Miller, S.E. (1986). Assessment for instructional planning. *Exceptional Children, 52,* 501-509.

# 4
# Cognitive Strategy Instruction in Written Language for Learning Disabled Students

**Steve Graham and Karen B. Harris**

This chapter will review the work we are presently conducting on teaching writing to learning disabled (LD) students. First, we will examine what we know about the writing of school-age learning disabled students. This will provide a backdrop for the work we have conducted on teaching LD students strategies for improving their composing.

## The Writing of Learning Disabled Students

Learning disabled students have been characterized as having severe and persistent writing problems (Graham & MacArthur, 1987). For example, even learning disabled students who attend college have considerable difficulty with writing in comparison to their nondisabled college peers (cf. Gajar, 1989; Gregg, 1983; Vogel, 1985; Vogel & Moran, 1982). While we currently lack longitudinal data regarding the development and progression of LD students' writing difficulties, enough cross-sectional studies have been conducted that we can at least draw some tentative conclusions regarding their written products. Unfortunately, we know much less about the process by which they write, their knowledge of how to write, and their perceptions of their own writing capabilities. We will briefly examine the available evidence for each of these areas. It should be noted that information on sex of subjects in the studies reviewed will be provided whenever possible, but such information will not be repeatedly presented for the same study in text. As Vogel (1990) has noted LD students' sex may be an important factor in LD students' performance.

### LD Students' Written Products

Much of what we know about learning disabled students' writing is limited to their production of narrative text, primarily creative stories. We have only recently begun to analyze the performance of LD students on expository writing tasks such as opinion essays, explanations, or descriptions. Not surprisingly, researchers have expended most of their efforts on cataloguing indices such as the length, vocabulary diversity, and syntactic complexity of LD students' compositions. Difficult to measure attributes such as quality have been virtually ignored. While the current literature does not allow for the construction of a complete or integrated picture of the characteristics of LD students' written products, it is possible to pinpoint with a reasonable degree of confidence several differences between the writing of LD and normal students.

*Fluency.* Perhaps the most consistent finding across studies is that LD students' compositions are shorter than those written by their normally achieving peers (Barenbaum, Newcomer, & Nodine, 1987; Bryson & Siegel, 1986; Deno, Marston, & Mirkin, 1982; Graham & Harris, 1989a; Meltzer, Fenton, Persky, 1985; Moran, 1981; Myklebust, 1973; Nodine, Barenbaum, & Newcomer, 1985; Poteet, 1979). For example, Nodine and her colleagues (1985) reported that the stories of eleven-year-old learning disabled students (16 males and 14 females) were approximately 54 words long; their normal counterparts wrote stories that averaged 104 words in length. Similarly, when writing an expository paragraph, secondary LD students (16 males and 10 females) produced an average of 70 words; normally achieving students averaged 92 words (Moran, 1981).

*Errors.* In addition to writing comparatively short compositions, LD students' papers contain an inordinate number of errors. Weiner (1980) noted that the eight- to twelve-year-old LD boys participating in her study averaged 52 errors (graphic, orthographic, phonological, syntactic, and semantic errors) per 100 words; normally achieving students committed only 15 errors in the same number of words. Thomas, Englert, and Gregg (1987) obtained similar results; the third, fourth, sixth, and seventh grade LD students (21 males and 15 females) in their study, made significantly more errors in spelling, handwriting, and syntax than normally achieving students. Many of the LD students' papers were "uninterpretable because of spelling or syntactical problems" (p. 27).

One category of errors that is especially salient in LD students' writing is mechanical errors. In comparison to normally achieving students, they make considerably more spelling, capitalization, and punctuation errors (cf. Moran, 1981; Poteet, 1979). For example, LD students misspell approximately 10 to 20% of the words they use in their writing; normal students only misspell about 5% of the words they write (Bryson & Siegel, 1986; Deno et al., 1982; Hermreck, 1975; MacArthur & Graham, 1987; MacArthur, Graham & Schwartz, 1988; Moran, 1981). Furthermore, MacArthur and Graham (1987) and MacArthur et al. (1988) found that LD students at both the elementary and secondary level averaged a capitalization and a punctuation error in 30 to 40% of the sentences they produced.

Information on handwriting problems that interfere with the legibility of LD students' written products are surprisingly scarce. While there is considerable agreement among practitioners and clinicians that the quality of LD students' penmanship is poor (Graham, Boyer-Schick, & Tippets, 1989), we were only able to locate three studies that addressed this issue. Meltzer et al. (1985) noted that in comparison to normal achievers, the written products of nine- to fourteen-year-old students with learning difficulties (equal distribution of males and females) exhibited more problems with important attributes of penmanship such as letter formation, alignment, and spacing. Similar findings have been reported by Graham et al. (1989) and MacArthur, Graham, and Skarvold (1986). They found that the legibility of the compositions produced by upper elementary-age LD students was poorer than that of their same-age peers. Furthermore, the LD students (31 males and 20 females) in the Graham et al. (1989) study evidenced considerable difficulty with letter formation, alignment, spacing, size, and neatness. It must be pointed out, however, that handwriting problems do not appear to be problematic for all LD students. There was a small group of students in the Graham et al. (1989) study who produced compositions as legible as those produced by average students.

Learning disabled students also appear to make more errors involving the conventions of written language than do normal students (cf. Moran, 1981). Conventions include those features of written expression that are governed by oral and written language rules, including verb markers for tense, noun markers for plurality, possessive forms of nouns and pronouns, and subject-predicate agreement. We suspect that errors of convention are not, however, as prevalent in the writing of LD students as are their mechanical errors. MacArthur and Graham (1987) found that upper elementary-aged LD students (6 males and 5 females) made, on the average, only three convention errors per 100 words when composing with either handwriting or word processing.

*Structural adequacy.* Another area that has been of considerable interest to researchers is the basic structural adequacy of LD students' written products. Within the narrative domain, investigators have used several different methods to analyze the structure of students' stories. One set of procedures involves analyzing structural adequacy in global terms. This has included rating the general structural adequacy of papers (Montague, Maddux, & Dereshiwsky, 1988), determining if papers meet the basic requirements for a story-setting plus conflict plus resolution (Bryson & Siegel, 1986), or classifying compositions along a continuum ranging from expressive writing to story writing (cf. Nodine et al., 1985).

In general, the results from research involving global evaluations have been fairly consistent; LD students were not as successful as normal students in meeting the structural requirements of a story (Barenbaum et al., 1987; Bryson & Siegel, 1986; Montague et al., 1988; Newcomer, Barenbaum, & Nodine, 1988; Nodine et al., 1985). The findings from several of these experiments, however, need to be clarified. While Montague et al. (1988) found global differences between LD and normal students attending fourth through eleventh grade, they further reported that 75% of the LD students included at least one complete episode (starter event/goal/action/ consequence) in their stories. Second, results from the Barenbaum et al. (1987) and Newcomer et al. (1988) studies were somewhat equivocal. In both investigations, LD and normal students wrote an equivalent proportion of papers that were classified as stories (setting/conflict/resolution) and primitive stories (beginning/middle/end). The most striking difference involved papers not classified as stories. Normal students were more likely to write papers that contained an action sequence, while LD students were more likely to write a description or to simply express thoughts about the topic.

A second means for analyzing the structural adequacy of LD students' stories has involved noting and/or rating specific structural elements included in students' papers. Graham and Harris (1989a) and Montague et al. (1988) both found that LD students' stories contained fewer basic elements than those written by normal students. Nonetheless, LD students' stories contained important story elements such as the main character, time, locale, action, and ending; what was commonly lacking was a focus on initiating events, goals, motives, thoughts, and feelings (Graham & Harris, 1989a; MacArthur & Graham, 1987; MacArthur et al., 1988; Montague et al., 1988).

Only a couple of studies have examined the structural adequacy of LD students' expository products. Englert and Thomas (1987) found that third through seventh grade LD students (21 males and 15 females) were less likely to produce papers that conformed to the topic and text structure requirements of different expository writing tasks when compared with those written by their normally achieving peers. MacArthur et al. (1988) reported that while the opinion essays of LD students in junior high school (29 males and 11 females) usually contained a premise as well as supporting reasons and elaborations, a concluding statement was absent in almost half of the students' papers.

Based on the results of the studies reviewed, LD students appear to be less adept than their normal counterparts in producing papers that meet the basic structural requirements for common narrative and expository writing tasks. This should not be interpreted to imply that their papers lack text structure. Most of the LD students participating in the reviewed studies produced at least a rudimentary, if not fully developed, structure in their compositions.

*Organization and quality.* While the available literature provides support for the assertion that LD students' writing is inordinately brief, error prone, and may be missing basic text elements, it is much more difficult to draw any firm conclusions regarding the cohesion, coherence, or quality of the content included in LD students' papers. To date, only four studies have investigated compositions of school-age LD students in terms of cohesion and/or coherence. Nodine and her colleagues (1985) indicated that 45% of the eleven-year-old LD students in their study wrote stories that were classified as either incoherent, confusing, or contained unclear referents; only 26% of the normals from their control group exhibited similar problems. They failed, however, to replicate these differences using the same measure in a study conducted with third, fifth, and seventh grade students (Newcomer et al., 1988). Montague et al. (1988) investigated cohesion by establishing a rating relative to the number of structural elements that were connected within the students' text. They reported that stories produced by normal students were significantly more cohesive than those of fourth through eleventh grade LD students. Finally, Bryson and Siegel (1986) found that eight-to fifteen-year-old LD students had more difficulty than normal students in the use of cohesive between-sentence ties and hierarchically ordering episodic information; for example, explicitly marking or noting cause and effect relationships.

Based on the studies reviewed, we suspect that organizational problems are evident in LD students' text. Furthermore, the best means for investigating these are the fine-grain type of analyses used by Bryson and Siegel (1986).

Evidence on the quality of the content included in LD students written products can, at this point, only be viewed as suggestive; studies examining this issue are scarce and replication of obtained findings is nonexistent. In an early study, Poplin, Gray, Larsen, Banikowski, and Mehring (1980) found that LD students in fifth through eighth grade registered lower scores on the Thematic Maturity subtest of the Test of Written Language than did normally achieving students. The Thematic Maturity subtest reportedly measures whether a story efficiently conveys meaning in a logical and sequence mannered. Thomas et al. (1987) indicated that the third through seventh grade LD students participating in their study were more likely than their normal peers to produce irrelevant and redundant content in their writing. Graham and Harris (1989a) reported that the overall quality of fifth and sixth grade LD students' stories was poorer than that of normal students; however, these results must be interpreted cautiously since the stories developed by the two groups were generated in response to similar but different pictures.

*Vocabulary and syntactic complexity.* There are several important writing variables on which LD and normal students' compositions do not differ. First, differences in writing vocabulary have not been established in terms of number and proportion of different words, number of large words, or word types (Barenbaum et al. 1987; Deno et al., 1982; Moran, 1981; Poplin et al., 1980). While Morris and Crump (1982) found that nine- to fifteen-year-old male LD and normal students' papers differed in terms of the corrected type/token ratio (a measure of word variety), no differences were found when using a vocabulary intensity index that involved the computation of such factors as vocabulary difficulty, diversity, or number of multisyllabic words. In addition, Deno et al. (1982) noted that normal students used more "mature words" in their writing than did third through sixth grade LD students. Their conclusions regarding this variable are misleading, since normal students' papers were longer than those written by LD students. When we reexamined their data in terms of proportion of mature words to total words, differences between the two groups disappeared.

Another variable that does not appear to yield any meaningful distinctions between LD and normal students' are measures of syntactic fluency. Differences have not been found in average T-unit length, number of T-units, or number of complex T-units (Barenbaum et al., 1987; Deno et al., 1982; Hermreck, 1975; Moran, 1981; Morris & Crump, 1982; Nodine et al., 1985). A T-unit is a single independent clause (single) plus what ever subordinate clauses or non clauses are attached to or attached or embedded in it. Somewhat similarly, elementary and secondary LD students have been reported to use the same types of sentences as their normally achieving peers (Hermreck, 1975; Moran, 1981). Moran (1981), however, reported that almost 20% of the sentences produced by secondary LD students in her study were run-ons.

*Influence of writing task.* Most of the research involving LD students' written products has been limited to one genre, story writing. Nevertheless, the type of writing task that LD students are assigned can affect what is written. For example, MacArthur et al. (1988) reported significant differences in the length of junior high school LD students' stories and essays, while Blair and Crump (1984) indicated that the syntactical complexity and distribution of sentence types differed when sixth through tenth grade male LD students wrote a description versus an argument. In contrast, MacArthur et al. (1988) found that junior high school LD students' stories and essays were similar with regard to quality of handwriting, proportion of mechanical errors, and pattern of revisions. Clearly more research is needed to examine the impact of topic on the written products of LD students.

## Composing Behavior of LD Students

In a recent review of literature, Graham and Harris (1989b) put forth the proposition that LD students have particular difficulty with important cognitive processes underlying effective writing. This supposition will be illustrated by examining the literature presently available.

*Generating content.* Learning disabled students have a great deal of difficulty finding enough to say; i.e., as mentioned earlier their compositions are inordinately short. While their content generation problems may be due to a lack of knowledge about the topics they are asked to write about, some recent evidence suggests that they don't necessarily use the knowledge they have. For instance, Graham (1989) found that simply encouraging fourth and sixth grade LD students (15 males and 8 females) to produce more after they had ostensibly stopped writing doubled to tripled their output on an argumentative essay. While not quite half of the newly developed text was redundant with previously generated content or was irrelevant, the proportion of text that was functional resulted in an increase in the number of reasons that supported a writer's premise and considerably more elaboration on specific points within a student's paper.

Englert and her colleagues (Englert & Raphael, 1988; Englert, Raphael, & Anderson, 1986; Thomas et al. 1987) have argued that LD students have difficulty with content generation because they are not adept at employing strategies for self-directed memory search. To illustrate, Thomas et al., (1987), found that third through seventh grade LD students evidenced difficulty in sustaining their thinking about topics; they failed to produce multiple statements about familiar subjects. Englert and Raphael (1988) suggest that these results indicate that LD students have distinct problems in retrieving ideas and using relevant schemas to maintain their writing in generative ways.

*Framing text.* Framing text involves the active process of developing an ongoing structure for a composition by using knowledge of genre patterns or other discourse schemas to regulate what will go where. As was indicated in the previous section, LD students are less likely than normal students to produce text that conforms to the common text structures found in different types of discourse. Two possible explanations can be put forward to account for these differences: their knowledge is incomplete and/or they have difficulty gaining access to or using all of the structural knowledge they possess. As Garner and Gillingham (1987) indicate, it is difficult to assess students' knowledge of the structural properties of text and, not surprisingly, the veracity of each of these propositions or their interaction has not been adequately established. Nonetheless, some support for the proposition that LD students have difficulty using genre patterns to frame text can be obtained from applied research. Several studies have shown that LD students' written products can be improved by teaching them specific genre patterns and a strategy for using these patterns for generating writing content (Graham & Harris, 1989a; Graham & MacArthur, 1988; Sawyer, Graham, & Harris, 1988).

*Producing text.* Having to consciously attend to the lower level skills of getting language onto paper (handwriting, spelling, and so forth) may interfere with higher order cognitive processes such as planning and content generation (Graham, 1982). For instance, the laborious production of individual letters may disrupt the associative processes involved in generating content or cause the writer to forget ideas or plans already developed (MacArthur & Graham, 1987). While mastery of mechanics appears to be sufficiently developed for upper-elementary age normal student so that interference is not a serious problem (Scardamalia, Bereiter, & Goelman, 1982), this does not appear to be the case for LD students. In a study by MacArthur and Graham (1987), fifth and sixth grade students generated longer and better stories when the mechanical requirements of composing were removed via dictation. Graham (1989) partially replicated these results with fourth and sixth grade LD students when he found that they generated qualitatively better essays when composing via dictation versus handwriting; differences in length of essays across the two modes of composing were not found, however. Basically, the handwritten and dictated essays were very short. Nevertheless, the dictated essays contained more functional elements and were more coherent. These latter two findings provide a possible explanation for the obtained differences in quality.

Graham (1989) also provided additional evidence in his study on the effects of mechanics on LD students' writing. This was accomplished by adding a third composing condition which Scardamalia et al. (1982) have termed slow dictation. This new condition required that the scribe take dictation at the same rate that LD students wrote their essays. By comparing handwriting and slow dictation, the effects of mechanical interference were isolated while the effects of speed were controlled. Correspondingly, the effects of speed were isolated by comparing dictation and slow dictation while the effects of mechanics were removed. Based on these comparisons, Graham found that mechanics had a negative effect on fourth and sixth grade LD students' writing; slow dictation resulted in longer and qualitatively better essays than handwriting. The effects of speed on LD students' written products were not so clear cut; dictated and slow-dictated essays did not differ in quality, but slow dictated essays were longer. These obtained differences in length were due, at least in part (though not entirely), to the generation of more nonfunctional information during slow dictation.

*Planning text.* Not much is known about how LD students plan their compositions. MacArthur and Graham (1987) noted that even though they prompted the fifth and sixth grade LD students in their study to plan their stories in advance, the average amount of advanced planning time was less than one minute.

Englert and her colleagues (Englert & Raphael, 1988; Thomas et al., 1987) have suggested that LD students' planning can best be described as what Scardamalia and Bereiter (1986) have termed *knowledge-telling*: convert the writing tasks into simply telling whatever one knows. Thomas et al. (1987) provide support for this proposal in a study examining the errors that LD and normally achieving students committed while composing different types of text. The results of the study were consistent with several of the characteristics that Brown, Day, and Jones (1983) indicated exemplify the knowledge-telling strategy. For example, third through seventh grade LD students were more likely than normally achieving students to include redundant and irrelevant information in their writing, reflecting a lack of interconnectedness and suggesting that one sentence may be as deletable as the next, two key features of the knowledge-telling strategy. Moreover, many of the LD students converted the writing assignments into a question-answering task; telling whatever came to mind and then terminating their response or answering in short choppy phrases. While there is not enough evidence to determine if the knowledge-telling strategy provides a cogent description of LD students' planning, the model is not inconsistent with the evidence available.

*Revising.* Only two studies have taken an in-depth look at LD students' revising behavior. In one of the studies (MacArthur & Graham, 1987), fifth and sixth grade LD students wrote and revised two stories: one on the word processor and one via handwriting. In the second study (MacArthur et al., 1988), LD students in junior high school wrote and revised two compositions: one was a story and the other was an essay. While some differences were noted between word processing and handwriting in terms of timing of revisions, LD students' overall approaches to revising in the two studies were very similar. First, LD students made a number of changes when directed to revise their first draft. These changes ranged from an average of 9 to 19 revisions per 100 words, depending on the mode of composing or the genre of writing. Second, their basic outlook and approach to revising was to detect and correct mechanical and stylistic errors. The most frequent revisions involved surface-level (for example, spelling or capitalization) or word changes; close to 80% of all revisions fell into these two categories. Third, LD students' revisions were not very effective.

Reductions in the proportion of mechanical errors from first to second drafts were not found in either study. Furthermore, when revisions involved larger units of text, such changes more often than not failed to result in significantly better or even altered units of text. LD students' revisions, also, did not affect the length or overall quality of their written products. Nonetheless, MacArthur et al. (1988) indicated that revising did result in a small increase in the legibility of LD students' written products. This is consistent with the view that the mechanical features of text drive the revising process for LD students.

## Knowledge of the Writing Process

Effective writing requires more than the development of effective strategies for the cognitive processes of planning, drafting, and revising text; it is also dependent on executive procedures for putting these strategies into use at the proper time (Scardamalia & Bereiter, 1986). The development of efficient executive procedures may well be hindered if students lack the metacognitive knowledge to recognize what strategies are needed and to successfully regulate implementation. According to Englert, Raphael, Fear, and Anderson (1988), LD students are less aware than normally achieving students about how to write. The fourth and fifth grade LD students in their study (6 males and 4 females), were less likely than normal controls to be knowledgeable about the writing process, including awareness of the steps in writing, strategies for presenting ideas, and procedures for selecting and integrating information from multiple sources. Furthermore, LD students were less knowledgeable about how to control and regulate the writing process, use organizational patterns to generate or organize ideas, and monitor the quality of text. Our preliminary examination of the data from a metacognitive interview we have conducted with junior high school students (Graham, MacArthur, & Schwartz, 1988), would also support the contention that LD students are less knowledgeable about writing than are their normally achieving peers.

# Perceptions of Writing Capabilities

The ability to assess one's own capabilities is an important metacognitive skill (Flavell & Wellman, 1977). There is increasing evidence that young children and learning disabled students have significant difficulties with predicting/assessing their performance (Flavell & Wellman, 1977; Harris, Graham, & Freeman, 1988). In relation to writing, Graham and Harris (1989a) reported that fifth and sixth grade LD students consistently overestimated their ability to write creative stories. Similarly, Graham et al. (1988) indicated that LD students were as confident as their normal peers in terms of their capabilities to write reports and stories and to engage in the various cognitive processes (e.g., idea generation, organizing information, or revising) considered central to effective writing. LD students' unrealistically high expectations in writing may be due to faulty self-knowledge, employment of a self-protective coping strategy, comprehension deficiencies, selective attention to mastered instead of unmastered task elements, or a developmental delay in the ability to match task demands to ability levels (Graham & Harris, 1989a; Harris et al., 1988).

## Summary

Our analyses of the literature have lead us to develop a hypothesis that one or more of the following three factors account for the difficulties LD students have with writing. One, their problems with text production may interfere with the execution of other important cognitive processes such as content generation, planning, or revising. Two, their lack of knowledge and/or their inability to gain access to the knowledge they possess may have a very pervasive impact on the operation and deployment of the cognitive processes considered central to effective writing, resulting in texts that are impoverished, incomplete, and/or inconsiderate of the needs of the reader. LD students may have difficulty with knowledge related to topic, audience, context, and genre. Furthermore, they may have difficulty in assessing their own capabilities and being able to recognize what strategies and processes are needed and how to regulate their use. Third, the cognitive moves or strategies that LD students employ when engaging in a cognitive process such as planning may be ineffective.

Our own research along with that of our colleagues at the University of Maryland has addressed, at least in part, each of these three factors. We have been involved in a series of studies that will be described in the next section that have involved strategy training and, in some instances, acquisition of genre-specific knowledge. In addition, we have conducted several studies (that will not be reviewed here) examining (a) alternatives to the traditional methods of text production (see MacArthur & Graham, 1987; Graham, 1989), and (b) the use of self-monitoring procedures during writing or writing instruction as a means for improving productivity and on-task behavior (Harris, 1986; Harris & Stern, 1988).

## Self-Instructional Strategy Training

Our strategy training studies have utilized a consistent instructional framework that we have labeled self-instructional strategy training (Graham & Harris, 1987, 1989b; Graham, Harris, & Sawyer, 1987; Harris & Graham, 1988). Seven basic but flexible, steps provide the format for this strategy training regimen: (a) pretraining, (b) review of current performance level, (c) description of the strategy, (d) modeling of the strategy and self-instructions, (e) mastery of the composition strategy, (f) controlled practice of the strategy and self-instructions, and (g) independent performance. Procedures for promoting maintenance and generalization are embedded throughout the training steps.

We have commonly used the seven training steps in the following manner. First, preskills important to understanding, acquiring, or executing the targeted strategy that are not already in the student's repertoire are taught. Second, the instructor and student examine and discuss prior performance and any strategies that the student presently uses. The significance and potential benefits of the proposed training are then discussed, and a commitment to participate as a partner and to attempt the strategies is solicited from the student. Also, negative or ineffective self-statements that the student currently uses are discussed, and specific self-regulation procedures are introduced at this point. Third, the instructor describes the strategy, its purposes, and outlines how and when to use it. Fourth, the instructor models the strategy and appropriate self-instructions (including problem definition, self-evaluation, coping and error correction, and self-reinforcement) using language suitable to the characteristics of the student. Following a discussion of the model's performance, the student generates and records specific self-statements for each type of self-instruction. Fifth, strategy steps are memorized, and each may be paraphrased as long as the original meaning is maintained. To aid in memorization of strategy steps and other pertinent material, students practice memorizing with and then without cue cards. Sixth, the student practices using the strategy and self-instructions. Instructor guidance and any physical prompts such as strategy charts are faded as the student independently reaches criterion during subsequent practice sessions. Furthermore, criterion levels for performance are gradually increased until the instructional objective is met. Self-regulation procedures such as goal-setting, self-assessment, or self-recording are used throughout this step. Seventh, the student is encouraged to use independently and covertly the strategy and self-instructions. Self-regulation procedures are usually continued at this point, but may be faded. Finally, the students' performance in independently using the strategy over time is monitored. Procedures for promoting maintenance and generalization, that are incorporated in the training regimen include, but are not limited to, the instructor and student discussing opportunities to utilize the strategy and self-instructions in other tasks and settings, asking teachers and parents to comment on the student's success in using the strategy, and encouraging teachers to prompt the use of the strategies in their mainstream classrooms.

It is important to note that training is criterion based; students do not progress to a new training step until the previous step is mastered. We have used the self-instructional strategy training format with both individuals and small groups of students. Moreover, this training regimen has proven to be an effective method for strategy instruction in general as it has been used to teach LD students strategies for handwriting (Graham, 1983), spelling (Graham & Freeman, 1986; Harris et al., 1988), composing (cf. Harris & Graham, 1985), and mathematics (Case & Harris, 1988).

## Developing and Teaching Composition Strategies

Before strategy instruction begins, careful learner and task analyses need to be conducted to determine training goals, select training tasks, and establish both the strategy(s) to be taught and a sequence of learning activities (Harris, 1982). These principles have guided our research efforts in using strategy training to improve LD students' writing performance.

*Learner analysis.* In designing and teaching selected composition strategies, we have primarily directed our efforts at improving specific components of the writing process that LD students generally have difficulty with (for example, revising). We have also directed our attention at carefully considering characteristics of our LD subjects such as their age, language development, cognitive capacity and competence, attributions and beliefs, expectations and attitudes, initial knowledge state, and current strategy usage. For example, if the students we are working with have severe written language deficits, the selection and construction of training activities is affected. This may include the use of prolonged pretraining, more explicit training procedures and components, simpler strategies, and/or more externally based and frequent reinforcement. Similarly, subjects who exhibit maladaptive attributions, negative self-perceptions, and/or poor attitudes receive instruction on using self-statements aimed at developing an internal locus of control and a stronger sense of self-efficacy.

*Task analysis.* In conjunction with the learner analysis, we conduct a careful analysis of the targeted composition task (e.g., revising). This includes not only specifying the goals of training (e.g., doubling the number of revisions and increasing the proportion of revisions that positively affect text meaning), but also determining the psychological demands of the task as well as the sequential, organized cognitions that the student must engage in in order to perform the task successfully (i.e., the strategy). In addition, we also consider the complexity of the resulting strategy and the level of frustration likely to be induced by training. Such considerations may result in a strategy mnemonic, charts, or worksheets to help alleviate or moderate anticipated demands.

*Characteristics of training.* Results from the learner and task analyses not only provide us with the necessary information to select or devise appropriate strategies and self-regulation procedures, but also (as can be seen from the above discussion) yield information on what components should be used to facilitate the acquisition and deployment of the strategies. While we have used the general framework of the self-instructional training model, the training components used in individual studies have differed slightly depending on who participated in the study, the targeted composition task, where the study took place, or the strategy selected.

*Evaluation of training.* In conducting specific experiments, we have evaluated strategy and skill development as well as other affective, cognitive, and behavioral changes that may occur (Harris, 1985). Evaluation of the effect of teaching LD students specific composition strategies has included (a) validation of instructional manipulation either through observation or concrete proof that the strategy was employed, (b) examination of pertinent changes in students' writing performance, (c) inspection of changes in students' cognitions (most often self-efficacy) or attitudes toward writing, (d) social validation of the strategy and training procedures by teachers and students, and (e) collection of evidence on maintenance and generalization (across settings and tasks) of observed effects. Most if not all of these evaluation components have been included in the composition strategy training studies conducted to date.

## Strategy for Increasing Vocabulary Diversity

Several investigations have shown that the type of vocabulary students include in their compositions is a powerful predictor of teachers' ratings of the quality of their writing (Grobe, 1981; Steward & Grobe, 1979). While LD students as a group do not appear to have much difficulty in using a variety of words in their writing (see previous discussion), some individual learning disabled students do evidence such difficulties; for example, their story writing may lack color because they fail to use descriptive words. In our first investigation examining the effectiveness of strategy training in improving LD students' compositions (Harris & Graham, 1985), we sought to increase the number and diversity of action verbs, adverbs, and adjectives in the creative stories written by sixth grade LD students (1 male and 1 female). The subjects in this study were selected because they commonly failed to use a variety of different and colorful words in their compositions, and their writing was brief and generally of poor quality.

The targeted vocabulary items were taught using a strategy instructional package that included mastery of a five-step composition strategy, self-instructional statements, and self-regulation procedures centered around goal setting. The composition strategy, illustrated here with action words, directed the student to (a) look at the picture (stimulus item) and write down good words, (b) think of good story ideas to use my words in, (c) write my story–use good action words and be sure my story makes sense, (d) read back over my story and ask myself–did I write a good story), and (e) fix my story–can I use more good action words? The self-instructional statements included prompts to facilitate generation of the target items through brainstorming (e.g., "Think of good words; let my mind be free"), problem definition (e.g., "What is it I have to do? What kinds of words do I need to use?"), self-evaluation (e.g., "Am I doing a good job? Have I included all the word types?"), and self-reinforcement (e.g., "I'm doing good work. My story is going to be good."). The self-regulation component of training was introduced after the students memorized the strategy and self-instructional statements. Prior to writing, students were taught to set specific goals regarding the number and diversity of vocabulary items they would include in their stories. Once the composition was finished, students graphed and evaluated their performance and set a new goal for their next story.

Stories written by the LD students after training demonstrated substantial increases above baseline levels in number and diversity of the three target items:

action verbs, adverbs, and adjectives. Posttraining stories were also much longer and received higher quality ratings than pretraining stories. Furthermore, increases in story length did not appear to be due solely to increases in the target vocabulary items. Training procedures resulted not only in the production of more action verbs, adverbs, and adjectives, but in an increase in the generation of other story content as well. Thus, the process of listing vocabulary words before writing may stimulate further content generation by supplying students with an executive strategy for carrying out a self-directed memory search (Graham & Harris, 1989b). In addition, increases in story length and vocabulary diversity may have been partially responsible for changes in story quality. MacArthur and Graham (1987) found that both of these indices were related to the overall quality of stories composed by learning disabled students.

We also found that generalization from the training setting to the students' special education resource room occurred and that the obtained effects were maintained for up to six weeks. However, on a follow-up probe collected 3 1/2 months after training, long-term maintenance and transfer were found for only one of the three vocabulary variables. Since the students did remember all of the strategy steps and the different vocabulary items, the application of a booster session would likely have returned performance rates to their initial posttraining levels.

The utility of a strategy is based not only on its effectiveness, but how well it can be adapted to different tasks. We believe the basic framework for the strategy in the Harris and Graham (1985) study can be modified to adequately meet this second criterion. For example, the strategy could be adapted to other types of vocabulary items or the generation of words or ideas that students will use in their compositions. To illustrate, Scardamalia and Bereiter (1986), found that having students generate words that they think they might use in their writing resulted in increases in content generation.

## A Planning Strategy Emphasizing Goal Setting

One of a number of recommendations made by Graham & Harris (1988a) on teaching writing to exceptional students is that educators should assist students in the development of goals for improving their written products. Goal setting may not only improve LD students' writing performance, but at the same time may promote the development of the cognitive processes central to effective writing. As Scardamalia and Bereiter (1986) have indicated, students who know what they are striving for and how successful they are in obtaining their goals are more likely to develop the cognitive processes necessary for component performance.

According to Flower and Hayes (1980), planning in writing includes three subprocesses: generating (retrieving relevant information), organizing (structuring useful information), and goal setting (developing goals and establishing means for meeting goals). In a study by Graham, MacArthur, Schwartz, and Page

(1989) each of these subprocesses were emphasized, but the process of goal setting received particular attention. Fifth grade LD students (3 males and 1 female) were taught a strategy that involved setting a limited number of specific and realistic writing goals (i.e., product goals) and establishing plans for how each goal would be met (i.e., process goals). Gaa (1979) reported that goal setting had a positive effect on reading performance and that the effectiveness of product goals can be enhanced by establishing process goals. A second component of the strategy included the generation and sequencing of writing notes prior to actually writing. Furthermore, subjects were encouraged to continue the process of planning as they drafted their paper. Finally, they evaluated their written product to determine if they successfully met the goals they established.

More specifically, the strategy involved three steps: (a) do PLANS (Pick goals; List ways to meet goals; And make Notes; and Sequence notes); (b) write and say more; and (c) test goals to see if they have been met. Goals were limited to three areas: purpose (e.g., "to make it fun"), content (e.g., "include all parts"), and length (e.g., "write a paper x words or longer"). Before the start of the study, students were taught to identify and generate the parts of essays and stories.

Prior to training in the strategy, the LD students included approximately three to four essay elements in each of their essays. Following training, students' included two to three times as many elements as were generated during baseline. In addition, essays written after training were considerably longer and received higher scores on overall quality. The amount of time spent planning essays also increased meaningfully. Prior to training, students usually spent less than 30 seconds planning. Following training, this increased to approximately 10 minutes per student.

The observed results were maintained over a twelve-week period, and we further examined whether or not training would have a positive transfer effect to a second genre, narrative stories. At the conclusion of training, students had discussed with the examiner how to use the three-step strategy to write a story. For one of the students, there was an increase in number of story elements, length, and quality following training. Two of the other students failed to show significant posttreatment gains, while the final student applied the strategy incorrectly when writing stories. Consequently, these three students received a short booster session in which the strategy was modeled with story writing. Following the booster session, all three of the students evidenced improvement in number of story elements, length, and quality across several story probes.

Evidence that students used the three-step strategy was also obtained. Moreover, students and teachers both reported that the strategy improved performance and should be taught to other LD students.

The three-step strategy used in the Graham et al. (1989) investigation could easily be adapted to other aspects of the writing task. For example, the procedure could be modified so that students set product and process goals for revising their written products. Furthermore, the goal-setting components could be activated by the teacher during individual writing conferences instead of through strategy instruction.

## Strategies Involving Structural Framing

As Graham and Harris (1988a) have indicated, students need to be able to activate and use knowledge relevant to the kinds of writing tasks they are assigned. For example, the development of a written argument requires knowledge of the purpose, conventions, and strategies pertinent to this genre. In two different studies (Graham & Harris, 1989a,c), we have provided LD students with direct instruction in the structural elements representative of specific genres as well as training in how to use this knowledge to frame or structure their compositions. This instruction was designed to provide LD students with prefabricated plans that could be used to shape their compositions.

In the first study (Graham & Harris, 1989a), fifth and sixth grade LD students learned to use a strategy for developing and writing a narrative story. The steps of the strategy were (a) look at the picture (stimulus item), (b) let your mind be free, (c) write down the story part reminder (Who-When-Where; What = 2, How = 2), (d) write down story part ideas for each part, and (e) write your story—use good parts and make sense. The mnemonic in the third step included seven self-generated questions designed to prompt the production of content relevant to common story elements. The questions were (a) Who is the main character, who else is in the story?  (b) When does the story take place?  (c) Where does the story take place?  (d) What does the main character do?  (e) What happens when he/she tries to do it?  (f) How does the story end? and (g) How does the main character feel?  Students used the generated content as a schematic blueprint for their stories. They also learned to use self-instructional prompts (in conjunction with the strategy) for promoting brainstorming, problem definition, self-evaluation, and self-reinforcement. Finally, half of the students were taught explicit, self-regulation procedure, including goal-setting (i.e., number of elements to be generated), self-assessment, and self-recording using a graph.

Mastery of the strategy resulted in meaningful improvements in creative writing behavior. First, the structure of stories written after training evidenced significant improvement; only 36% of LD students' stories written prior to training included at least six common story elements, while 86% of stories written after training met this same criteria. Furthermore, LD students were significantly less adept than their normally achieving peers at incorporating story grammar elements into their compositions prior to training. However, following training their performance in terms of number of story elements was indistinguishable from that of same-age, skilled writers. Second, posttraining stories received significantly higher quality ratings than did pretraining stories. Third, students' confidence (self-efficacy) in their ability to write a good story also improved. Fourth, training effects generalized to a new classroom setting and were maintained two weeks after treatment. Some of the students also reported using or adapting the strategy for other types of writing assignments, for reading stories, and for writing outlines. Finally, students who used the self-assessment and graphing procedures evaluated them enthusiastically; nonetheless, the explicit self-regulation procedures did not produce augmented effects on any of the measures of writing performance or on self-efficacy.

In the second study (Graham & Harris, 1989c), LD students (1 male and 2 females) were again taught a strategy for generating content in relation to the structural requirements of a specific genre; argumentative essays were chosen as the focal point for this investigation. Students were further directed to evaluate their writing content by considering the potential reader(s) of their text as well as reasons for writing their compositions. Students were also encouraged to expand on their prewriting notes while actually writing their essays.

The strategy in the Graham and Harris (1989c) study consisted of three steps: (a) think, who will read this and why am I writing this; (b) plan what to say using TREE (note Topic sentence, note Reasons, Examine reasons, note Ending); and (c) write and say more. Moreover, students developed and practiced self-instructional prompts for brainstorming, problem definition, self-evaluation, and self-reinforcement.

The strategy was effective in improving sixth grade LD students' essay writing. Following training, students wrote essays that were judged to be qualitatively better, and their essays generally included all of the components (premise, reasons, and conclusions) central to a complete argument. The amount of material relevant to a student's paper increased, while content tangential or unrelated to the author's basic premise decreased. Essays were usually longer and the text that students produced was coherently ordered. Use of the strategy by the students was documented and when they used the strategy they were much more likely to spend time generating ideas and notes prior to writing. Furthermore, the obtained effects were maintained over time and transferred to the students' classroom. Associated with the changes in writing performance were changes in students' affect; two of the three students became more confident in their ability to write an essay. The students and their teacher reported that the strategy was effective and should be taught to other students. Finally, some evidence for transfer of training effects to a second genre, story writing, was obtained. However, for two of the students a booster session was implemented; they received practice in using the mnemonic SPACE (note Setting, Purpose, Action, Conclusion, and Emotion) during the second step of the strategy. Following the booster, their stories improved considerably.

The strategies developed in the two experiments just reviewed can also be adapted to other tasks. Story element questions similar to the ones used in the Graham and Harris (1989a) study, were used by Short and Ryan (1984) to facilitate comprehension of appropriate reading material. Furthermore, teachers can adapt the three-step writing strategy in Graham and Harris (1989c) to other writing genres by providing students with a specific aid (like SPACE) to help them generate content relevant to the genre under consideration.

## Strategies For Revising

As discussed in a previous section of this chapter, LD students' primary outlook and approach to revising tends to center around simply detecting and correcting mechanical and stylistic errors (MacArthur & Graham, 1987, MacArthur et al., 1988). Consequently, in a study by Graham and MacArthur (1988), fifth and sixth grade LD students (2 males and 1 female) were taught a revising strategy for not only detecting and correcting mechanical errors, but also for improving the clarity and cohesiveness of their argumentative essays. In addition, the strategy included self-directed prompts for adding relevant textual material, and it was designed to be used when working on a word processor.

The revising strategy included the following six steps: (a) read your essay; (b) find the sentence that tells what you believe–is it clear?; (c) add two reasons why you believe it; (d) SCAN each sentence (does it make Sense, is it Connected to my belief, can I Add more, Note errors); (e) make changes on the computer; and (f) reread the essay and make final changes.

The effectiveness of the revision strategy was clearly demonstrated. Following training, there was a positive change not only in the number of revisions students made but also in the type of revisions completed; revisions that altered textual meaning and involved larger units of text increased. Associated with the change in student's revising behavior were changes in writing performance and affect. Students' essays became longer and were judged to be qualitatively better. In addition, students reported that they were more confident in their ability to write and revise an essay. The obtained effects in terms of both revising behavior and writing performance were maintained over time and students were able to successfully adapt the strategy when composing with paper and pencil. Validation of instructional manipulations was documented by examining students' use of the strategy; observations by the instructors and classification of revisions according to purpose revealed that students consistently used the revision strategy. They did, however, make some modifications in the inculcated strategy (i.e., tended to drop first and last steps) and some steps were more salient than others (i.e., steps for adding material). Students also exhibited little difficulty in learning the strategy and reported that they enjoyed the training procedures.

A second revising study has just recently been completed by one of the first author's doctoral students, Barbara Stoddard, and one of our colleagues, Charles MacArthur. In their study (Stoddard & MacArthur, 1988), seventh and eight grade LD students were taught two strategies: one for initially editing a peer's paper primarily in terms of content, and another that focused on editing the peer's paper with regard to mechanics and grammar.

The strategy that focused on content included the following steps: (a) listen and read along as your editing partner reads his/her paper; (b) tell your partner what you like best about the paper; (c) reread the paper to yourself; (d) ask yourself the following four revision questions and make notes (Parts–does it have a good beginning, middle, and end?  Order–does it follow a logical sequence? Details–is there anywhere that more details could be added? Clarity–is there any part that you do not understand?); and (e) share your suggestions with your partner.

The follow-up strategy that concentrated primarily on polishing the peer's paper included the following steps: (a) listen and follow along as your partner reads his/her revised paper; (b) react to the changes your partner made and decide if further changes are necessary; (c) reread each sentence of your partner's paper; (d) ask yourself the error-monitoring questions and make editing marks (Sentences–is this a complete sentence? Punctuation–does it have punctuation in the right place? Capitalization–are first words and proper names capitalized? Spelling–is everything spelled correctly?); and (e) discuss your changes with your partner.

During the study, each of the participating LD students both gave and received feedback following the procedures outline above. Furthermore, they composed and revised their papers while working on a word processor. The strategy training procedures had a significant impact on students' revising behaviors as well as their written products. Total number of revisions rose dramatically and, more importantly, the number of revisions that had a positive impact on textual meaning increased. In addition, the length and quality of papers written after training were superior to those written during baseline. Finally, the obtained effects were maintained over time and generalized to a paper and pencil writing assignment.

We would also like to note before concluding this section, that the revising strategy developed by Graham and MacArthur (1988) could be modified so that it was useful across a variety of writing tasks. For example, the sentence revising strategy SCAN could be adapted as follows: SCAN each sentence (does it make Sense; is it Connected to my central idea; can I Add more detail; Note errors).

## Final Comments

In a recent review of instructional recommendations for teaching writing to exceptional students, we made 10 suggestions that we think are especially pertinent to improving LD students' skills in composing (Graham & Harris, 1988a). The strategies presented in this chapter address four of these suggestions directly. First, *teachers can help LD students gain competence in the processes central to effective writing* (e.g., planning, production, and revising) by teaching them appropriate task-specific and metacognitive strategies. Second, the acquisition of such strategies should *assist LD students in pursuing goals that are slightly beyond their current capabilities*; this is a necessary prerequisite to facilitating the development of more mature and complex composing behaviors. Third, teachers should *assist LD students in developing goals for their written products* as was done in the study by Graham et al. (1989). Fourth, *students need to develop explicit knowledge about the characteristics of good writing*, and they can be taught to use such knowledge to shape their compositions as was done in the Graham and Harris (1989a,c) studies.

The reader should not assume that we are suggesting that the only way that LD students can meet the above goals is through strategy training (see Graham, 1982 and Graham & Harris, 1988a, 1988b for other suggestions). Moreover, we don't believe that strategy instruction should supplant traditional writing pedagogy or other remedial methods that have been shown to be effective (Graham & Harris, 1989b). Rather, strategy instruction should be incorporated as an integral component of a broad instructional regime aimed at alleviating LD students' writing problems.

Other components of an effective writing program that we have identified (Graham & Harris, 1988a) include the recommendations that students should write at least four days a week, and they should be exposed to a broad range of writing tasks aimed at promoting the use of writing to meet social, recreational, and occupational needs. Whenever possible, writing tasks should be directed at an authentic audience and serve a real purpose. In addition, it is important that students learn to write in an atmosphere that is supportive, pleasant, and nonthreatening. Students will also need considerable help in automatizing the skills for getting language onto paper. Procedures for developing handwriting fluency and spelling skills have been outlined by Graham and Miller (1979, 1980). It is further recommended that writing not be treated as a separate language activity; instead, instruction in the language arts should be integrated. Finally, teachers should avoid instructional practices that do not result in improved writing performance. Workbook exercises devoted to grammar and usage do not improve students' skills at writing text. These skills are best developed within the context of real writing tasks. Overemphasizing students' writing errors should also be avoided. Intensive concentration on students' errors may make them more aware of their limitations and less willing to write.

# References

Barenbaum, E., Newcomer, P., & Nodine, B. (1987). Children's ability to write stories as a function of variation in task, age, and developmental level. *Learning Disability Quarterly, 10,* 175-188.

Blair, T., & Crump, D. (1984). Effects of discourse mode on the syntactic complexity of learning disabled students' written expression. *Learning Disability Quarterly, 7,* 19-29.

Brown, A.L., Campione, J.C., & Day, J.D. (1981). Learning to learn: On training students to learn from texts. *Educational Researcher, 10,* 14-21.

Brown, A., Day, J., & Jones, R. (1983). The development of plans for summarizing texts. *Child Development, 54,* 968-979.

Bryson, M., & Siegel, L. (1986, June). *The development of written language production in normally achieving and learning-disabled children.* Paper presented at the Annual Meeting of the Canadian Psychological Association, Toronto,

Case, L.P., & Harris, K.R. (1988, April). *Self-instructional strategy training: Improving the mathematical problem solving skills of learning disabled students.* Paper presented at Annual Meeting of the American Educational Research Association, New Orleans.

Deno, S., Marston, D., & Mirkin, P. (1982). Valid measurement procedures for continuous evaluation of written expression. *Exceptional Children, 48,* 368-371.

Englert, C. & Raphael, T. (1988). Constructing well-formed prose: Process, structure, and metacognition in the instruction of expository writing. *Exceptional Children, 54,* 513-520.

Englert, C., Raphael, T., & Anderson, L. (1986, December). *Metacognitive knowledge and writing skills of upper elementary and student with special needs: Extensions of text structure research.* Paper presented at the National Reading Conference, Austin, TX.

Englert, C., Raphael, T., Fear, K., & Anderson, L. (1988). Students' metacognitive knowledge about how to write informational texts. *Learning Disability Quarterly, 11,* 18-46.

Englert, C., & Thomas, C. (1987). Sensitivity to text structure in reading and writing: A comparison between learning disabled and non-learning disabled students. *Learning Disability Quarterly, 10,* 93-105.

Flavell, J.H., & Wellman, H.M. (1977). Metamemory. In R.V. Kail, Jr., & J.W. Hagen (Eds.), *Perspectives on the development of memory and cognition* (pp. 3-33). Hillsdale, NJ: Erlbaum.

Flower, L., & Hayes, J. (1980). The dynamics of composing: Making plans and juggling constraints. In L. Gregg & E. Steinberg (Eds.), *Cognitive processes in writing* (pp. 31-51). Hillsdale: LEA.

Gaa, J. (1979). The effects of individual goal-setting conferences on academic achievement and modification of locus of control orientation. *Psychology in the Schools, 16,* 591-597.

Gajar, A. (1989). A computer analysis of written language variables and a comparison of compositions written by university students with and without learning disabilities. *Journal of Learning Disabilities, 22,* 125-130.

Garner, R., & Gillingham, M. (1987). Students' knowledge of text structure. *Journal of Reading Behavior, 19,* 247-259.

Graham, S. (1982). Composition research and practice: A unified approach. *Focus on Exceptional Children, 14,* 1-16.

Graham, S. (1983). The effects of self-instructional procedures on LD students' handwriting performance. *Learning Disability Quarterly, 6,* 231-234.

Graham, S. (1990). The role of production factors in learning disabled students' compositions. *Journal of Educational Psychology, 82,* 781-791.

Graham, S., Boyer-Shick, K., Tippets, E. (1989). The validity of the Handwriting scale from the Test of Written Language. *Journal of Educational Research, 82,* 166-171.

Graham, S., & Freeman, S. (1986). Strategy training and teacher- vs. student-controlled study conditions: Effects on LD students' spelling performance. *Learning Disability Quarterly, 9*, 15-22.

Graham, S., & Harris, K.R. (1987). Improving composition skills of inefficient learners with self-instructional strategy training. *Topics in Language Disorders, 7*, 66-77.

Graham, S., & Harris, K.R. (1988a). Instructional recommendations for teaching writing to exceptional students. *Exceptional Children, 54*, 506-512.

Graham, S., & Harris, K.R. (Eds.). (1988b). Written language instruction and research [Special issue]. *Exceptional Children, 54*(6).

Graham, S. & Harris, K.R. (1989a). A components analysis of cognitive strategy training: Effects on learning disabled students' compositions and self-efficacy. *Journal of Educational Psychology, 81*, 353-361.

Graham, S., & Harris, K.R. (1989b). Cognitive training: Implications for written language. In J. Hughes & R. Hall (Eds.), *Cognitive behavioral psychology in the schools: A comprehensive handbook* (pp. 247-279). New York: Guilford.

Graham, S., & Harris, K.R. (1989c). Improving learning disabled students' skills at composing essays: Self-instructional strategy training. *Exceptional Children, 56*, 201-214.

Graham, S., Harris, K.R., & Sawyer, R. (1987). Composition instruction with learning disabled students: Self-instructional strategy training. *Focus on Exceptional Children, 20*, 1-11.

Graham, S., & MacArthur, C. (1987). Written language of the handicapped. In C. Reynolds & L. Mann (Eds.), *Encyclopedia of special education* (pp. 1678-1681). New York: John Wiley & Sons.

Graham, S., & MacArthur, C. (1988). Improving learning disabled students' skills at revising essays produced on a word processor: Self-instructional strategy training. *Journal of Special Education, 22*, 133-152.

Graham, S., MacArthur, C., & Schwartz, S. (1988). [Learning disabled and normally achieving students' knowledge of the writing process]. Unpublished raw data.

Graham, S., MacArthur, C., Schwartz, S., & Page, T. (1989, April). *Improving LD students' compositions using a strategy involving product and process goal-setting.* Paper presented at Annual Meeting of the American Educational Research Association, San Francisco.

Graham, S., & Miller, L. (1979). Spelling research and practice: A unified approach. *Focus on Exceptional Children, 12*, 1-16.

Graham, S., & Miller, L. (1980). Handwriting research and practice: A unified approach. *Focus on Exceptional Children, 13*, 1-16.

Gregg, N. (1983). College learning disabled writers: Error patterns and instructional alternatives. *Journal of Learning Disabilities, 16*, 334-338.

Grobe, C. (1981). Syntactic maturity, mechanics, and vocabulary as predictors of quality ratings. *Research in the Teaching of English, 15*, 75-85.

Harris, K.R. (1982). Cognitive behavior modification: Application with exceptional students. *Focus on Exceptional Children, 15*, 1-16.

Harris, K.R. (1985). Conceptual, methodological, and clinical issues in cognitive-behavioral assessment. *Journal of Abnormal Child Psychology, 13,* 373-390.

Harris, K.R. (1986). Self-monitoring of attentional behavior versus self-monitoring of productivity: Effects on on-task behavior and academic response rate among learning disabled children. *Journal of Applied Behavior Analysis, 19,* 417-423.

Harris, K.R., & Graham, S. (1985). Improving learning disabled students' composition skills: Self-control strategy training. *Learning Disability Quarterly, 8,* 27-36.

Harris, K.R., & Graham, S. (1988). Self-instructional strategy training: Improving writing skills among educationally handicapped students. *Teaching Exceptional Students, 20,* 35-37.

Harris, K.R., Graham, S., & Freeman, S. (1988). The effects of strategy training and study conditions on metamemory among learning disabled students. *Exceptional Children, 54,* 332-338.

Harris, K.R., & Stern, R. (1988). [Self-monitoring of attention versus self-monitoring of productivity: Effects on on-task behavior and fluency among LD children on story writing]. Unpublished raw data.

Hermreck, L. (1975). *A comparison of the written language of learning disabled and non-learning disabled elementary children using the inventory of written expression and spelling.* Unpublished Master's Thesis, University of Kansas, Lawrence, KS.

MacArthur, C., & Graham, S. (1987). Learning disabled students' composing with three methods: Handwriting, dictation, and word processing. *Journal of Special Education, 21,* 22-42.

MacArthur, C., Graham, S., & Schwartz, S. (1988). [The stability of LD students' revising behavior across writing tasks]. Unpublished raw data.

MacArthur, C., Graham, S., & Skarvold, J. (1986). *Learning disabled students' composing with three methods: Handwriting, dictation, and word processing.* Technical Report #109. College Park, MD: Institute for the Study of Exceptional Children and Youth, 49 pages.

Meltzer, L., Fenton, T., & Persky, S. (1985, April). *A developmental study of the components of written language in children with and without learning difficulties.* Paper presented at Annual Meeting of the American Educational Research Association, Chicago.

Montague, M., Maddux, C., Dereshiwsky, M. (1988, April). *Story grammar and learning disabled students' comprehension and production of narrative prose.* Paper presented at Annual Meeting of the American Educational Research Association, New Orleans.

Moran, M. (1981). *A comparison of formal features of written language of learning disabled, low-achieving and achieving secondary students.* (Research Report No. 34). Lawrence, KS: University of Kansas Institute for Research in Learning Disabilities.

Morris, N., & Crump, D. (1982). Syntactic and vocabulary development in the written language of learning disabled and non-learning disabled students at four age levels. *Learning Disability Quarterly, 5*, 163-172.

Myklebust, H. (1973). *Development and disorders of written language, Vol. 2: Studies of normal and exceptional children.* New York: Grune & Stratton.

Newcomer, P., Barenbaum, E., & Nodine, B. (1988). Comparison of the story production of LD, normal-achieving, and low-achieving children under two modes of production. *Learning Disability Quarterly, 11*, 82-96.

Nodine, B., Barenbaum, E., & Newcomer, P. (1985). Story composition by learning disabled, reading disabled, and normal children. *Learning Disability Quarterly, 8*, 167-181.

Poplin, M., Gray, R., Larsen, S., Banikowski, A., & Mehring, T. (1980). A comparison of components of written expression abilities in learning disabled, reading disabled, and normal children. *Learning Disability Quarterly, 8*, 167-179.

Poteet, J. (1979). Characteristics of written expression of learning disabled and non-learning disabled elementary school students. *Diagnostique, 4*, 60-74.

Sawyer, R., Graham, S., & Harris, K.R. (1988). [Improving learning disabled students' composition skills with story grammar strategy training: A components analysis of self-instructional strategy training]. Unpublished raw data.

Scardamalia, M., & Bereiter, C. (1986). Written composition. In M. Wittrock (Ed.), *Handbook of research on teaching* (3rd ed., pp. 778-803). New York: Macmillan.

Scardamalia, M., Bereiter, C. & Goelman, H. (1982). The role of production factors in writing ability. In M. Nystrand (Ed.), *What writers know: The language, process, and structure of written discourse* (pp. 173-210). New York: Academic Press, Inc.

Short, E.J., & Ryan, E.B. (1984). Metacognitive differences between skilled and less skilled readers: Remediating deficits through story grammar and attribution training. *Journal of Educational Psychology, 76*, 225-235.

Steward, M., & Grobe, C. (1979). Syntactic maturity, mechanics of writing and teachers' quality ratings. *Research in the Teaching of English, 13*, 207-215.

Stoddard, B., & MacArthur, C. (1988). [Teaching LD students to revise their writing: A word processing and peer editing strategy training approach]. Unpublished raw data.

Thomas, C., Englert, C., & Gregg, S. (1987). An analysis of errors and strategies in the expository writing of learning disabled students. *Remedial and Special Education, 8*, 21-30.

Weiner, E. (1980). The Diagnostic Evaluation of Writing Skills (DEWS): Application of DEWS criteria to writing samples. *Learning Disability Quarterly, 3*, 54-59.

Vogel, S. (1985). Syntactic complexity in written expression of LD college writers. *Annals of Dyslexia, 35*, 137-157.

Vogel, S. (1990). Gender differences in intelligence, language, visual-motor abilities and academic development in males and females with learning disabilities: A review of the literature. *Journal of Learning Disabilities, 23*(1), 44-52.

Vogel, S., & Moran, M. (1982). Written language disorders in learning disabled college students: A preliminary report. In W. Cruickshank & J. Lerner (Eds.), *Coming of age: The best of ACLD* (Vol. 3). Syracuse: Syracuse University Press.

# 5
# Effective Interventions: Using Both Hemispheres in Math

Joyce Steeves

## Effective Interventions for Dyslexic Students: Using Both Hemispheres in Mathematics

This chapter will attempt to address the need for the use of both hemispheres of the brain in the effective teaching and efficient learning of mathematics specifically for dyslexic junior high and high school students. Interest in mathematical cognition is not new in the field of psychology, but very little has been written concerning mathematical processing in educational research. Ginsberg (1983) noted that even in psychology there was a lapse of some thirty years until interest was rediscovered in the 1970s, and this was brought about through the influential work of the Genevan School, particularly that of Piaget on conservation. Developmental psychologists have thus begun to discover a wider set of topics in mathematical cognition.

### Curriculum

Many teachers in graduate programs relating to Special Education express an enormous sense of surprise if they are asked to differentiate between mathematics and arithmetic. This is partly because, in the educational system as a whole, despite the fact that every curriculum insists that children are scheduled to learn mathematics, mostly what is taught in the early years is arithmetic. One definition of arithmetic is the study of how positive numbers are added, subtracted, multiplied, and divided, while one dictionary defines arithmetic as the science of numbers, or the art of computation by figures or numerals. It is clear that, until the pre-algebra skills of the seventh grade curriculum are introduced, this is often exactly what children in math classes are studying. Education systems tend to ignore the beauty of the whole study of mathematics, that science dealing with pattern, form, quantity, measurement, and arrangements, and in particular with methods for discerning by concepts and symbols the properties and interrelationships of shapes, quantities, and magnitudes. Teachers have until now tended to focus attention on what they could see and measure.

Recently educators have been looking closely at the implications of what brain scientists are finding about hemispheric differences for ways in which instruction may be made more effective for potentially able students who are not succeeding in school. This scrutiny has led to the belief that the whole system of instruction is primarily a "left-brained" one with input mainly through reading and listening, and output, or performance, expected to be primarily written and only occasionally spoken. This is just as true in math as in any other content area. In math, however, students who are primarily left-brained processors often appear to be much more successful than their predominantly right-brained peers. This is because they tend to do better at "pushing the numbers around," especially in the elementary grades. Even left-brained children with learning handicaps are able to perform fairly well when the numbers are small and the examples all of one kind. Worksheets that are neatly set out with correct answers are parent and teacher pleasers, so it is natural for children to try to do well. It is not uncommon for mothers of left-brained dyslexic children to report that their children are "very good" at math, although usually this is only in contrast to their reading prowess. What it means is that they appear better because they are keeping up with their peers in math, whereas in reading they are way behind. Right-brained dyslexic students, on the other hand, do not fare so happily. They are not good pencil-pushers; what they are made to write on paper has little or no meaning for them, and the symbols they inscribe with such difficulty certainly do not reflect their good thinking. Yet these are the students who should be succeeding in mathematics.

Research in these fields strongly suggests that in this left-brain–based system both kinds of learners are being deprived of appropriate mathematical instruction. The left-brained learners because they are learning what to do and how to do it, but not why they are doing it, and the right-brained learners because they understand about concepts, but they cannot do what is expected of them with pencil and paper. What the authorities appear to want, it seems, is to create a nation of "performers," rather than a nation that is truly educated in mathematics. The left-brained learner without any learning problems may survive and do very well in a left-brained system, but it becomes increasingly difficult for the learning disabled student. There is a significant positive relationship between memory and mathematical computation (Steeves, 1983) and, in the scope and sequence of any math curriculum, increasing demands are made upon memory and sequencing as students progress to higher grades. Failure sets in for many left-brained dyslexic students when numbers become larger or the sequencing of written algorithms is more complex. Right-brained dyslexic students are able to compensate for some of their weaknesses in computation when they reach the stage of being allowed to use their inherent abstract reasoning or good spatial abilities. Written and timed tests, however, are always very difficult for them, and they seldom perform as well as expected.

Levy (1983) denies that standard school curricula are biased in favor of the left hemisphere, saying that all content areas depend equally on both hemispheres and on the synthesis of specialized inherent abilities. Although this is true, cognitive styles that are usually associated with L/R cortical hemisphere preference in virtually all right-handed people and two-thirds of left-handers, undoubtedly influence teachers in the way they teach. Methods of introducing material differentially arouse one hemisphere rather than the other, so that teaching styles may certainly affect "learning styles." Both instructors and students have dominant processing styles which may or may not be matched in the mathematics classroom.

The left-hemisphere–dominant person processes information in a sequential, linear, analytic manner, which plays a primary role in computation. Unless they suffer from learning disabilities, these people are usually highly verbal, logical, organization-oriented individuals who master the required recipe and are precise in carrying it out. Teachers who are predominantly left-hemisphere processors will teach in a sequential fashion, and students who process in a similar fashion will learn in their classes to perform in a left-hemisphere–dominant mode. In higher level math courses they may arrive at the correct answer but often they have no way of knowing whether they are correct because the answer has no meaning for them. The right-hemisphere–dominant math student specializes in a nonverbal, simultaneous, and holistic approach to information that is for the most part physical, intuitive, and creative. These individuals have their own special pathways to learning and to organizing their thinking, although they may not be the ways advocated by teachers or systems.

## Dyslexia and Mathematical Ability

In his biological studies of left-handedness Norman Geschwind reported (1983) that, in examining the brains of fetuses, he found the right side of the brain developing more rapidly than the left. He considered this noteworthy since it relates to a very important principle concerning the development of the brain. If there is injury, insult, or delayed development of one hemisphere in fetal life, there is compensatory growth of the corresponding regions of the other hemisphere. It is reasonable to think, then, that the rapid growth of the right hemisphere indicates some slowing of the left, together with an increase of left-handedness and the development of other superior right-hemisphere skills. As left-handedness, learning disorders, and superior right-hemisphere skills are more common in males than in females, Geschwind proposed that it might be some factor connected with the male sex that retarded the growth of the left hemisphere in intrauterine life. He suggested the possibility that the production of testosterone in enormous quantities in the male fetus might be responsible. He described this phenomenon, however, as "a funny mechanism." If you get it just right, you have superior right-brained talents including mathematical ability, but if it is overdone, trouble may result.

This possible link with mathematical talent caused other researchers in this field to look again at some of their data. Among these were Camilla Benbow and Julian Stanley of Johns Hopkins University. In their *Study of Mathematically Precocious Youth* they found that 20% of their highly talented youngsters were left-handed (Kolata, 1984) which made them twice as likely to be left-handed as the general population. This in itself is sufficiently interesting to make those educators who work with dyslexic youth having a similar high incidence of left-handedness suspect that there is an identifiable group of dyslexic children who can be considered to have mathematical potential equal to that of already identified nondyslexic gifted children (Steeves, 1983). These students, however, tend not to perform in a manner commensurate with that potential.

It used to be thought that many such students did not succeed because they were unmotivated. Many children report being called lazy or careless in school, when in fact they care very much and work extremely hard to try to reach the level of their less talented but non-disabled peers. In a study of identified gifted students who were not achieving as expected, Okabayashi and Torrance (1984) postulated that these students' inability to achieve in a manner commensurate with measures of intelligence and other indicators of academic promise may be associated with preferred styles of processing information. It was also conceived that these students were not yet ready for self-directed learning. The nonachieving students were in grades 4-7, and were compared with two similarly identified groups, one achieving in a manner commensurate with potential and the other achieving beyond expected levels.

The researchers found no significant difference between the groups in readiness for self-directed learning. They reported that the lowest-achieving group indicated a stronger preference for using the right-brained style of processing, whereas the highest-achieving group seemed to have developed an integrative style of processing. This means they were able to use the specialized cerebral functions of the left hemisphere in conjunction with those of the right hemisphere simultaneously, or they were able to switch from one to the other efficiently as befits the nature of the task.

How many of us have wished for the intelligent adolescent to "just get it all together"? But how many teachers have changed their style of teaching in mathematics to accommodate the necessity for using both hemispheres of the brain? Human brains are built to be challenged. They operate at optimal level when cognitive requirements are sufficiently complex to activate both sides of the brain and to facilitate integration of simultaneous hemispheric activities. When emphasis is placed on lower level cognitive skills such as memorization of facts interest wanes, especially for the intelligent student who might be solving problems in other ways if given the opportunity.

Vitale (1982) illustrated a pleasantly simplified table showing the "modes of consciousness" as they relate to the separate hemispheres.

| LEFT HEMISPHERE | RIGHT HEMISPHERE |
|---|---|
| linear | holistic |
| symbolic | concrete |
| sequential | random |
| logical | intuitive |
| verbal | nonverbal |
| reality-based | fantasy-oriented |
| temporal | nontemporal |
| abstract | analogic |

It is obvious from this table that the hemisphere-specific functions of both sides of the brain are essential for efficient output in the math performance demanded of students in our educational system.

It is interesting to note that teachers of gifted children are being encouraged to help them learn how to use both hemispheres in conjunction for the processing of information. It is also interesting that there has been a sudden upsurge in programs for teaching "thinking skills." Should not all education be concerned with thinking? And should not all children have the right to the most efficient and effective ways of learning? Why do we have special problem-solving programs that are unrelated to the curriculum?

There are many schools in this nation where only the highly able and achieving students are introduced to programs entitled "Creative Problem Solving." In these programs we are told that students constantly move from left to right styles of thinking in order to understand a problem, define it, develop alternative solutions, evaluate these alternatives, and finally develop a plan for implementation of the best solution. What could be wrong with this form of learning/teaching throughout the curriculum and for all students?

It must be clearly stated that not all dyslexic students are gifted. It must also be understood that not all dyslexic students have superior right-brained talents. We are certain, however, that all dyslexic students have a specific language difficulty which may interfere with learning across the curriculum. We also know that many dyslexic students have difficulty with organization and sequencing. How beneficial it will be for these students if they are taught creative problem solving in order to deal with the difficulties they encounter in school and in life. Self-directed learning, self-monitoring skills, and initiative should all be fostered in the early life of these children. Problem solving does not belong only in the math texts at the end of each chapter under the title "Word Problems." Indeed, although many teachers of learning disabled children will tell you that their students "cannot do" word problems, for the specific dyslexic they often present no problem at all. These are the students who cannot read the word problems, so they do not attempt to. They know that they have been working on a certain type of problem for the last week, or in the last few pages in the book, so they use good generalization strategies to simply pull out the numbers and proceed to operate on them in a similar fashion. The solution of real problems is important in the lives of dyslexic children at all levels, and they are often "unavailable" for content area learning until some basic problems are dealt with.

Let us imagine a disorganized fourth-grader arriving late, as always, for math class:

| | |
|---|---|
| Student: | (enters but says nothing) |
| Teacher: | Why are you late? |
| Student: | I was looking for a pencil. |
| Teacher: | Here's a pencil. Sit down and begin your work. |

Ostensibly the problem is solved. This is the easy way, but what message is it giving to the student? (a) You don't need to worry, someone will always provide what you need. (b) It doesn't matter that you are late for class. (c) You may repeat the same performance tomorrow and no one will care. The student has been absolved of all responsibility for solving his problem, but the problem has not been solved.

Consider the alternative scenario:

| | |
|---|---|
| Student: | (who has been instructed to greet the teacher on entry) Good morning. I'm sorry I'm late, I was looking for a pencil. |
| Teacher: | Oh, then you have a problem. Class, please stop what you are doing so that we can help S. with a problem. Tell us about it, S. |
| Student: | I don't have a pencil. |
| Teacher: | What are some solutions to this problem? |
| Pupil 1: | He could ask you for one just for today. |
| Teacher: | Good! Any more suggestions? |
| Pupil 2: | I could lend him one. |
| Pupil 3: | You could give him one. |
| Teacher: | Good, thank you. Any more? (several more are suggested) |
| Teacher: | S., which do you think is the most efficient solution? |

| Student: | I'll borrow a pencil from you. |
|---|---|
| Teacher: | Good. Here you are. For how long are you going to need this? |
| Student: | Just for today. |
| Teacher: | If you had it just for this period, what would happen? |
| Student: | I'd be in trouble next period. |
| Teacher: | That's true. So you have this pencil for today. What will happen at the end of the day? |
| Student: | I will give it back to you. |
| Teacher: | Then what about tomorrow? |
| Student: | I will have to bring one from home. |

What messages has this student received? (a) You are capable of fulfilling expectations on arrival for this class. (b) You are an important member of this class. (c) You are capable of stating a problem. (d) Your teacher and your peers really want to help you. (e) You are capable of making a decision. (f) You must evaluate, face consequences, predict, and be responsible for your behavior.

All of the above are important lessons to learn and are at the heart of good problem solving. Sometimes, with the learning-handicapped child, real problem solving must begin at this basic level. But what are the skills used in the above technique? Do they have any bearing on the use of both hemispheres in problem solving? Yes! The affective side of learning often prevents the development of cognition. Affective needs must be addressed so that the student develops a good sense of "self"—a recognition of his own worth as a person of merit. In involving the class the teacher was allowing the student to be aware of himself in the larger context, using his right hemisphere. In stating the problem the student was using the left-hemisphere language function. In listening to the possible solutions the student had to switch again to the *gestalt* or the big picture relating to people and objects, which is a right-hemisphere function. He used the logic and language of the left hemisphere again to evaluate, choose, predict, and make some decisions. The final solution may not be accomplished the next day, or even the next week, but that student would at least be on the way to empowerment. He was developing not only the intent but the means to achieve in class, and, it is hoped, to solve real-life problems.

How can we as educators empower the students in math classes to achieve at the level of their full potential? In an article entitled "Right-brained kids in left-brained schools," Madeline Hunter, as long ago as 1976, advocated presenting information in such as way that students can practice integrating it from both of their hemispheres (Hunter, 1976). She also stated that research findings suggest that whenever a student is not "getting it" teachers should augment the stimulus that they are already using with one to the other hemisphere; that they should also adopt practices that facilitate the use of each hemisphere singly or "in concert." She believes that this can be done easily by using such strategies as doing an example on the chalkboard while giving a verbal explanation, or having a model perform the act while others are hearing directions.

Davidson and Marolda (in press) have identified two types of mathematical learners that relate very closely to right and left hemispheric differences. Their manipulative math programs have gone a long way towards improving the learning of mathematics for many students. One of their most important principles is that, for the child who does not have a sense of geometric properties, spatial ability and spatial reasoning must be taught. Unfortunately, even the most willing and caring teachers do not know how to teach these skills because most of the teachers themselves have been poorly taught. It is a sad indictment of our teacher training systems that for so many years children in elementary schools have been taught math by teachers who were mandated to teach math, but who themselves were either lacking in preparation or afraid of math. This latter condition often leads classroom teachers to be wedded to a prescribed text, unable to meet the needs of the students because they have no confidence in their own ability to deviate from the book and still be able to teach math.

Fortunately there are some mathematicians who also possess expert pedagogical skills, and who have realized for several years that workshops, conferences, and college courses may help to relieve math phobics of some of their anxieties. In her book entitled *When Children Don't Learn*, Diane McGuinness expresses the opinion of many educators when she says that fear is overcome not be sympathy or hand-holding, but by instilling competence (McGuinness, 1985). It is hoped the teachers in these workshops may benefit to the extent that they will go back to their students with renewed confidence and enthusiasm, setting the major goals of their math classes as, first, acceptance of individual learning styles, and second, the generating of confidence and competence. We are wrong to label children as underachievers if we have not given them the means of achieving. The students who have not learned the skills necessary to achieve are *underskilled*, but are achieving as well as they are able to without the requisite skills. It is incumbent upon educators to empower students by teaching them the necessary skills in the way in which they learn.

## Children's Learning in Mathematics

Possibly no other human being has provided as much insight in the logico-mathematical learning of children as Jean Piaget. He was criticized by many who said that he was not interested in individual differences, but only in developmental stages. Yet it is through the knowledge of these developmental stages, of what children can and cannot do, that some educators have based their most successful teaching strategies. Davidson, among others, asserts that Piaget was right (McGuinness, 1985). Piaget's great love of children was evident in the charm and patience noted in observations of his working with young students. He, in turn, criticized the training of elementary school teachers, saying that educators were more interested in teaching than in children. This situation is still evident today in some systems where teachers are mandated to cover curriculum content to the extent that they "teach the book" instead of teaching the children.

Piaget stated very clearly that the relationship between brain development and abilities is not one-way, but interactive. The child learns by using his developmental abilities to interact with his environment, surely a right-brained function, including movement as well as thinking. There is no learning unless the child *acts* upon his experiences. Experiences facilitate neural development, and neural development facilitates higher levels of learning. In one of his later books (Piaget, 1976), Piaget pointed out that a child may perform an arithmetic operation, such as addition or multiplication, correctly but not be really conscious of what is going on. Being able to perform the necessary actions correctly may precede understanding of a mathematical concept by as much as six years.

In his book *How Children Learn Mathematics*, Copeland (1979) lists the ages at which mathematical concepts develop (Appendix II). The first concept that is appreciated by young children (4-7 years) is topological space, closely followed by simple classification, seriation and ordering, and then the concepts of conservation of number, length, and area. These concepts develop during the Preoperational stage. All of them must be integrated and securely in place before children are able to understand addition of classes and numbers. Such concepts do not develop until the first period in the Concrete Operational stage (about 7-9 years). This writer's more than thirty years of testing, talking to, and observing children in math situations bear this out.

There must be a rationale somewhere for the ignoring of these truths in the design of many math curricula. Scope and sequence charts tend to begin at the Concrete Operational stage, apparently trying to bypass the necessity of pattern-building, categorization, and classification among other right-brained skills inherent in those early concept developments. How much time do we allow our young children in math classes to experiment with their own position in time and space? What would be the reaction if a small child informed his teacher that a doughnut is the same as a tractor tire? Yet a topologist or a professor of mathematics might prove the wisdom of that observation. Sadly, we rush our infants through the early stages, forcing them into situations where they are expected to use skills that are, for the most part, not yet possible for them.

Geometry, with its concomitant right-brained accomplishments, is reserved until much later, when it is taught as a separate subject. Many high schools, both private and public, choose to teach Algebra I for one year, switch to Geometry for one year, then switch back to Algebra II for another year. This *may* be an appropriate approach for students who are not learning handicapped in any way, but it penalizes those who have memory problems, as well as failing to integrate the hemispheric learning inherent in those topics. Mathematics should be regarded as a whole, with its parts being related and relevant.

Experienced tutors/teachers of mathematics can describe numerous encounters with failing adolescents who will tell them, "I just did what the teacher told me to do. Sometimes it worked, sometimes it didn't. But I never understood what I was doing." These are frequently cases where the concept has been introduced before the student was developmentally ready, and the student learned "how" before he learned "what" or "why." This is very frustrating for the subject who is intelligent enough to recognize that an answer does not make sense but who is unable to do anything about it because he has been instructed to perform an algorithm without thought or meaning, and does not know how to change the situation without falling foul of "the system."

An example of this is a bright, mildly dyslexic senior in high school who has been passed through the system because he is hard-working, conscientious, and charming. Forced to take an advanced mathematics course to gain the final three credits necessary for graduation, this handsome young man stood outside the room and cried from frustration. When he was seen for assessment he said that he used to like math, and he *is* able to think things out for himself, but he had never understood anything the teachers had told him. He was able to add, subtract, multiply, and divide whole numbers fairly easily, until the numbers got larger. But even if the numbers were small, after about five written examples he began to be confused and to make errors. Because what he has been writing since elementary school has been for the most part meaningless, he had developed the idea that written arithmetic is not *intended* to have any meaning unless it is directly related to word problems, and then the student supplies the meaning. When completing a word problem that necessitated that he add two sums of money, he completed the addition then moved the decimal point four places to the left, and immediately said, "That doesn't make sense." On being asked to explain he said, "Well, I started with $37.85, and added some to it, and I haven't even got that much now." Asked if he would like to change his answer he declined. The reason he gave for moving the decimal point four places was that the teacher had told him to do it, and so he had to. He was obviously perseverating on the written algorithm for multiplication of decimals. The concepts are in place in his mind, but there has been no attempt to link what he writes with how he thinks.

McGuinness (1985) agrees that children must be taught to become literate, to acquire numeracy, and to respond appropriately to social context, but is equally adamant in affirming that children must not be punished for failing to conform to these cultural demands. Neither should educators impose unnecessary psychological pressures upon children because of the failure to understand how children learn, and consequently, how educators should teach. Is "normalization" becoming increasingly valued as a cultural necessity? Are this nation's children being forced to accept the notion that the only "good" learning is that which takes place when they are seated in rows of desks listening to an adult? The student mentioned in the last paragraph had been passed through school doing just that, but he had not learned, and he certainly did not feel good about his experiences or about himself.

## Is Language the Link?

It is generally accepted that children learn in four steps: concrete, pictorial, symbolic, abstract. This suggests that we believe learning begins in the right hemisphere and remains predominantly right-brained throughout the first two stages, concrete and pictorial (or iconic or representational, as it is sometimes called). There is a switch to the left-hemisphere during the symbolic period, and then another switch occurs at the abstract stage, back to the right. Is it possible that educators have been missing a vital step, that of integration? Many children do not or cannot form the relationship between what they learn experientially, and the symbolic codes that are often presented too soon for them to understand. To make the link between input and output children should be encouraged to record what they have learned in ways that are *understandable and most appropriate for them*. If they cannot write the symbols, then they should be encouraged to draw, or even to make some other representation. All the concrete manipulatives in the world are not going to make the necessary transition for the child. Neither will they teach him the written algorithms necessary for the efficient solution of problems on paper. Only when children have recorded their findings in the simplest and most meaningful way for them, and when they have compared them with others and talked about the similarities and differences, are they ready to generalize and see the necessity for a common method, of communication. The language of the teacher should be the bridge between the language of the student and this common method, which is the written algorithm and which should relate to all individual experiences.

Consider the class where addition of single-digit numbers is being taught through the use of place value blocks. Each unit is a centimeter cube. The children are placing sets of cubes on their desks and adding them by putting them together. There is a movement, a kinesthetic element, that clearly illustrates the addition concept *in that context*. If, at this juncture, the teacher writes the horizontal addition statement $3 + 2 = 5$ on the blackboard, one could say that learning is taking place in both hemispheres. But how can we guarantee that? If the symbols on the blackboard have no meaning, the left hemispheres of many children will not even respond to that written equation. The teacher might even *read* what she/he writes on the blackboard so that the children can *hear* the addition sentence. Surely that is a multi-sensory approach that must succeed. Unfortunately research has not found this to be so. Unless the children understand that the numeral 3 represents the three cubes they have placed on the desk, but can also represent three of any other items in another situation, the written algorithm remains meaningless and unconnected to the experience. All children have an inalienable right to learn as they are comfortable learning and to show what they know in their own inimitable way at first, and we must give them the time to do this.

In the above example, there will be children who, when instructed to record what they were working on, *in any way they can*, will simply take more blocks and repeat the process. They are still at the concrete stage, and will need to continue to manipulate objects until they are ready to illustrate what they have been learning. The child who draws three cubes, trying to make them three-dimensional, is probably at the early pictorial stage, whereas the child who draws the three cubes as three squares is probably indicating that he knows that this is just a representation and is more ready for the symbolic step. The child who draws three lines, or three dots, but who can tell you that they "stand for" three cubes is ready to move into the symbolic stage. This recording stage of learning is the great linking step for children. It is the third step, not only desirable, but essential to bridge that gap between the hemispheres and confirm the newly acquired knowledge. This bridging, however, cannot take place successfully without language. Many good teachers believe that dyslexic children fail in mathematics because mathematics is yet another language to be learned. They will plead that the language of mathematics must be taught directly to these children, with much emphasis placed on terminology. They will tell you that learning-handicapped students fail in math because they cannot do "word problems." This may well be true, but it is more likely that these are the "symptoms" rather than the "disease." Experience frequently shows that the missing link is that the child is not given the opportunity to use his *own language* to state what he has been learning, and what he has understood. The student's own language, no matter how inefficient at the time, is more meaningful to him. His words, though they may be ill-chosen, are the bridge to comprehension. The teacher's job is to "channel" that information into the expected mathematical terms.

The American Association for the Advancement of Science report of mathematics for project 2061 (Blackwell & Henkin, 1989) devotes section 5 to Mathematics and Language. Speaking of the need for use of mathematical language the report states: "We do not have in mind an elaborate symbolism replete with formulas full of esoteric characters. Rather, we mean the *careful use of natural language*, clarified by certain conventions that eliminate ambiguity, and supplemented by the use of variables and carefully defined terms." This "careful use of natural language" depends greatly upon opportunity for use of the child's own language.

The two important elements for the learning of mathematics for all students, then, are *involvement* and *language*. Children do not learn passively. Ultimately they are held accountable for their own learning, so they must be involved. Teachers who care about their students tell them that they must be responsible for their own learning. This can only be brought about by creating a classroom climate where they are allowed the opportunity and the time to integrate their learning.

Teachers often complain that they are willing to help children if the children ask for help. They say, "Do you understand?" and the child says, "Yes." They say, "Raise your hand if you do not understand," and no hand is raised. They say, "Stay behind after class if you need help," and nobody stays. Often children do not know that they do not understand, because they do not know that what they are doing on paper is supposed to be meaningful. Sometimes the children are floundering so badly that they do not know how to explain what they don't understand. Telling them to ask for help is placing the onus unfairly. Teaching should be a diagnostic cycle with teachers continually checking for comprehension. Instead of asking, "Do you understand?" the child should be requested to tell in his own words what he has just heard. If several children are given this opportunity, a common terminology can be found that then can be channeled back into the teacher's words or the mathematical formulae.

Consider the case of six high school students in the same school system who were reported as having difficulty with mathematics, specifically geometry. Two of the students were in the same school but with different teachers. All understood the concept of congruent triangles, and when asked why the triangles were congruent, each one was able to point to the two triangles and say, "Well, this equals that, and this equals that, and this is the same as that." In each case they pointed to two sides and the included angle. Asked how they would like to show that proof, they drew two small triangles and marked the equalities. What had to happen in their classrooms, however, was different for each one. To prove this particular congruence the following had to be written:

Student 1:    The S.A.S. theory

Student 2:    The Side Angle Side Theorem

Student 3:    Theorem 11.2, page 57, the S.A.S. theorem

Student 4:    If two sides and the included angle of one triangle correspond to two sides and the included angle of anoth er triangle, then the triangles are congruent.

Student 5:    (All of the above explanation, plus the theorem number and its title.)

Student 6:    Every SAS correspondence is a congruence.

It is small wonder that some students pass that unit, while others fail. Many students are so busy learning the exact words to please the teacher that that is where they focus their energy. These students report that most schools have two "tracks" in Geometry: Formal and Informal. Informal Geometry is nicknamed "Dummy Geometry" and does not appeal to many students who are able to understand and enjoy geometry at the conceptual level. Yet these students fail in

Formal Geometry, which appears to be unnecessarily complicated by the mandatory memorization of about 200 theorems and 20 postulates. The question must be asked, Do they need to fail? It might appear that some students are failing teacher preference, rather than mathematics.

## Teaching Techniques

How then do we teach in order to access both hemispheres of the brain and involve the students in their own learning? It is vital to follow the steps that are essential for learning for all students:

- Concrete    (a) supply as many different manipulatives as students need to learn and *integrate* the new concept; (b) encourage students' language in peer or teacher interaction.

- Pictorial    (a) provide different representations of the same object; (b) have students talk about other representations of the same concrete objects; (c) use students' own language to discuss "numberness."

- Linking    (a) encourage students to talk about what they have worked on or learned; (b) allow them to record and demonstrate in a way that is meaningful to them; (c) link directly with the language of mathematics or the written algorithm.

- Symbolic    when presenting the written algorithm or other symbolic language, do not ask students if they understand. Allow them to demonstrate comprehension by (a) talking or (b) demonstrating (drawing, pointing, replicating). Also, model for the students, but do not end there. It is essential that students model for themselves and each other. As a true test of comprehension ask students to construct some similar examples for themselves rather than always depending on a text. If students can abstract from the examples of others, make inferences and form conclusions so that they can make up examples for themselves, it is almost a certainty that they have full comprehension. If they cannot, then they are not ready to proceed.

- Abstract    (a) teach the steps for problem solving with alternate solutions; (b) give time and opportunity for problem solving in novel or creative ways within the structure of a well-defined system; (c) give attention to the higher cognitive skill of problem finding.

# Standards for the Teaching/ Learning of Mathematics

The new *Standards for Curriculum and Evaluation* from the National Council of Teachers of Mathematics (1989), describes standards for the teaching of mathematics for the levels K-4, 5-8, and 9-12. These standards, which have been studied for two years by a team of expert teachers of mathematics, offer more than a ray of hope for all students, and have a decided effect on what pencil and paper skills students need to learn. The introduction addresses changes in society that dictate differing mathematical skill needs, and the philosophy of problem solving is emphasized throughout all the standards at all levels.

Naturally, the authors have much to say about technology, with the major thrust being how to *teach* with the tools that are available in this technological age. Teachers are advised that they cannot plan to teach without the use of calculators and computers. They must make appropriate and ongoing use of calculators and computers in problem solving in all grades and at all levels. Some of the recommendations are:

Calculators should be available at all times to all students.

Every classroom should have at least one computer for demonstration purposes.

Every student must have access to a computer whenever it is needed.

Students must learn to use the computer as a tool for processing information and for calculating in order to solve problems.

At the middle school levels, available calculators must be of the scientific variety with functions that will enable students to complete all tasks inherent in middle school mathematics.

At the high school level, computers with graphing and calculating capabilities must be available at all times.

The Chief States School Officers have also sanctioned the use of calculators and computers during standardized examinations, *but only in the problem-solving sections.* Through this they imply that they still endorse the necessity for children to learn the basic skills of mathematics, and we cannot argue with that. The children themselves want to be efficient in those skills to the best of their abilities, so long as the difficulties they encounter at this lower level of cognitive functioning do not interfere with their success at the higher levels of cognition. In problem solving, students will be encouraged to ask themselves the questions:

Is a calculator needed? Is it better to use mental computation, a calculator, or a computer? Do I need an exact or an approximate answer? If approximate, can I use mental calculation only?

It is hoped the 1990s will see an improved school situation for students who are good right-brained problem solvers, but who do not meet the requirements of pencil and paper assignments and tests.

## Computer Assisted Instruction

Educators will do well to obey the mandates of the promised standards for the use of computer assisted instruction (CAI) in mathematics. Computers will not go away, and students have a right to their use for the achievement of educational goals. Research has been conducted into the optimum conditions for the use of CAI with learning-handicapped students, and though very little is conclusive, some studies may provide guidelines for some teachers. Software must be carefully chosen in order to be congruent with the Individualized Education Program (IEP) or curriculum goals of the student (Steeves, 1988). Grouping arrangements should be appropriate for optimal learning. Givner and Berlin (1988) found that for the use of drill and practice CAI, a learning-handicapped student at the elementary level could work satisfactorily alone, but did even better in a dyad when working with a more efficient peer. The implications for the teacher are that she/he must orchestrate the grouping with care. The more efficient student must be sensitive and have the necessary social interaction skills to make pairing successful, or these skills must be directly taught beforehand. The teacher must also choose instruction packages that are sound in design and that structure the learning situation. These researchers found that with drill and practice programs three students grouped around one computer was not satisfactory, as the student with the greatest need was the least likely to succeed. For problem-solving programs, however, they discovered that three students working together was very successful. There was more task-related discussion and the students shared the appointed tasks very efficiently.

## Counting Strategies and Automaticity of Recall

In a well-meaning attempt to lessen anxiety-producing tension for dyslexic students in math, many teachers, tutors, and parents (this writer among them) have encouraged children to develop their own counting strategies when unable to recall math facts on demand. It seemed preferable to arrive at the correct answer more slowly than not at all or incorrectly. Recent research suggests, however, that such counting strategies may interfere with the learning of higher level math skills, so, once again, automaticity of recall becomes an enviable state. It is believed by cognitive scientists that most people have a limited capacity for information processing. As basic facts become more automatic, less of this limited capacity is used for performing basic skills, so more of it may be devoted to understanding higher level concepts.

Educators generally have agreed that the solution to developing automatic recall of math facts in children is through the consistent use of considerable amounts of drill and practice (Ashcraft, 1985; Gagne, 1983). When it was realized that one way of delivering large amounts of drill and practice in a carefully monitored yet motivating environment was through the use of a computer, technology was hailed by many classroom teachers as a panacea for all ills. Commercial software vendors had introduced a plethora of computerized drill and practice programs, especially in math. Both regular and special education teachers welcomed these into their classrooms as a boon for children who needed to practice their math facts.

The unique needs of students who are gifted, and/or dyslexic, or otherwise disabled can be addressed by the flexibility and power of the computer's resources. The computer is an "equalizer" (Male, 1988) in that it has the capacity to bypass the specific difficulties that contribute to failure in academic achievement. Great care must be taken, however, to ensure that both hardware and software are appropriate for each individual. As we identify a piece of software that enables students to accomplish something that was previously out of reach, we must be sure that the achievement is meaningful and relevant to their needs. Research has shown that computer-based drill and practice can be successful in developing automaticity, but only when specific criteria are met. If these specific criteria are not met, the data indicate that there is little or no improvement in the recall performance of learning-handicapped students (Hasselbring et al., 1988; Howell & Gracia, 1985; Reith, 1985).

From studies with both elementary and secondary level students, it can be seen that neither pencil and paper drill and practice nor computer-based drill and practice is sufficiently powerful in and of itself to bring about improvement in automaticity of recall of basic math facts for learning-handicapped students. What is essential for making these methods work is that the subjects have been provided with appropriate, individualized instruction to establish a declarative knowledge network before providing them with drill and practice programs. But even this will not bring about the desired outcome unless the teacher links the CAI (computer assisted instruction) to her/ his own teaching practices (Steeves, 1988). Teacher involvement is vital to the success of CAI. Hasselbring and his colleagues (1988) have described several instructional principles that may be applied in establishing this network:

> Determine the learner's level of automaticity.
> Build on existing declarative knowledge.
> Instruct on a *small* set of target facts.
> Use controlled response times.
> Intersperse automatized with target nonautomatized
> > facts during instruction.

If there is no existing declarative knowledge base, then drill and practice of any kind is useless for the purpose of developing automatic recall. Instruction must begin with a very small set of unknown facts--ideally, two--and must focus intently on these two facts and their commutative opposites until they are memorized. When some facts are able to be recalled from memory, they must be practiced and reviewed repeatedly; then this knowledge base must be expanded by introducing a new set of two facts. Learning-handicapped students will benefit from drill and practice in any format only if they can respond correctly from memory about 80% of the time. Hofmeister (1983) supports these statements when he states, "Drill and practice activities that are used as a substitute for the necessary teaching of the underlying concepts, and drill and practice that is not followed by meaningful applications of the skills, are inappropriate uses of drill and practice, regardless of whether a computer is used or not" (p. 42).

The right-brained, intuitive, mathematical thinker who is unable to remember basic facts may well become bored with drill and practice at the computer. He may be resentful of programs that not only place unnecessary demands on his memory, but either continue with the next screen before he has remembered the fact, thus indicating that he is "wrong," or are unable to progress until he has provided the correct response, which leads him either to revert to counting strategies or to pressing keys at random. In either case, student self-concept is lowered, and no learning takes place.

All of the above may suggest that, for the bright dyslexic, a more appropriate use of technology in the math classroom must be simulations and problem solving. Some excellent commercial programs can be found to satisfy both of these needs, but perhaps the most important use of all for the child who is failing is to teach him how to use the computer as a tool to meet his own needs. For example, the child who has trouble with sequencing and direction in long multiplication, as well as being unable to remember multiplication facts takes a long time to compute even one problem. Teaching him just enough Basic computer language to enable him to input the problems on the computer showing his partial products (multiplication by ones, tens, etc., then adding together the partial products) will ensure that he develops the correct sequencing. Not having to worry about remembering the facts will allow him to proceed more quickly, and consequently, more examples will be completed, thus allowing better integration of the format of the written algorithm. Periodically students should be encouraged to transfer successful learning to pencil and paper. The visual repetition of correctly computed facts will, it is hoped, encourage recall of the facts and more correct responses should result.

Even more importantly if students are provided the opportunity to use technology to foster their good problem-solving skills, then it should be possible for the talents of these students to be recognized, and more appropriate education and consequently greater academic achievement should result.

# Conclusion

In a study to assess the effects of "metacognitive" instruction on reading comprehension, Haller, Child, and Walberg (1988) found that metacognition facilitates comprehension, and that the effect sizes were greatest at the seventh and eighth grades. There seems to be some agreement about the mental activities inherent in metacognition. These comprise three clusters of skills relating to awareness, monitoring, and regulating.

**Awareness skills:**

- searching for the source of the difficulty
- recognition of implicit as well as explicit information
- responsiveness to various textual components

**Monitoring skills:**

- goal setting to facilitate comprehension
- self-questioning, paraphrasing, and summarizing
- integrating prior knowledge with content information
- confirming assumptions and making predictions

**Regulating skills:**

- compensatory strategies to redirect and bolster faltering comprehension
- backward and forward search strategies
- self-questioning
- contrasting textual information with prior knowledge
- comparison of ideas

These metacognitive skills are equally important for math comprehension as they are for reading comprehension. I venture to suggest, however, that although metacognitive *skills can be taught*, if a student does not have the innate ability to understand the concept that is being taught, he will not understand it without experience and direct explanation. What the metacognitive learning will provide is a more linear, organized, readiness for the performance of written tasks. So, once again, we are forced into the realization of the need for the synchronization of the right- and left-brained activities. The final word must come from Piaget. Children learn through the development of three abilities. These are:

**Assimilation:** wherein the child takes in all the knowledge and information in his environment, including that directly taught.

**Accommodation:** the child fits that knowledge into his own schemata, integrating it until it is his own.

**Reflective Abstraction:** when the child is able to look back, take that information from one situation and, fully understanding it, use it to solve a new problem either in its original form or changed to fit the new situation.

The teacher's role must be one of facilitator. She/he must ensure that from the first planning stage to the final implementation and evaluation the instructional environment is appropriate for the students' needs. If this chapter has implied any criticism of teachers, let me hasten to add that it is the system that is at fault, not the individuals. The classroom teacher is the key to all successful learning. She/he is the catalyst who will provide the bridging of the hemispheres, thus encouraging a nation of true learners, rather than sedentary classrooms of "performers."

Much great talent is being lost, but there *is* hope for our students in mathematics, if we practitioners listen to the children and act upon research findings. Recently, caring people in the medical professions as well as those in academia have been concerned by the sufferings of children as well as by lost talents. A quote by H.J. Morowitz (1986) from the journal *Hospital Practice* sums up the essence of this chapter's message. "I have the gut feeling that we are standing on the threshold of an era when computer technology can substantially ameliorate the lives of a large segment of our society affected by disabilities of one kind or another. I'm elated by the concept of using this technology to convert the disabled into the able."

Technology alone is not the answer, however. The training of teachers in methods of instruction that will utilize both sides of their brains in order to arouse both hemispheres of their students' brains in learning is an imperative for all in the next decade. It is doubly important for meeting the needs and fulfilling the potential of dyslexic students who not only could be, but should be the future successful students in mathematics.

# References

Ashcraft, M.H. (1985). *Children's knowledge of simple arithmetic: A developmental model and simulation.* Unpublished manuscript, Cleveland State University.

Blackwell, D., & Henkin, L. (1989). *Mathematics: Report of the project 2061 Phase 1 mathematics panel.* Washington, DC: American Association for the Advancement of Science, Inc.

Copeland, R.W. (1979). *How children learn mathematics.* New York: Macmillan.

Davidson, P.S., & Marolda, M.R. (in press). *The neuropsychology of mathematics learning.* Menlo Park, CA: Addison-Wesley.

Gagne, R.M. (1983). Some issues in the psychology of mathematics instruction. *Journal for Research in Mathematics Instruction, 14*(1), 7-18.

Geschwind, N. (1983). Biological associations of left-handedness. *Annals of Dyslexia,* (33), 29-40.

Ginsberg, H.P. (1983). *The developmental mathematical thinking.* New York: Academic Press.

Givner, C.C., & Berlin, M.S. (1988). *Student performance on CAI within various grouping arrangements.* (Technical Report) Baltimore: The Johns Hopkins University, Center for Technology and Human Disabilities.

Haller, E.P., Child, D.A., & Walberg, H.J. (1988). Can comprehension be taught?: A quantitative synthesis of "metacognitive" studies. *Educational Researcher, 17*(9), 5-8.

Hasselbring, T.S., Goin, L.I., & Bransford, J.D. (1988). Developing math automaticity in learning handicapped children: The role of computerized drill and practice. *Focus on Exceptional Children.* Denver: Love Publishing Co.

Hofmeister, A. (1983). *Microcomputer applications in the classroom.* New York: Holt, Rinehart, & Winston.

Howell, R.D., & Graica, J. (1985, July). *The effects of computer use on the generalization of learning with a learning disabled student.* Paper presented at the Research Symposium on Special Education Technology, Washington, DC.

Hunter, M. (1976). Right-brained kids in left-brained schools. *Today's Education,* November-December, 46-48.

Kolata, G. (1984). Math genius may have hormonal basis. *Science, 222,* 1312.

Levy, J. (1983). Research synthesis on right and left hemispheres: We think with both sides of the brain. *Educational Leadership,* January, 66-71.

Male, M. (1988). *Special magic: Computers, classroom strategies, and exceptional students.* Mountain View, CA: Mayfield Publishing Co.

McGuinness, D. (1985). *When children don't learn.* New York: Basic Books.

Morowitz, H.J. (1986). Hardware, software. *Hospital Practice,* September 15, 37-40.

Okabayashi, H., & Torrance, E.P. (1984). Role of style of learning and thinking in self-directed learning readiness in the achievement of gifted students. *Journal of Learning Disabilities, 6*(2), 104-107.

Piaget, J. (1976). *The grasp of consciousness: Action and concept in the young child.* Cambridge, MA: Harvard University Press.

Reith, H. (1985, July). *An analysis of the instructional and contextual variables that influence the efficacy of computer-based instruction for mildly handicapped secondary school students.* (Technical Report) Baltimore: The Johns Hopkins University, Center for Technology and Human Disabilities.

Steeves, K.J. (1983). Memory as a factor in the computational efficiency of dyslexic children with high-abstract reasoning ability. *Annuals of Dyslexia, 33,* 141-152. Towson, MD: The Orton Society, Inc.

Steeves, K.J. (1988). *The impact of instructional variables on the effective integration of computer assisted instruction for students with mild handicaps*

(Technical Report). Baltimore, MD: The Johns Hopkins University, Center for Technology and Human Disabilities.

Vitale, B.M. (1982). *Unicorns are real: A right-brained approach to learning.* Rolling Hills Estates, CA: Jalmar Press.

# Part 3
## On the Cutting Edge

# 6

# In the Spirit of Strategies Instruction: Cognitive and Metacognitive Aspects of the Strategies Intervention Model

## B. Keith Lenz

Over the past fifteen years, the notion of direct strategy instruction has moved steadily from the laboratory settings of researchers into the classroom settings of teachers. Publishers have begun to produce strategy-labeled materials, and sessions on strategy-related interventions have become common at many professional conferences related to education and learning. However, the translation between research and practice has often been a poor one. While the research on strategies used by individuals with learning disabilities and their response to novel strategy instruction has been ongoing since the mid to late 1970s (e.g., Torgesen, 1977; Wong, 1979), the translation of this research into effective practice has been relatively limited, and where a translation of the research has been attempted, the nature of these various strategy-training efforts has often been quite varied. As a result, many of the strategy-labeled programs and materials have not always resulted in an improvement in student performance.

A number of specific strategy-training efforts have been empirically developed and implemented by researchers interested in improving the performance of students with learning disabilities and other students performing poorly in school (e.g., Deshler & Schumaker, 1986; Lloyd & deBettencourt, 1982; Palincsar & Brown, 1984). In general, these strategy-training efforts have included teaching, guiding, or prompting the student to "establish goals, select appropriate procedures, and monitor progress towards achieving goals" (Mayer, 1987, p. 418) in order to meet task demands. In these efforts, a strategy or set of strategies is identified that will enable students to meet a specific problem. The teacher then initiates strategy training. These strategy-training efforts have generally required instruction over time (six weeks to a year) and with small groups of students (e.g., one to six).

Probably the most fully researched and developed approach to direct strategy training for students with learning disabilities is represented by the Strategies

Intervention Model developed by the staff at the University of Kansas Institute for Research in Learning Disabilities. Under the direction of Dr. Donald D. Deshler, a core research and development staff, consisting of Drs. Jean B. Schumaker, Frances L. Clark, B. Keith Lenz, Daryl F. Mellard, Stephen J. Hazel, and Janis Bulgren and a national network of research associates have worked together on various research projects on the identification and intervention issues related to adolescents with learning disabilities and other adolescents and young adults judged to be low-achieving or at risk for educational failure. Research and development efforts have focused on identification and assessment issues, continued validation and replication of various components of the model, materials development and dissemination, and various efforts related to teacher training and the infusion of the model into educational programs.

The purpose of this chapter is to identify some of the major concepts and themes that have been infused throughout the Strategies Intervention model as it has evolved over the past ten years. Many of the aspects of the model discussed in this chapter may be different from perspectives that were presented in some earlier descriptions of the model. The concepts and themes discussed reflect a number of perspectives that have evolved as a result of the continuing validation and development of the model. This ongoing research and development focus has been required to meet the ongoing concerns of parents and professionals who continue to challenge educators to meet the needs of the student with learning disabilities.

In order to understand some of the basic themes and concepts related to the Strategies Intervention Model and how this model may compare to other strategy-training efforts, this chapter has been divided into two sections. The first section is a short discussion of a number of general issues related to strategies instruction. This section includes a definition of a strategy, differentiates strategy instruction from some other types of skill instruction, and describes a number of different perspectives on the instructional procedures that are used in promoting strategy acquisition. The second section describes features across four dimensions of a strategy intervention that have been identified as contributing to the "strategicness" of the intervention. The features described in this section represent many of the quality control checks that have been applied in the development of the strategies included in the Strategies Intervention Model.

## Strategy Intervention Issues

*What is a strategy?* The definition for a strategy (the definition of a strategy presented by Deshler and Lenz 1989) that has been described for the development of the Strategies Intervention Model is as follows:

*An individual's approach to a task is called a strategy; it includes how a person thinks and acts when planning, executing, and evaluating performance on a task and its outcomes.*

Clearly, the orientation of a strategy, as conceptualized in the Strategies Intervention Model, is on the *approach* used by a person to complete a task. The approach includes both cognitive (what goes on in a person's head) and behavioral (what the person actually does) elements that guide student performance and evaluation of the task. In addition, the strategy must assist the student in evaluating the results of the effort that has been applied in performing the strategy.

While a strategy refers to an individual's approach to a task, it is clear that the approaches employed by students do not always lead to success. Therefore, some strategies are successful and some strategies are unsuccessful. The goal of strategy *development* is to identify strategies that are optimally effective (i.e., will help the student meet the demands of both current and future tasks) and efficient (i.e., will help the student meet the demands of the task in a manner that is appropriate, timely, resourceful, judicious, etc.). The goal of strategies *instruction* is to teach the strategies in a manner that is effective (i.e., the strategy is learned and generalized by the student) and efficient (i.e., the strategy is learned to an optimal level with a minimum amount of effort by both the teacher and the student).

***How is strategy instruction different from instruction in basic academic skills or study skills?*** A strategy is different from a basic skill or a study skill. Although it is possible to think of a strategy as a skill, in most school curricula a basic skill or a study skill usually consists of a set of steps or a procedure related to meeting a specific setting demand. This concept of a skill is often operationalized and taught through the specification of a behavioral task analysis. For example, the steps that must be demonstrated in long division or to complete an outline can be listed and observed, and usually lead to a very specific outcome that documents completion of a task or some element of a task. On the other hand, a strategy consists of critical guidelines and rules related to selecting the best skill or procedure and how to make decisions about its use. Therefore, while a strategy relies on some type of skill knowledge, the focus is on  the individual's approach to the task. The strategy must guide the appropriate selection and use of skills and the background knowledge that the individual has about the task.

***How is strategy acquisition promoted?*** Current strategy training efforts have approached training primarily through direct or indirect teaching tactics. The indirect approach focuses on prompting student use of strategies through modeling, questioning, shaping, correcting, and interactively guiding student response to the task. An expert guides the student through the task and, as instruction progresses, gradually guides the student to take responsibility for effective and efficient completion of the task. In some cases, the teacher never presents a "best" strategy, but helps the student discover the best approach to the task. The direct teaching approach focuses on identifying an effective and efficient system for accomplishing a specific task and training the student in the strategy. Once the strategy is identified, the teacher instructs the student in the necessary skill prerequisites, presents the strategy, models and demonstrates the strategy, and provides direct practice and feedback related to the student's application of the strategy. The primary difference between these two approaches is in the role of the teacher. In the indirect approach, the teacher leads the student to knowledge and use of the strategy, whereas in the direct teaching approach the strategy is made explicit and taught by the teacher.

The training approach used in the Strategies Intervention Model has changed over the years. Initially, the focus of the instructional process was on the direct delivery of the strategy through a direct teaching approach. Since the content of each strategy had been heavily researched and refined, it was believed that the power of the strategy would result in the intended outcomes. However, while it was found that students could be taught the strategy, some students did not see the benefits of the strategy, were not highly motivated to learn the strategy, and were not generalizing the strategies for academic success and personal use. As a result, the instructional procedures have been changed to include an increased level of student involvement, participation, control, and commitment in the instructional process. Therefore, the instructional procedures utilized in the Strategies Intervention Model may best be described as a direct strategy training approach incorporating planned opportunities for the student to (a) become involved in the instructional process and (b) to discover ways in which the strategy can be personally empowering.

## Dimensions of Strategies Instruction

The difficulty of many applied research efforts in the area of strategies instruction is that the intervention effort usually does not consist of a single strategy, tactic, or condition, but is actually a string of strategies, tactics, and conditions that are put in place to meet the logistical requirements of the classroom setting (e.g., a strategy designed to help a student develop mnemonic devices to help remember information is only practical if the student has understood the information and has a method for accurately identifying and organizing the important information that needs to be remembered). Therefore, when an intervention effort brings about a significant and practical magnitude of change (i.e., a change that parents, students, teachers, and administrators all recognize as satisfactory improvement), it is very difficult to selectively identify which aspects of the intervention are contributing to specific improvements in student performance, which aspects make no contribution, which aspects are actually inhibiting improvement, and which elements could have been added that

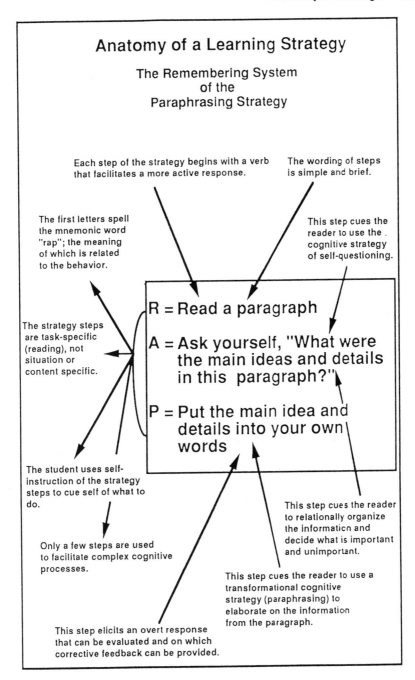

Figure 6.1. From Ellis, F.S. and Lenz, B. K. (in press). *TACTIC: Procedures for developing strategy interventions.* Lawrence, KS: Edge Enterprises, Inc.

would have contributed to an even greater magnitude of improvement. Therefore, validation of strategy-training efforts are actually validation of a combination of intervention dimensions that are arranged according to the concepts or spirit of strategies instruction.

The key steps of the remembering system of the *Paraphrasing Strategy* (Schumaker, Denton, & Deshler, 1984) from the Learning Strategies Curriculum of the Strategies Intervention Model can be used to illustrate the many features that can be embedded in a strategy intervention. Figure 6.1 illustrates how the *Paraphrasing Strategy* has been analyzed (Ellis, Lenz, & Clark, in press) for its strategic qualities. Note that while there are various strategic qualities that have been included as part of the intervention, the cognitive strategy of "paraphrasing" is only one of these aspects. Therefore, more often than not, a strategy intervention does not consist of a single strategy, but incorporates several cognitive and metacognitive strategies arranged in a manner that leads to completion of the task. As a result, the interventions in the Strategies Intervention Model are actually systems of strategies arranged in a manner that creates a strategic approach to meeting a demand. Yet, throughout the steps of each intervention, a spirit of strategies instruction is maintained.

The *spirit* of strategies instruction that has been created in the Strategies Intervention Model can be made apparent by examining the model across four major dimensions related to a strategies-training effort. These dimensions include (a) the nature or content of the strategy that is to be learned, (b) how the strategy content is organized or designed for learning by the student, (c) the usefulness or transfer-ability of the strategy in meeting demands and problems that the student must face, and (d) the procedures used to facilitate student acquisition and generalization of the strategy. Knowledge of these four dimensions is useful when a strategy intervention is being compared with another intervention, when a strategy is being developed, or when a strategy is being considered for use with students. Ellis and Lenz (1987) have identified a number of critical features across these four dimensions that should be considered when judging whether the spirit of strategies instruction is present in a direct strategy-training intervention. These four major dimensions and their associated features are described below.

# Strategic Content

The "content features" of the strategy relate to how well the process of meeting the demand has been specified in terms of both mental and physical actions. The critical features that must be considered under this dimension generally relate to the degree to which the strategy has incorporated principles of learning that have been found to facilitate a more effective and efficient response to meeting a demand. Although a strategy intervention may not contain all of these features, the intervention is more likely to be strategic if the following features are included in the intervention.

*1. The strategy should contain a set of steps that lead to a specific and successful outcome.* A strategy is not a collection of unorganized rules, characteristics, and guidelines that result in separate outcomes. A strategy consists of a set of steps that organizes the approach to a task and results in the successful completion of that task. While individual units of performance may be evaluated, there is always one outcome that is used to judge the success of the strategy (e.g., Did the strategy help the student pass the test?). The individual can then examine the result of his or her effort and begin to evaluate the effectiveness of the strategy.

*2. The steps of the strategy should be sequenced in a manner that leads to an efficient approach to the task.* A strategy is not a collection of good ideas organized into a set of steps. A strategy taught to students must be a collection of the "best" ideas organized into the "best" sequence that lead to the "best" mental and physical actions for the task. A strategy that simply leads to completion of the task is not enough. However, what an adult thinks is the "best" approach to a task may not be "best" for the student. For example, whereas adults often stop to check comprehension after chunks of reading passages consisting of multiple paragraphs, school-age individuals struggling to improve comprehension often must stop at the end of much smaller chunks to induce comprehension (e.g., at the end of each paragraph or even several times within a paragraph). Indeed, many adults find that stopping frequently to check comprehension often feels unnatural and inefficient. However, for immature readers, this is often the "best" approach.

*3. The steps of the strategy should cue the student to use specific cognitive strategies.* Most strategy interventions are really "strategy systems" that include many cognitive strategies such as paraphrasing, clustering, imaging, etc. If the strategy does not include cues and explanations related to using cognitive strategies to approach tasks, it is likely that the strategy is simply a procedure with few strategic qualities. For example, a variety of cognitive strategies are cued in the *Paraphrasing Strategy* illustrated in Figure 6.1.

*4. The steps of the strategy should cue the student to use metacognition.* The process of reflection on and evaluation of the way that a task is being approached and accomplished is often difficult to identify in our own behavior. Therefore, these metacognitive processes are often not directly specified when we develop interventions. It is important to include these (e.g., self-questioning, self-evaluation, goal-setting, checking, reviewing, self-monitoring) behaviors in the steps of the strategy when they are important to completing the task. These behaviors must be embedded in the steps of the strategy and explained to students.

*5. The steps of the strategy should cue the student to select and use appropriate procedures, skills, or rules.* A key function of a strategy is to guide the student to select the procedures, skills, and rules that are most appropriate for meeting the demands for a task. Therefore, the strategy must specifically inform the student as to which resources need to be applied and where. The strategy should name the appropriate procedure, skill, or rule and, if appropriate, include it as part of the strategy acquisition and generalization process. For example, if a student should use a specific computation procedure as part of a strategy to manage and organize time, then this procedure should be specified along with specific instructions about how to think and make decisions about the procedure.

*6. The steps of the strategy should cue the student to take some type of overt/physical action.* A strategy must cue both mental and physical actions. An absence of physical actions from the strategy steps will make it difficult for the individual and the teacher to evaluate application of the strategy and monitor progress towards meeting the setting demand. Indeed, the actions, comments, and products that result through completion of a task are the only sources of information that the teacher has in determining whether the student is learning the strategy. These behaviors serve as the basis for providing elaborated feedback to the student as part of the instructional process. The student must learn to associate how their thoughts affect their behavior. Therefore, this must be included as part of the content of the strategy.

*7. All of the overt/physical actions should be supported by a clear explanation of the associated mental actions that need to take place.* Every critical physical action should be associated with mental actions. Explanations or information about mental actions provide guidance related to decisions about the best way to meet the demand. For example, if the steps of the strategy cue the student to take notes, then the explanation for that cue should provide guidance in how to make decisions about what information should be written as notes.

*8. All of the steps of the strategy should be able to be performed by an individual in a limited amount of time.* The steps of the strategy need to be balanced in relation to when they are to be performed. Usually, a strategy must be performed in a reasonably short period of time. Strategies that must be performed over an extended period of time often undermine the self-instruction process (are forgotten) and can be ineffective. Frequently, strategies that have been developed that cover tasks that extend over a long period of time, such as one or two days, often suffer from insufficient analysis of the task or demand. Strategies that attempt to address such tasks, such as homework completion, must take into consideration that there are probably many strategies involved, not just one strategy, and are very complex.

*9. Unnecessary steps or explanations should be eliminated.* The number of steps and the amount of explanation in the strategy should be no more than what is needed to enable the individual to learn the strategy and meet the setting demand. Therefore, the content must be reviewed, and information that might be trivial to the task or unnecessarily increase the amount of information that must be remembered may need to be omitted. Cues to pick up the pencil, turn the page, etc., are examples of steps that may be unnecessary.

*10. Information related to why to use the strategy, when to use the strategy, and where to use the strategy should be included.* The knowledge of the situational conditions under which the strategy should be used is as much a part of the strategy as the specific steps. Rationales for use and nonuse of the strategy should be taught. In addition, identifying the characteristics of situations where the strategy should be used and the cues that will help the student identify these situations will help to promote appropriate use and subsequent generalization of the strategy.

*11. In general, does the strategy include guidelines related to how to think and act when planning, executing, and evaluating performance on a task and its outcomes?* While the features described above should accomplish this, the whole strategy should promote overall task completion and awareness of effort. It should guide the individual's approach to the task while promoting strategy flexibility that will enable the student to meet unexpected circumstances that may surround a task. The teacher should review the entire strategy and evaluate whether sufficient attention to the content features described above has accomplished this. If not, then the strategy may need to be modified to meet these conditions.

## Strategic Design

The content of the strategy should be designed in a manner that successfully organizes the content of the strategy for optimal learning and use by the student. The critical features that are addressed under this dimension relate to how understanding and memory of the strategy are facilitated through the arrangement of the strategy content. Although a strategy intervention may not meet all of these conditions, a strategy intervention is more likely to be acquired and generalized if the following design features are included in the intervention:

*1. Entry level skills should be clearly specified or taken into consideration as part of the steps of the strategy.* A strategy often informs an individual of how to apply skills. Therefore, the skills or skill levels that are assumed or required in order for the strategy to be effective must be clearly specified. Any skills that are not specified as a prerequisite should be addressed somewhere in the intervention process. The teacher must decide either to teach any entry level skills that are required so a particular strategy can be taught or to implement another intervention. For example, if the strategy requires the use of a dictionary or a glossary, should the student be taught how to use a dictionary or glossary before instruction in the strategy begins or should this instruction be a part of the strategy?

*2. A remembering system should be incorporated into the intervention to facilitate memorization of the strategy steps and explanations.* There are always two aspects of each step in a strategy. The first reality consists of a full explanation of all of the guidelines, cues, rationales, procedures, rules, processes, exceptions, etc. that are important to the successful performance of a strategy. This is the content of the strategy. The second aspect of each step consists of the set of key action words that an individual learns and memorizes that trigger the appropriate associations or explanations related to successful performance of a strategy. This is the remembering system of the strategy. Since the content of a strategy can be quite extensive, and many individuals who require direct strategy training need assistance in learning and remembering information, the design of the strategy must facilitate the memorization process. Therefore, the content of the strategy should bc organized for ease in remembering, and a mnemonic device may need to be developed as part of the strategy intervention. This design feature can reduce the memorization load and allow the student to focus on understanding and applying the strategy.

*3. Each step of the remembering system should be short.* As each step of the remembering system is formulated, unnecessary words should be eliminated. Every attempt should be made to select a few key action words that will facilitate a direct association to the critical cognitive and physical actions that are necessary for completion of the step and that have have already been presented to the individual as part of the full explanation of that strategy step. The steps of the *Paraphrasing Strategy* presented in Figure 6.1 demonstrate this feature.

*4. Each step of the remembering system should begin with a verb or a key word directly related to the mental or physical action that the step is designed to cue.* Beginning each strategy step with a verb helps promote an active approach to the task. In addition, the steps are often more easily remembered when each step begins with an action word. Steps that begin with words such as "the," "if," "then," and "which" do not have the power of words such as "write," "find," "look," "ask," and "choose." It is also helpful if all the steps use a parallel language structure. For example, all the steps should begin with a verb and should be written in the first person, singular.

*5. There should be seven or less key steps in the remembering system for the strategy.* The memory load of a strategy increases as the number of steps in a strategy increases. Therefore, it is best to limit the number of steps to seven or less. However, some tasks require a much more sophisticated strategy and, as a result, more steps are required. If this occurs, then ways of embedding a substrategy or a mini-strategy within a general set of steps might be helpful. For example, there may be five steps to a strategy; however, in the fourth step of the strategy there may be a cue to perform a short three-step mini-strategy before going on to the fifth general step of the strategy. The use of this tactic more efficiently organizes the strategy and makes the strategy easier to remember and perform.

*6. The remembering system should relate to the overall process that the strategy is designed to address.* When a mnemonic device is used to promote remembering of the strategy, it is helpful if the mnemonic word or image is closely related to the strategic process desired. For example, a strategy related to homework with an mnemonic device centered around the word "ASSIGN" may more easily be remembered and trigger the appropriate strategy than a mnemonic centered around the word "BOAT." Although many strategies have been developed and are successful without taking this into consideration, this feature can make the mnemonic easier to learn and remember for some students.

*7. The language structure used to convey the strategy steps and explanations should be uncomplicated and familiar.* As in any intervention, the words and sentences selected to teach the strategy should be carefully selected. The words generally should be familiar and easy to understand. However, it is critical that the remembering system consist of words that are powerful and meaningful to the student. If this is not possible, then specific concepts and language prerequisites critical to the understanding of the strategy should be included as part of the teaching process.

## Strategic Usefulness

A strategy should guide the approach used by a student to meet a specific need or demand or to solve a specific problem that the student might face. Therefore, while the strategy content may already be developed, the selection of the strategy and its relevance to the needs of the student are an important part of the strategy intervention process. The critical features that must be considered under this dimension generally relate to the potential use and transferability of the strategy across materials, people, settings, situations, and time. Although a strategy may not meet all of these conditions, an intervention is likely to be successful if the following conditions related to the usefulness of the strategy are met:

*1. The strategy should address a key problem that is found in settings that the student must face.* Strategies that are immediately useful and that the benefits of their use are readily apparent to everyone tend to be learned and generalized more quickly than strategies that are useful only in future circumstances. While reading comprehension is an important overall skill, if the student is not expected to read to obtain information in regular classes (i.e., the content is presented primarily through lectures), the student is not likely to be motivated to learn reading strategies. The student must see (or be taught to see) the relationship between the effort applied to strategy learning and his or her success in settings in which performance is continually being evaluated.

*2. The strategy should relate to a demand that is frequently required across settings.* The more opportunities that a student has to apply the strategy, the more likely the student will be to learn the strategy quickly, see the benefits of the strategy, attribute success in meeting specific demands to application of the strategy, and habitualize its use. Therefore, when selecting which strategies should be developed or taught to students, a key consideration is the degree to which the student will have an opportunity to apply the strategy and integrate it into his or her overall approach to solving problems.

*3. The strategy must be generalizable across a variety of settings, situations, and contexts.* A strategy can be developed for a very specific situation. However, those strategies that have the greatest generalization potential will be those that can be used across situations and settings. For example, the *Paraphrasing Strategy* can be applied in almost every setting and content area that requires reading. Therefore, the *Paraphrasing Strategy* is very generalizable. However, the *Paraphrasing Strategy* could be altered in such a way as to make the steps relate only to reading and paraphrasing science content. While the strategy may be very effective for reading science material, the application of the strategy to other content areas becomes more difficult.

*4. The strategy should relate to future demands that the student will encounter that are similar to those for which the strategy was originally taught.* While it is important that the strategy meet current demands, the strategy should be powerful enough to have long-term uses and benefits across many aspects of the individuals life in the near-future and into adulthood. Therefore, a careful balance between current and future needs must be sought when deciding the efficacy of a particular strategy intervention. Instruction in goal setting to facilitate assignment completion becomes more important when viewed in the context of the goal setting skills needed for career and life planning.

# Strategic Instruction

Once the content, design, and usefulness of the strategy have been determined, the strategy must be taught to the student. Strategic instruction promotes the active participation of the student in the learning process. In general, the goal is to immerse the student in an instructional situation in which learning is seen as a vehicle to realize personal goals. The student is involved in making decisions about what is to be learned and how fast learning will occur. Specific stages for promoting successful strategy acquisition and generalization have been developed by researchers at the University of Kansas Institute for Research in Learning Disabilities. The eight stages of this instructional process are presented in Figure 6.2.

These stages attempt to achieve a balance between the control of the teacher and the control of the student over the learning process. Other strategy training efforts may emphasize one type of control over another. However, while strategy learning may be achieved through instruction that is more teacher directed or through instruction that is more student directed, the following general instructional features appear to be central to successful strategy instruction:

*1. The student should be committed to learn the strategy and fully understand the purpose and benefits of the strategy.* The student's understanding of the potential impact of the strategy and the consequences of continued use of ineffective and inefficient strategies should be the first step in the instructional process. The student should be committed to learn the strategy and understand how it can have an immediate impact on success. Therefore, the teacher must be responsible for informing the student of the goals of the strategy and obtaining a commitment from the student to learn it. Likewise, the teacher must demonstrate to the student that he or she is committed to assisting the student to acquire and generalize the strategy.

*2. The physical and mental actions covered in the strategy should be fully described and explained.* The student must be informed of what to do and how to think about each step of the strategy. The full content of the strategy should be made apparent to the student. Examples and circumstances relevant to the student's experiences should be incorporated into the presentation, and the student should play an active role in exploring and commenting on the strategy and its uses. In addition, the teacher should ensure that students understand when and where to use the strategy and how to identify cues that signal appropriate and timely use.

*3. The student should be informed of how to use the remembering system incorporated in the strategy intervention to facilitate the process of self-instruction.* Once the content of the strategy has been presented to the student, the teacher should demonstrate how the strategy can be easily remembered using the remembering system included in the intervention. The teacher should explicitly relate the steps of the remembering system to the intended physical and mental associations, and teach the student how to use the remembering system to guide the student in the self-instruction process. This step enables the teacher

A Working Model for Teaching Learning Strategies

**Stage 1:  Pretest and Make Commitments**
Phase 1:  Orientation and pretest.
Phase 2:  Awareness and commitment.

**Stage 2:  Describe the Strategy**
Phase 1:  Orientation and overview
Phase 2:  Present strategy and remembering system

**Stage 3:  Model the Strategy**
Phase 1:  Orientation
Phase 2:  Presentation
Phase 3:  Student enlistment

**Stage 4:  Verbal Practice**
Phase 1:  Verbal elaboration
Phase 2:  Verbal rehearsal

**Stage 5:  Controlled Practice and Feedback**
Phase 1:  Orientation and overview
Phase 2:  Guided practice
Phase 3:  Independent practice

**Stage 6:  Advanced Practice and Feedback**
Phase 1:  Orientation and overview
Phase 2:  Guided practice
Phase 3:  Independent practice

**Stage 7:  Posttest and Make Commitments**
Phase 1:  Confirm and celebrate mastery
Phase 2:  Forecast and commit to generalization

**Stage 8:  Generalization**
Phase 1:  Orientation
Phase 2:  Activation
Phase 3:  Adaptation
Phase 4:  Maintenance

Figure 6.2.  The stages of strategy acquisition and generalization.

to address the possible memory difficulties exhibited by many low-achieving students.

*4. The student should understand the process of learning the strategy and should participate in goal-setting activities in order to anticipate and monitor learning.*    The student should (a) be informed of the acquisition and generalization process, (b) understand the goals and vocabulary associated with each step, and (c) set goals for mastery of each step. As instruction proceeds, the student evaluates completion of each step to determine if specified learning goals have been met. If not, the student initiates feedback to the teacher on which aspects of learning goals have not been met. Figure 6.2 illustrates the stages of strategy acquisition and generalization that comprise the strategy instructional process. During the instructional process, the student should become an active facilitator and evaluator of the successfulness of the instruction. In addition, the student must be taught to become a collaborator in identifying and addressing failures in strategy learning.

*5. Multiple models of the strategy should be provided; an appropriate balance between the physical and mental activities involved in the strategy should be achieved.* The heart of strategic instruction is in the "think aloud" model that must be presented by the teacher. This model must present an accurate and complete demonstration of the application of the strategy. While a complete and thorough initial model is critical, additional modeling episodes should be inserted throughout the instructional process. In each of these models, the physical activities must be demonstrated as the associated mental activities are made apparent in an overt "think aloud" depiction of the strategy. However, while it is important to thoroughly model the "thinking" aspects of the strategy, careful consideration should be given to avoid bogging down the instructional process and overwhelming students with teacher talk. The strategy must remain a crisp depiction of an effective and efficient approach to a task.

*6. The student should be enlisted in the model and become a full participant in guiding the strategy instructional process.* While the modeling phase of instruction begins with the teacher, it should end with student participation and experience with the modeling process. The teacher should gradually include students in the model. Initially, the teacher should enlist the students in the self-instructional statements of the model, providing the "think aloud" aspects of the strategy and gradually prompting and guiding students to comment and provide thoughts on completion of each step. Students should eventually be able to perform the strategy while providing many of the key mental actions associated with each step.

*7. The strategy should be fully understood and memorized before practice in the strategy is initiated.* Sufficient rehearsal of the strategy steps should be provided before the student is asked to perform the strategy from memory. Before applied practice of the strategy begins, students should know the remembering system, be able to demonstrate how they can use the remembering system to guide the self-instruction process in applying the strategy, paraphrase or explain what is involved in each step, provide personal rationales for learning and using the strategy, and accurately answer questions about uses and misuses of the strategy across various conditions. During the forthcoming practice phase the student must be confident in his or her knowledge of the strategy and be able to concentrate on the application of the strategy and not have to focus unnecessary mental effort on remembering the strategy steps.

**8. Practice should begin with controlled guided practice and ultimately conclude with advanced independent practice.** The goal of the initial practice stage should be on mastering the strategy without having to struggle with content or situational demands. Therefore, practice should be provided under conditions in which the student feels comfortable or knowledgeable. As the strategy is learned, conditions that approximate actual setting and task demands should be gradually introduced. While general principles of effective teaching should be applied, the most important teaching behaviors during strategy practice appear to include communicating expectations, ensuring intensity of instruction, requiring mastery, and providing elaborated feedback.

**9. A measurement system should provide ongoing information that will demonstrate to the student and the teacher that strategy is being learned and used and that the demands of the setting are being met.** Knowledge of progress and performance is a critical part of the learning process. The measurement system should provide information to the student on whether the strategy is doing what was promised in terms of promoting success in meeting a demand. However, the measurement system should also provide information related to the students mastery of the strategy. Progress in learning the strategy should eventually relate to an increase in the student's ability to meet a setting demand or some aspect of a setting demand. The student should be able to see this relationship and attribute success to mastery and application of the strategy.

**10. While generalization should be promoted throughout the strategy acquisition process, specific efforts to promote generalization should follow strategy acquisition.** After the strategy has been mastered, the student should once again make a commitment. However, this time commitment should be focused on generalizing the strategy. In the generalization stage, the teacher and student must work together to identify where the strategy can be used across settings and conditions, identify modifications in the strategy to make it more generalizable, and program use of the strategy across settings. In addition, the generalization process can be greatly enhanced through the cooperation of as many teachers and other facilitators as possible.

## Conclusion

The issues and dimensions of direct strategy training that have been described represent one strategy training method. However, these features could be viewed as representing a rather limited perspective on strategies training. It can be viewed as limited because the spirit of strategies instruction has really only been considered at the single intervention level. That is, these features focus on how the spirit of strategies instruction might be manifested in a specific strategy-labeled intervention. However, it could be argued that the key to delivering a truly strategic intervention is to stop conceptualizing strategies instruction as consisting of a single strategy intervention, or several strategy interventions, or even a well-developed strategies curriculum. It may be more beneficial to begin thinking about strategies interventions as consisting of the creation of environments in which everything that is done is done in a strategic manner. A strategic environment should promote, model, guide, and prompt effective and efficient  learning and performance across all settings, not just in settings providing services for the learning disabled.

Currently, the focus of research and development on the Strategies Intervention Model is directed at identifying the critical features of a strategic environment and how the environment can affect the various dimensions of strategies instruction. It is apparent that even though we are beginning to have a clearer idea of the nature of strategy-related interventions, it is likely that the goal of student success that is sought  in direct strategy training cannot be achieved through specific and isolated strategy training. It is more likely that this goal may be achieved when strategic curricula are being delivered through strategically rich instruction in an environment that promotes teamwork and shared responsibility for the learning and performance of all students.

# References

Deshler, D.D., & Lenz, B.K. (1989). The strategies instructional approach. *International Journal of Disability, Development, and Education, 36*(3), 203-224.

Deshler, D.D., & Schumaker, J.B. (1986). Learning strategies: An instructional alternative for low-achieving adolescents. *Exceptional Children, 52*(6), 483-590.

Ellis, E.S., & Lenz, B.K. (1987). A component analysis of effective learning strategies for LD students. *Learning Disabilities Focus, 2*(2), 94-107.

Ellis, E.S., & Lenz, B.K. (in press). *TACTIC: Procedures for developing strategy interventions.* Lawrence, KS: Edge Enterprises, Inc.

Lloyd, J., & deBettencourt, L. (1982). *Academic strategy training: A manual for teachers.* Charlottesville: University of Virginia Learning Disabilities Research Institute.

Mayer, R.E. (1987). *Educational psychology: A cognitive approach.* Boston: Little, Brown.

Palincsar, A.S., & Brown, A.L. (1984). Reciprocal teaching of comprehension fostering and monitoring activities. *Cognition and Instruction, 1,* 117-175.

Schumaker, J.B., Denton, P.H.., & Deshler, D.D. (1984). *The learning strategies curriculum: The paraphrasing strategy.* Lawrence: The University of Kansas Institute for Research in Learning Disabilities.

Torgesen, J.K. (1977). Memorization processes in reading-disabled children. *Journal of Educational Psychology, 79,* 571-578.

Wong, B.Y.L. (1979). Increasing retention of main ideas through questioning strategies. *Learning Disability Quarterly, 1*(2), 42-47.

# 7
# Using Computers to Assist in Reading Instruction for Children with Learning Disabilities

**Joseph K. Torgesen and Neal M. Horen**

Most educators who understand recent advances in computer technology would agree that computers have enormous potential to help teachers educate children more effectively. Even those who are pessimistic about current instructional uses of computers (e.g., Woodward & Carnine, 1988) are optimistic that future developments may prove much more effective. Although there is general agreement about the potential of computers as an educational tool, there is considerable controversy surrounding the question of which specific uses of computers with young children will prove most effective over the long-term.

In the field of special education, perhaps the most frequently cited controversy concerns the use of computers to provide drill and practice exercises to students. For mildly handicapped children in elementary school, this is currently the most common way that computers are being used. In fact, the use of drill and practice programs in special education settings appears to be significantly higher than in regular classrooms, which tend to expose children to a greater variety of software (Cosden, Gerber, Semmel, Goldman, & Semmel, 1987).

In the drill and practice mode, the computer essentially provides repeated learning or practice trials to assist children in the acquisition of basic facts and skills. In the area of reading, some programs provide practice identifying letter names and sounds, others allow children to practice identifying phonetic patterns in words presented in isolation, while others provide support for practice in reading complete text. Although drill and practice programs sometimes have the capacity to teach new responses (learning new spelling words, acquiring new sight vocabulary), their most common use is to supplement teacher instruction by providing practice to consolidate, or increase the fluency of, responses that are originally taught elsewhere.

Educators or researchers who propose other uses of computers in education frequently criticize the use of drill and practice programs as "simple minded," "dull and uninteresting," or as merely "electric flashcards or electronic page turning." These critics suggest that drill and practice programs do not take advantage of the capabilities of computers to provide interesting, novel instruction that may enhance more complex thinking and problem-solving skills in young children. Often, the implication of these arguments is that drill and practice applications are second class, or not innovative, when compared to uses that may enhance higher-order thinking skills. The preponderant use of drill and practice applications with special education students is sometimes viewed as depriving them of important opportunities for intellectual growth that are available to children in the regular classroom (Cosden et al., 1987).

In more traditional instruction, it is now well documented (Brown, Palincsar, & Purcell, 1986) that poor readers are subject to an instructional environment different from that of good readers, almost from the beginning of elementary school. Children who easily master the decoding aspects of reading are given much more instruction and practice focused on comprehension of written material than are poor readers. As a result of this extra practice and instruction, they become more able to engage in the complex strategies required to comprehend text than do children who have difficulties mastering word-reading skills. Thus, by the time they reach the late elementary years, many poor readers have a double problem in reading: not only do they have continuing difficulties decoding individual words, but also, because of lack of instruction and practice, they have not developed a repertoire of active processing strategies to help them comprehend text.

It is easy to see how something similar to the reading instruction scenario might occur within the realm of computer assisted instruction (CAI). Because the basic skill deficiencies of learning disabled (LD) children are so obvious, computers are primarily being used to provide remediation in this area, rather than as a means to provide other kinds of learning opportunities. Another factor that probably contributes equally toward influencing the heavy use of drill and practice programs in special education classrooms has been the unavailability, until recently, of credible and educationally relevant software that purports to provide other kinds of instruction. However, apart from the availability issue, it is easy to justify the use of good drill and practice programs with learning disabled students, given the proven effectiveness of computers in providing this type of learning experience for children with learning problems (Torgesen & Wolf, 1986). These types of programs are also supported by modern learning theory. Current conceptualizations suggest that practice is the most effective way to build fluency in component skills so that they can contribute to effective performance on more complex tasks (Goldman & Pelligrino, 1987).

In a recent, comprehensive discussion of the effect of early reading failure on subsequent academic achievement, Stanovich (1986a) argued persuasively that children with reading difficulties need more opportunities for practice in basic reading skills. Because they cannot independently execute basic word recognition processes, they receive much less practice (both in school and at home) in reading than do children who learn to decode the written word easily from the beginning of instruction. This lack of practice, in concert with the cognitive difficulties that made reading difficult for them to begin with, insures that many LD children acquire word identification skills very slowly and retain these difficulties in high school (Warner, Schumaker, Alley & Deshler, 1980). While it is often difficult for teachers to provide the extra practice in reading that LD children need, Stanovich was optimistic about the use of recently developed computer technology to provide such practice.

We would not want to be interpreted as suggesting that LD children should not be given the opportunity to interact with computer programs that are designed to enhance creativity, teach complex concepts, or build strategic problem-solving skills. However, we are concerned that the use of such programs be supported by sound research on both the appropriateness of the activity for LD children (Woodward & Carnine, 1988), and the generality of the learning they produce (Torgesen, 1986). In the meantime, we view it as a serious mistake to suggest that drill and practice programs are somehow second class, or less innovative than other types of programs. Because of their unique learning needs, specifically the need for extended practice opportunities in the acquisition of fluent component skills (Stanovich, 1986a), learning disabled children have more of a need for drill and practice exercises on the computer than do children who learn normally. In the best of all worlds, LD children would be given sufficient practice time on computers, as well as the opportunity to learn from other types of software.

Consistent with this introduction, the body of this chapter will be devoted to a discussion of drill and practice programs designed to enhance reading skills in children with learning disabilities. We will further focus specifically on programs designed to increase word reading, or decoding skills. This focus is dictated not only by the fact that the primary reading problems of learning disabled children appear to involve the acquisition of fluent word identification skills (Stanovich, 1986b), but also because most recent research has focused on this area. For purposes of this chapter, our definition of word identification skills includes all the processes and knowledge required to translate the printed representation of a word into speech or meaning. Words are identified in several different ways (Perfetti, 1984) during reading, and the programs we discuss address various aspects of the word identification process. The discussion is divided roughly into three broad sections. First, we will describe recent efforts to use computers in training phonological awareness in young children as a prereading skill. Then we will discuss research with programs designed to build various context-free word identification skills, and finally, we will describe work that focuses on increasing the fluency of decoding while reading connected text.

Although this chapter is meant to identify information useful for the instruction of learning disabled children, some of the studies we review examined the use of computers with children who were not explicitly identified as learning disabled. In all cases, however, the children were delayed in the acquisition of decoding skills, which is the target skill with which we are concerned. Whether or not these programs will work as well with learning disabled children as with the subjects in the studies we examine is a question that needs clarification in further research. However, the problem of generalization of findings from one sample to another in studies of learning disabled children is a ubiquitous one

(Torgesen, 1988), and is unlikely to be more severe for the studies we review in this chapter. In fact, there may be more generalization of instructional effects between samples of children identified by similar academic problems than might be found between samples identified by traditional psychometric criteria (Hallahan, Kauffman, & Lloyd, 1985; Paris, Jacobs, & Cross, 1987).

# Phonological Awareness Training

One of the most solidly established recent findings from research on the acquisition of reading skills is that phonological awareness is strongly related to success in the early stages of reading (Wagner & Torgesen, 1987). Phonological awareness refers to one's awareness and access to the phonology of one's language. It is demonstrated by performance on tasks such as segmenting, blending, and reversing syllables and phonemes in words.

There is now substantial evidence that it is possible to train phonological awareness in young children, and such training can have a beneficial effect on attainment of beginning reading skills. Training in phonological awareness has been shown to produce effects on the attainment of word recognition skills both when it is offered as an adjunct to reading instruction (Bradley & Bryant, 1985; Williams, 1980), and when it is offered prior to the beginning of reading instruction (Ball & Blachman, 1988; Lundberg, Frost, & Peterson, 1988). There is also evidence that some individuals may not develop phonological awareness without direct training (Bradley & Bryant, 1978), and that these individuals fail in reading to the extent that they are later identified as learning disabled (Gough & Tunmer, 1986).

Although efforts to develop computer-based training in phonological awareness skills are not very far along, they are mentioned here because of their direct relevance to reducing individual differences in the ease with which children learn to apply the alphabetic principle in decoding written words. In the programs discussed here, the computer is used to provide ample amounts of the type of analytic experience with words that will help children become more aware of their phonological structure.

The OVE-project, based in the Royal Institute of Technology in Stockholm and the University of Umea (Dahl, 1988) has employed a system in which synthetic speech and speech sounds are generated via a computer keyboard. Children engage in a series of activities with words (answering such questions as "which sound comes first?", "what is missing?", "which vowel is it?") in which they receive immediate feedback in the form of computer generated speech, concerning the correctness of their responses. They also have the opportunity to explore the structure of words in activities that allow them to hear the sound represented by each letter, or combination of letters, in words. This program does not make use of elaborate computer graphics, but maintains interest by providing a kind of feedback for reading and writing activities (phonemes corresponding to individual letters that are typed) that children have not previously experienced.

Because it requires typing and knowledge of letters, the program is not really suitable for prereading training in phonological awareness. It has been pilot tested with a group of Swedish children in the second to fifth grade who were experiencing severe reading difficulties (Dahl & Galyas, 1987). The children worked with the program in two 20-minute sessions per week for 12 weeks. Although no data were reported, the authors claimed that, in comparison to a control group, the children exposed to the program made substantial gains, not only in phonological awareness, but also in their motivation to read and write. A more extensive evaluation of the program is currently underway.

In contrast to the Swedish program, one in the United States (Foster, Foster, & Torgesen, 1990) is attempting to develop a phonological awareness program that will be suitable for children as young as four years of age. This program, being developed by OnTrack, Inc. in Provo, Utah, employs the extensive graphics and speech capabilities of the Apple IIGS computer to create a series of entertaining "games" that build phonological awareness in young children. The children receive training in accomplishing both phoneme analysis and blending on systematically organized word sets in order to build generalized skill in recognizing and manipulating the phonological structure of words. The child interacts with the program using a mouse, so the only skill required is the ability to move a cursor and "click" the mouse to make selections on screen. Individual words and word sounds are presented via high-quality digitized speech, while sentences and instructions are represented by synthetic speech.

Although this program has not yet been formally evaluated, initial reactions of children on which a prototype has been piloted have been very encouraging. The open game structure, as well as the high-quality graphics and sound that are provided by the IIGS, make the program very engaging for young children. If the programs prove to be instructionally effective as well as engaging, they will provide a means to make available high-quality training in phonological awareness to large numbers of young children.

## Context-Free Practice in Word Reading

There is now broad consensus (Anderson, Hiebert, Scott, & Wilkenson, 1985) that the best form of practice in reading involves reading meaningful text with the goal of understanding its message. In order to accomplish the ultimate purpose of reading, children must be able to coordinate a complex set of component skills fluently, and this requires extensive practice. However, for children with severe reading difficulties, reading meaningful text is often difficult and frustrating because of their problems in identifying individual words in text. The goal of the programs discussed here is to provide focused practice on deficient word reading skills that interfere with children's ability to read effectively for meaning. Such programs are potentially useful because they

(a) allow children to concentrate specifically on aspects of reading that are particularly difficult for them, and (b) provide for success experiences in "reading" during the *extended* process of acquiring reading fluency. We will consider programs in this section that provide practice on a variety of word recognition skills ranging from perception of subword letter units to automatic recognition of whole words.

Perhaps the most systematic evaluation of isolated word reading practice, as provided by the computer, has been carried out by Fredericksen and colleagues (Fredericksen, Warren, & Rosebery, 1985a,b). They developed a three-part training regimen that was based on a componential theory of reading (Fredericksen, 1982), as well as an analysis of the skills that are particularly deficient in poor readers. A componential theory of reading identifies a series of information-processing activities that interact with one another during the performance of the more complex task of text comprehension. Adolescent poor readers (not necessarily identified as learning disabled) were found (Fredericksen, 1981, 1982) to differ from good readers primarily in the speed or efficiency in which various components were executed, rather than in accuracy of performance. As with other work cited earlier, they found that poor readers were characterized by slow and inefficient decoding skills.

Their first computer training program was called SPEED. The goal of the program was to increase the efficiency (both speed and accuracy) with which students could identify multiletter units in words. The student was presented with a "target" multiletter unit (e.g., un, gen, th, ance) and then required to indicate whether the "target" was present in a series of rapidly presented words. The game itself used computer graphics to provide feedback about both response speed and accuracy, and both aspects of performance were important to success with the program.

SPEED was evaluated using five subjects ranging in age from 15 to 19 years of age (Fredericksen, Warren, & Rosebery, 1985a). These subjects were identified by their English/Reading teachers as poor readers, and they obtained total reading scores ranging from the 9th to 24th percentile on the Nelson-Denny Reading Test (Brown, Nelson, & Denny, 1973). IQ test scores were not reported. The students received extensive training in identifying from 60 to 80 different multiletter units using the SPEED game.

All subjects showed significant improvements in speed of identifying not only the multiletter units used in training, but also others that had not been trained. The overall pattern of results suggested that students had improved both in their ability to encode multiletter units, and in their ability to distribute attention across letter positions within words (as opposed to simply attending to the first and last letters of words). The results also showed that the skills acquired during SPEED training generalized to tasks involving word and pseudoword identification. Students who had been very inaccurate decoders improved significantly in accuracy, while students who had been accurate but inefficient decoders increased the speed of their decoding significantly.

Relying on somewhat the same principle as Fredericksen, Roth and Beck (1984) evaluated a program called *Construct-a-Word* (Beck & Roth, 1984a) with a group of inner city poor readers. The *Construct-a-Word* program provides practice in forming real words by matching beginning consonants and consonant blends (i.e., st, dr) with appropriate word endings (i.e., amp, ate, ot, eep, eaf, um). The program has two game options. One game, called "Words," challenges the child to form increasing numbers of words from the same set of beginning and ending subword parts. The second game option, called "Time," emphasizes forming these same words with ever-increasing speed. Thus, the program provides practice with a broad set of word beginnings and endings in a context that emphasizes both speed and accuracy of performance.

The evaluation compared the performance of fourth grade poor readers (grade level on the Word Attack subtest of the Woodcock Reading Mastery Test = 1.9) who received approximately 10 hours of practice with the program over a 4-month period, with that of a control group who did not receive the computer-based practice. On two separate dependent measures, the experimental group made substantially larger gains than the control group. For example, the speed with which the trained group could vocalize pseudowords composed of word parts practiced on the computer increased by 25%, while the control group showed no improvement. Further, on a task that required the children to judge whether a sentence presented on the computer was true or false, the experimental group showed an increase of 17% in reading speed, while the control group only improved 3%.

While the SPEED and *Construct-A-Word* programs are designed to help children use information about multiletter units in decoding print, another program called *Hint and Hunt* (Beck & Roth, 1984b) was developed to increase children's ability to fluently decode medial vowels and vowel combinations. This is a skill that is often extremely difficult for children with reading disabilities to master.

There are two basic instructional activities in the *Hint and Hunt* program. First, the vowel sounds are introduced and practiced in an "instructional mode" that employs a simple response format and does not emphasize speed. High-quality digitized speech is used to present the sounds associated with the different vowels. The second activity, called *Hunt*, employs a game format to provide extensive speed-oriented practice in recognizing words and nonsense syllables that contain the vowel sounds introduced in the instructional phase of the program. This game can be played at four different speeds to provide a continuous challenge as children become more fluent at recognizing the words being practiced.

The *Hint and Hunt* program was evaluated (Jones, Torgesen, & Sexton, 1987) with 20 learning disabled children in the 4th and 5th grades. The grade-level performance of the children on a test of word recognition (Peabody Individual Achievement Test) was 3.1. Half the children were randomly assigned to a practice group that worked with the *Hint and Hunt* program for 15 minutes a day over a period of approximately 10 weeks. The other 10 subjects were assigned to a control group that received equivalent experience with CAI on a program designed to help them learn their spelling words.

The most important dependent measure in the study was the speed with which children could read single-syllable words containing the vowels they practiced. Some of the words were identical to the ones practiced in the program (target words), while others contained the same vowels, but had different beginning and ending consonants (generalization words). The results for both speed and accuracy of reading individual words showed that the program was effective. The experimental group improved 27% in speed of response to generalization words, and their level of accuracy jumped from 80% correct to close to 100%. In contrast, the control group improved only 4% in speed and 5% in accuracy as the result of repeated testing. Another important finding was that the experimental group improved 35% in their oral reading speed for a paragraph containing many single-syllable words, while the control group's speed increased only 4%. Results from all the dependent measures suggest that practicing with the *Hint and Hunt* program was effective in increasing the generalized phonological decoding skills of the LD children in the experimental group.

The *Hint and Hunt* and *Construct-a-Word* programs are actually designed to be used together to increase decoding fluency in poor readers. The combined use of two levels of each program (levels I and II) over a substantial treatment period has been evaluated in two different studies. The first study, (Roth & Beck, 1987) employed inner city minority group children not diagnosed as LD but who showed serious delays in the acquisition of word identification skills. All the fourth grade children in one school received training on the decoding programs, while an equivalent group in another school was used as a no-treatment control group. Those receiving training practiced with the computer three times a week in 20-minute sessions over a period of 20 weeks. The results were analyzed separately for three groups differing in reading ability. We are concerned with results for the lowest group only, as they most closely resembled learning disabled children in the degree of their reading difficulties (grade level on the Word Analysis subtest of the Woodcock Reading Mastery Test = 1.7).

Improvement in reading skills over the course of treatment was measured by both experimental and standardized measures of reading. One of the most striking results was that the experimental group improved from the 1.7 to 3.0 grade level on the Word Attack subtest, while the control group only improved from the 1.6 to 2.0 grade level. Also, on the reading vocabulary subtest of the California Achievement Test, trained subjects improved from the 2.6 to 4.5 grade level, while those in the control group improved from the 2.6 to 3.5 grade level. On computer-based measures of naming speed for isolated pseudowords and real words, the experimental group also generally showed greater improvement than the control group. The experimental group also showed significantly greater gains in speed on a task that required children to read a sentence and decide whether it was true or false. The only task that showed no measurable effects from the treatment was the reading comprehension subtest of the California Achievement Test.

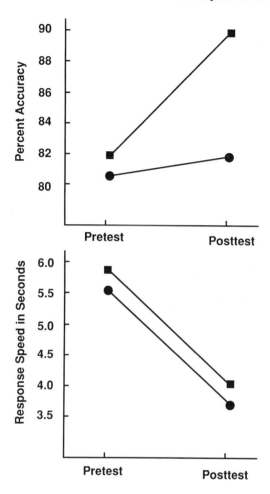

Figure 7.1. Speed and accuracy of performance on a comprehension task for experimental and control group children.

The second study (Torgesen, Greenstein, & Jones, 1990) evaluating the combined use of the *Hint and Hunt* and *Construct-a-Word* programs employed 43 ten-year-old learning disabled students. Twenty-eight subjects practiced in their resource rooms with the programs for 15 minutes a day over 80 training sessions. Children in the control group worked an equivalent amount of time on computer programs focusing on other academic skills. Dependent measures were similar to those employed by Roth & Beck (1987).

In contrast to the Roth and Beck (1987) study, however, children in the experimental and control groups did not differentially improve on standardized measures of reading. This was not because the experi-mental group failed to show significant improvement, but because the control group also improved substantially on these measures. For example, on the Word Attack subtest of the Woodcock Reading Mastery Test, the experimental group improved from the 2.7 to 4.1 grade level, while the control group improved from 2.3 to 3.7. The experimental group improved 1.1 grade levels on the Comprehension subtest, while the control group improved 0.8 grade levels. Results from a measure of sentence comprehension similar to the one employed by Roth and Beck are shown in Figure 7.1. As can be seen, both groups improved substantially in speed of response, while the experimental group made, at the same time, some significant improve-ments in accuracy of their judgments. Although the groups did not differentially improve in speed, again, the absolute amount of improvement made by the experimental group is very similar to that reported by Roth and Beck for their poorest readers.

Results for isolated reading of both real and nonsense words are reported in Figure 7.2. As can be seen, the training had its primary differential impact on speed and accuracy of decoding nonsense words. These results were also consistent with those of the earlier study in showing that the programs had their largest effects on ability to apply analytic, or phonological, decoding strategies to words that had not previously been encountered.

The overall results from the Torgesen et al. (1987) study were less impressive in terms of differential improvements between experimental and control groups than those reported by Roth and Beck (1987). One factor appears to be at least partially responsible for the different patterns of results. The control group in the former study was probably receiving more intensive instruction in reading skills as part of their resource room activities than was the control group in the Roth and Beck study. This latter group actually made very little improvement in reading over the course of an entire school year. Thus, the relatively small amount of extra practice provided by the computer programs did not provide as powerful an educational contrast with the regular program of instruction in the former study as in the latter.

The programs considered thus far were designed to have their primary impact on children's ability to use knowledge of the orthographic regularities within words, or specific letter-sound knowledge, to improve independent reading skills. In order to become fluent readers, children must also recognize large numbers of words as whole-word units, without having to engage in a "decoding" process (Perfetti, 1984). This type of word recognition occurs very rapidly, and it is the basis of fluent reading in good readers. The sight vocabulary of normal readers increases dramatically as a result of repeated exposure to words as they process text. However, the sight vocabulary of LD children increases more slowly than that of their peers, presumably because their weak decoding skills preclude large amounts of independent reading practice (Stanovich, 1986a).

Although there are many different microcomputer-based programs designed to build sight vocabulary using context-free practice, only two have been evaluated with learning disabled children. The WORDS (Torgesen & Torgesen, 1985) program was designed for children with essentially no, or only beginning, reading skills. The program is constructed so that children move from being able

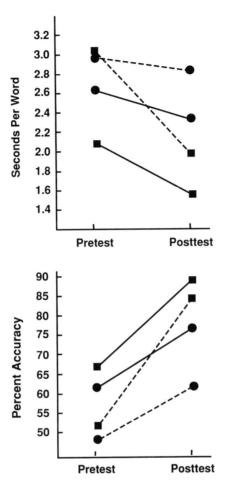

Figure 7.2. Speed and accuracy of reading real words and nonwords for experimental and control group children.

to read the words in their practice set accurately to being able to read them both accurately and quickly. The program uses graphic representations (pictures) toindicate the identity of a word being practiced. It requires the child to respond at a given level of accuracy on one type of study activity before moving to the next. The first practice activities emphasize accuracy of responding, while the final level requires the child to meet preset criteria for both accuracy and speed of responding.

Two separate studies have demonstrated that learning disabled children can learn to read previously unknown words both rapidly and accurately as a result of practice with the WORDS program. In one study (Torgesen, Waters, Cohen, & Torgesen, 1988), second and third grade LD children learned to rapidly recognize (out of context) about 70% of the words they practiced. A second study (Cohen, Torgesen, & Torgesen, 1988) showed that third and fourth grade students could add to their sight vocabulary at the rate of one word for every 6.7 minutes of study with the WORDS program.

As part of their more comprehensive attack on the reading deficiencies of adolescent poor readers, Fredericksen and his colleagues (Fredericksen, Warren, & Rosebery, 1985b) also developed a program to increase sight vocabulary. This program, called RACER, requires students to rapidly identify words presented out of context one at a time. Both speed and accuracy of word identification are emphasized by the game characteristics of the program. Phonological decoding rules are not taught, nor are elaborate correction procedures employed. However, words are arranged systematically in lists in order to enhance learning of various phonological patterns in words.

Six subjects received approximately 24 training sessions with this program, each lasting about 30 minutes. The training was organized so that students were exposed to lists of gradually increasing difficulty. Four of the subjects had previously served in the evaluation of the SPEED program mentioned earlier, and the two new subjects were of similar age and reading skill.

Training experience with the RACER program produced significant effects on the student's word identification skills. Not only did students improve in efficiency in recognizing the words practiced by the program, but they were also able to read pseudowords more efficiently. For example, average pronunciation times for two-syllable words decreased by 245 msec., while pronunciation times for two syllable pseudowords decreased by 297 msec. This finding is important because it suggests that students experienced generalized improvements in phonological decoding skills as a result of RACER training. In contrast to these effects on context-free word identification skills, there was no effect of RACER training on a passage comprehension task.

The failure to find immediate effects of improved decoding skills on a measure of reading comprehension are not surprising in light of the relatively weak generalization effects of other decoding programs already noted. However, in a third experiment that involved training to improve a specific comprehension skill, Fredericksen et al. (1985b) were able to show that improved decoding skills do generalize to comprehension tasks once some of the comprehension skills required on the task are directly trained.

The purpose of the SKIJUMP training program was to develop skill in using semantic information derived from context to gain access to word meanings. Earlier experimentation had determined that poor readers were not as efficient as good readers in using information in a context frame (e.g., a sentence) to activate a wide range of relevant concepts in semantic memory, which is a skill that facilitates good reading comprehension. The basic format of the SKIJUMP program involved determining whether a rapidly presented word fit appropriately into a previously presented sentence. Like the other programs in this series, this activity was embedded within a game that emphasized both speed and accuracy of performance.

Of the seven subjects in the study, four had been previously exposed to SPEED and RACER training. The other three were selected from the same high schools and by the same criteria. Their performance on a standardized measure of reading ranged from the 10th to 30th percentile. Training varied for individual subjects, ranging from 12 to 20 sessions lasting 30 to 45 minutes.

The pattern of performance on the SKIJUMP task itself suggested that it accomplished its purpose of training subjects to use information from context to gain access to a set of words or concepts that were consistent with that context. Whether or not subjects had received prior training on word identification skills did not make a difference in the size of the SKIJUMP training effect.

Subjects were also given the same comprehension task they had received after RACER training. This task required subjects to identify the correct conjunctive expression with which to begin the last sentence in a brief paragraph. The paragraph was written so that the conjunctive expression (i.e., "As a result") communicated the appropriate relationship between the content of the last sentence and the context established by the previous sentences in the paragraph. Subjects with prior training in word decoding showed improvements in both speed and accuracy of responding on this task. Although these findings must be considered tentative in light of the small number of subjects on which they are based, they do suggest that improvements in decoding proficiency before training in comprehension processes can enhance the effectiveness of the latter training. They support the idea of an interaction between decoding fluency and comprehension processes that is most clearly manifest when readers have begun to master the specific information processing activities required for good comprehension.

## Summary

Research to date has shown that microcomputers can be used effectively to enhance a variety of word recognition skills in learning disabled children. The programs considered here all provided practice in reading words out of context. Such practice has the advantage of providing a large number of repetitions of specific words and letter combinations in a short period of time. For practice on such component skills as fluent perception of subword units and fluent translation of specific grapheme-phoneme correspondences it may be very useful as a precursor to efficient context-based practice for LD children. It may also be helpful in creating an initial sight vocabulary during early stages of reading acquisition. One potential problem for these kinds of programs is that they can become repetitive and uninteresting for children unless they are placed within a meaningful context. Children do not receive the same  kind of intrinsic satisfaction from these activities that they do from reading meaningful text. Although the game-like format of these programs helps to maintain interest, over extended periods of use even the most interesting game can become repetitive. In order to help maintain the effectiveness of this type of practice, teachers should use a variety of different programs that build similar skills, and should also try to embed this type of practice within a meaningful context. One way to accomplish this is to move children as quickly as possible toward reading meaningful text.

## Practicing Reading in Context

One method that has frequently been used to increase reading fluency using noncomputer materials is the repeated reading technique (Moyer, 1982). This method involves having children reread a selection three or four times (Sindelar, 1987). Rashotte and Torgesen (1985) showed that computer-administered repeated-reading practice resulted in improved word reading fluency in fourth grade learning disabled children. In this study, the LD children enjoyed reading the same selections repeatedly, not only because the computer gave them immediate feedback about their improved speed of reading, but also because they simply enjoyed the experience of reading a passage fluently and without errors. This study showed that the primary effectiveness of the technique for dysfluent LD children was to increase the rate at which they identified specific words in the selections they practiced reading.

Since this initial study, we have completed three additional investigations of the repeated-reading technique with LD children. These studies used a computer format specifically designed to administer the repeated-reading technique, with colorful graphics and interesting feedback about reading rate. The program, called Lesson Master (Brezin & Wager, 1987), provides several different formats for practicing decoding skills, and it also allows complete customization of instructional materials. In all of our studies with this technique, children have reread selections orally, and have received correction of reading errors from a tutor listening to their performance. Although these studies have not been able to show *generalized* fluency increases (e.g., increased rate of reading words not practiced in the selections) as a result of repeated-reading practice, they provide extensive documentation that LD children's sight vocabularies are improved by the technique.

For example, in one of our studies (Greene, Torgesen, & Wager, 1988), third and fourth grade poor readers practiced different sets of words using either the repeated-reading technique, or a context-free method. In the repeated-reading condition, the target words were embedded within several different short stories that were each reread four times. Children's reading errors were corrected only during the first two story repetitions. The context-free method used was also part of the Lesson Master program, and used digitized speech to present words that were then chosen from a set of printed (on the computer screen) alternatives. The computer provided error correction feedback in this condition. The study used a posttest only design.

Figure 7.3 presents the percent of words that were fluently identified (accurate

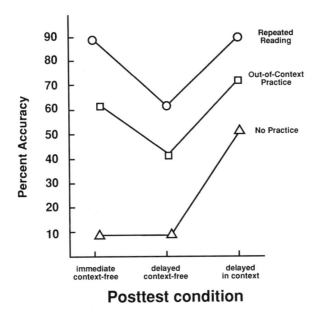

Figure 7.3. Effects of three practice conditions on children's ability to accurately identify words in less than 21 seconds.

in less than 2 seconds) after receiving either no practice, context-free practice, or repeated-reading practice. The immediate context-free test took place two days after a word set was studied, and the delayed test took place three weeks later. The in-context test measured how well subjects identified practiced words when they were encountered in a new story. The results from the no-practice conditionindicate that the words practiced in this study were difficult for the children--without practice, they could only recognize 10% of them out of context. The most effective condition was repeated reading, with approximately 90% of practiced words being recognized fluently on the immediate posttest. The data from the delayed in-context posttest suggest that these children were able to use context to aid in word recognition, but the effect of practice with the repeated-reading technique was still significant. We have observed similar effects on word recognition skill in two other studies of the repeated-reading technique with learning disabled children (Cohen & Torgesen, 1988; Selvey & Torgesen, 1989).

The major drawback of the repeated-reading technique as we have used it in our studies is that it requires a teacher, peer tutor, or aid, to provide correction of errors during the first readings of each selection. However, recent developments in computer-controlled speech suggest that this limitation may be overcome in future applications. Peter Rietsma (1988) reported the use of a computer-controlled tape recorder to allow children to request pronunciation of difficult words as they occurred in text. Seven-year-old children read different stories in which the same set of 20 target words had been included. They could request pronunciation of any word in the story simply by touching a pressure-sensitive pad on which the text was placed. Rietsma showed that poor readers improved significantly in their fluency of reading these difficult words as a result of a small amount of practice with this technique.

Perhaps the most sophisticated and flexible technique for providing speech feedback during reading has been reported by Olson and his colleagues (Olson, Foltz, & Wise, 1986; Olson & Wise, 1987; Olson, Wise, Conners, & Rack, 1990). These investigators have used high-quality computer-generated synthetic speech to provide several different kinds of auditory information about words as children encounter them in text. For example, their system, which uses a DECtalk speech synthesizer controlled by an IBM compatible computer, can aurally present either whole words or parts of words separately. When words are presented in segments, the auditory presentation of those segments can be timed to correspond with highlighting the corresponding orthographic segments on the computer screen.

One of the questions that Olson et al. have investigated in their research involves the specific type of feedback that is most effective in enhancing the word reading skills of poor readers. In their most recent study (Olson et al., 1990), they employed 46 reading disabled children in grades three to six as subjects. Thirty-six of the children were assigned to one of four treatment conditions, which involved different kinds of auditory and orthographic feedback when they requested help with a word while reading. The treatment conditions were (a) whole-word feedback, (b) syllable-level feedback, (c) subsyllable feedback (each syllable was broken into onset and rhyme parts), and (d) combined syllable and subsyllable feedback. The control children received no treatment intervention. Children in the different treatment conditions read stories that each contained several words that were difficult for them. Sessions lasted approximately 30 minutes and extended over the course of a semester, with an average total time on the system of 10 hours. Students were trained to use a "mouse" to select words on which they desired help from the computer. For these words, orthographic and speech feedback was given according to the assigned treatment condition. After every 4-8 pages in a story, the children answered one or two comprehension questions, and they also took a word recognition test on words they had targeted for help, or on other relatively difficult words in the story.

Across conditions, the children selected an average of approximately 70 target words for each hour spent reading the stories. There were no significant differences among conditions in number of words targeted for help. Overall improvement on a timed word recognition test was significant, with children in the subsyllable and whole-words conditions showing the greatest improvement. On a test of reading nonwords, children in all the segmentation conditions showed significant improvement, while those in the control and whole-word conditions did not. Across all dependent measures, children in the subsyllable segmentation condition showed the greatest gains from pretest to posttest.

Although in some cases, these differences did not reach statistical significance, the authors suggest that a longer treatment study might more clearly show the advantages of this condition.

Another issue not addressed in this study, but that might be addressed in future research, involves individual differences in the type of feedback that might be most helpful. Some children, for example, might profit more from whole-word feedback, while others might find subsyllable segmentation the most useful. Such a study would require a much larger sample of reading disabled children than those reported on thus far. As a final note, Olson et al. (1990) report that the type of practice provided by their system is highly motivating for children with reading problems. The opportunity to read interesting stories independently (with only the help of a computer) was very attractive for almost all of the subjects in their study. Teresa Rosegrant (1985) has also reported the development of a program called the "talking textwriter" that allows children to select words in text for pronunciation by the computer. Although the speech technology of this program is not as sophisticated as that employed by Olson et al., Rosegrant (1985) reports informal evidence that it can have a substantial impact on both the skills, and interest, of LD children in reading.

## Concluding Comments and Future Directions

From the material presented thus far, it is clear that microcomputers can be programmed to provide effective practice in a variety of prereading and reading skills. However, there remain large gaps in our knowledge about how to utilize the resources presently available to have the maximum long-term impact in overcoming the reading problems of poor readers. The problem with our information to this point is that it is based on relatively short-term studies of narrow treatment packages. These studies do not provide information about the long-term impact of this kind of practice in normalizing the reading skills of LD children, nor does it provide guidance about how the programs might be applied either sequentially, or in parallel, toward remediation of word-reading difficulties.

For example, one of the findings from an early study of Olson's reading practice program was that children who made a lot of oral reading errors did not profit from the program to the same extent as those who made fewer errors. In effect, these children were overwhelmed by the number of new words they had to learn in each selection. For these children, a period of practice to build either phonological decoding skills or a larger corpus of sight vocabulary words might be necessary before they can take maximum advantage of computer-aided reading of text. Such practice might most easily be provided using out of context methods to target the specific skills that are most deficient. On the other hand, it might also be possible to make the story, or paragraph selections easy enough so that this kind of out-of-context practice would not be necessary for many children.

A further issue is related to ways of making focused practice on component skills more meaningful to LD children so that their involvement in the practice can be sustained over substantial periods of time. One suggestion comes from Warren and Rosebery (1988), who employ the term *contextualization* to describe their method. Contextualization means "tying reading instruction explicitly to an understanding of purpose both in the context of the immediate instructional activity and in the larger context of learning" (p. 37). One way that this might be accomplished for reading disabled children is to employ both out-of-context and in-context methods in parallel. This would provide teachers with more opportunities to show children how practice on component skills is meaningfully related to the development of skill in processing complete text.

Another relatively unexplored area involves questions about ways to use computers to build skills (in addition to fluent decoding) that are required for efficient comprehension. Although we know that computers can be used effectively to enhance specific decoding skills, we still lack convincing evidence that such practice, by itself, can produce significant changes in children's ability to comprehend text. Both Roth and Beck (1987) and Torgesen, Greenstein, and Jones (1987) showed that increasing decoding fluency can have an effect on sentence-level comprehension, but neither obtained effects on passage-level comprehension. Further, a conclusion from the study by Fredericksen et al. (1985b) was that the effects of increases in decoding fluency on comprehension are most clearly seen *after* children are provided with practice to build the specific comprehension skills they lack. This same study provided one model of computer based comprehension training that involved direct practice in a component skill (gaining access to the meaning of words in text by utilizing previous context) that facilitates good reading comprehension. Other direct approaches might involve programs to build children's knowledge of the meanings of words. In fact, Beck, McKeown, and Roth (1988) have recently published software called *Word Wise I, II, and III: Better Comprehension Through Vocabulary* (1988) that incorporates many of the features of a successful noncomputer training program reported by Beck, Perfetti, and McKeown (1982). In contrast to many vocabulary building methods (Mezynski, 1983), Beck et al.'s program did produce significant effects on children's reading comprehension scores.

Another way of building poor readers' comprehension skills is currently being investigated by Warren and Rosebery (1988). This program, called *Reader's Assistant*, provides children with the opportunity to explicitly engage in many of the cognitive processes that are required for good comprehension, but that are not usually made explicit in reading instruction. It is consistent with the work of Palincsar and Brown (1984) in which they gradually taught children to use a variety of text comprehension strategies (asking questions, summarizing, clarifying) in a highly interactive context. *Reader's Assistant* provides a tool for children to engage in these otherwise covert mental activities by performing explicit activities on the computer, like attaching questions to certain locations in text, or making predictions about expected outcomes. Although this program has not been evaluated with LD children, noncomputer-based programs that teach similar strategies to young children have proven very effective in increasing reading comprehension skills.

A final way that computers may prove useful in improving reading comprehension is by providing detailed assessments of comprehension skills in support of teacher-led instructional programs (Brown & Palincsar, 1987). One of the most important characteristics of recently developed training programs for comprehension is the need for dynamic, ongoing assessments of emerging skills (Paris, Jacobs, & Cross, 1987). The development of increasingly explicit knowledge concerning the processes and knowledge required for good comprehension (Brown & Campione, 1986) will allow computers to play a more important role in both assessment of these skills and in providing practice to increase facility in executing them.

In conclusion, it is clear that substantial progress has been made in developing the microcomputer as a useful tool in reading instruction for LD children. Some of this progress has been directly fueled by recent technological advances (such as speech capabilities) that have given the computer additional capabilities important to reading instruction. We are also making some progress toward conceptualization of how computers might participate as part of an integrated program to facilitate reading acquisition in children with learning disabilities. Although we certainly need to continue developing effective software, it is on the integration problem that large amounts of work remain to be done. We have available a useful technology, and our challenge now is to demonstrate how different kinds of programs, focusing on different aspects of reading skill, can be co-ordinated with teacher-led instruction in ways that will have a substantial impact on the reading skills of individual LD children.

# References

Anderson, R.C., Hiebert, E.H., Scott, J.A., & Wilkenson, I.A.G. (1985). *Becoming a nation of readers*. Washington, DC: National Institute of Education.

Ball, E.W., & Blachman, B.A. (1988). Phoneme Segmentation Training: Effect on reading readiness. *Annals of Dyslexia, 38*, 208-225.

Beck, I.L., McKeown, M.G. & Roth, S.F. (1988). *Word Wise teacher's manual*. Allen, TX: Developmental Learning Materials.

Beck, I.L., Perfetti, C.A., & McKeown, M.G. (1982). Effects of long-term vocabulary instruction on lexical access and reading comprehension. *Journal of Educational Psychology, 74*, 506-521.

Beck, I.L., & Roth, S.F. (1984a). *Hint and Hunt teacher's manual*. Allen, TX: Developmental Learning Materials.

Beck, I.L., & Roth, S.F. (1984b). *Construct-A-Word teacher's manual*. Allen, TX: Developmental Learning Materials.

Bradley, L., & Bryant, P.E. (1978). Difficulties in auditory organization as a possible cause of reading backwardness. *Nature, 221,* 746-747.

Bradley, L., & Bryant, P. (1985). *Rhyme and reason in reading and spelling.* Ann Arbor: University of Michigan Press.

Brezin, M., & Wager, W. (1987). *Lesson Master Authoring System.* Tallahassee, FL: IDDEA, Inc.

Brown, A.L., & Campione, J.C. (1986). Psychological theory and the study of learning disabilities. *American Psychologist, 14,* 1059-1068.

Brown, A.L., & Palincsar, A.S. (1987). Reciprocal teaching of comprehension strategies: a natural history of one program for enhancing learning. In L. Borkowski & L.D. Day (Eds.), *Intelligence and cognition in special children: Comparative studies of giftedness, mental retardation, and learning disabilities* (pp. 81-132). New York: Ablex.

Brown, A.L., Palincsar, A.S., & Purcell, L. (1986). Poor readers: Teach, don't label. In U. Neisser (Ed.), *The school achievement of minority children: New perspectives* (pp. 105-143). Hillsdale, NJ: Lawrence Erlbaum.

Brown, J.I., Nelson, M.J., & Denny, E.C. (1973). *The Nelson-Denny Reading Test.* Boston: Houghton Mifflin.

Cohen, A., & Torgesen, J.K. (1988). *An evaluation of two methods for providing computer-assisted repeated reading training to reading disabled students.* Unpublished manuscript, Florida State University, Tallahassee, FL.

Cohen, A., Torgesen, J.K., & Torgesen, J.L. (1988). Improving speed and accuracy of word recognition in reading disabled children: An evaluation of two computer program variations. *Learning Disabilities Quarterly, 11,* 333-341.

Cosden, M.A., Gerber, M.M., Semmel, D.S., Goldman, S.R., & Semmel, M.I. (1987). Microcomputer use within micro-educational environments. *Exceptional Children, 53,* 399-411.

Dahl, I. (July, 1988). *The OVE project: Using computers to teach phonological awareness and reading.* Paper presented at meetings of the International Academy for Research in Learning Disabilities, Ann Arbor, MI.

Dahl, I., & Galyas, K. (1987). *Experiences with the use of computer programs with speech output in teaching reading and writing.* Paper presented at the European Conference on Speech Technology, Edinburgh, September.

Foster, K., Foster, D., & Torgesen, J.K. (1990). *Daisy quest.* Orem, UT: Ontrack, Inc.

Fredericksen, J.R. (1981). Sources of process interaction in reading. In A.M. Lesgold & C.A. Perfetti (Eds.), *Interactive processes in reading* (pp. 361-386). Hillsdale, NJ: Lawrence Erlbaum.

Fredericksen, J.R. (1982). A componential theory of reading skills and their interactions. In R.J. Sternberg (Ed.), *Advances in the psychology of human intelligence* (Vol. 1, pp. 125-180). Hillsdale, NJ.: Lawrence Erlbaum.

Fredericksen, J.R., Warren, B.M. & Rosebery, A.S. (1985a). A componential approach to training reading skills: Part 1. Perceptual units training. *Cognition and Instruction, 2,* 91-130.

Fredericksen, J.R., Warren, B.M. & Rosebery, A.S. (1985b). A componential approach to training reading skills: Part 2. Decoding and use of context. *Cognition and Instruction, 2,* 271-338.

Goldman, S.R. & Pellegrino, J.W. (1987). Information processing and educational microcomputer technology: Where do we go from here? *Journal of Learning Disabilities, 20,* 144-154.

Gough, P. & Tunmer, W. (1986). Decoding, reading, and reading disability. *Remedial and Special Education, 7,* 6-10.

Greene, E.C., Torgesen, J.K., & Wager W.W. (1988). *The effects of repeated reading and context-free instruction on increases in children's word recognition fluency.* Unpublished manuscript, Florida State University, Tallahassee, FL.

Hallahan, D.P., Kauffman, J.M., & Lloyd, J.W. (1985). *Introduction to learning disabilities.* Englewood Cliffs, NJ: Prentice-Hall.

Jones, K., Torgesen, J.K., & Sexton, M.A. (1987). Using computer guided practice to increase decoding fluency in learning disabled children: A study using the Hint & Hunt I Program. *Journal of Learning Disabilities, 20,* 122-128.

Lundberg, I., Frost, J., & Peterson, O. (1988). Effects of an extensive program for stimulating phonological awareness in pre-school children. *Reading Research Quarterly, 23,* 263-284.

Mezynski, K. (1983). Issues concerning the acquisition of knowledge: Effects of vocabulary training on reading comprehension. *Review of Educational Research, 53,* 253-279.

Moyer, S.B. (1982). Repeated reading. *Journal of Learning Disabilities, 45,* 619-623.

Olsen, R., Foltz, G., & Wise, B. (1986). Reading instruction and remediation with the aid of computer speech. *Behavior Research Methods, Instruments, & Computers, 18,* 93-99.

Olsen, R., & Wise, B. (1987). Computer speech in reading instruction. In D. Reinking (Ed.), *Computers and reading: Issues for theory and practice* (pp. 156-177). New York: Teachers College Press.

Olsen, R., Wise, B., Conners, F., & Rack, J. (1990). Organization, heritability, and remediation of component word recognition and language skills in disabled readers. In T.H. Carr and B.A. Levy (Eds.). *Reading and its development: Component skills approaches.* Orlando, FL: Academic Press.

Palincsar, A.S., & Brown, A.L. (1984). Reciprocal teaching of comprehension-fostering and comprehension-monitoring activities. *Cognition and Instruction, 1,* 117-175.

Paris, S.G., Jacobs, J.E., & Cross, D.R. (1987). Toward an individualistic psychology of exceptional children. In J.G. Borkowski & J.D. Day (Eds.), *Intelligence and exceptionality: New directions for theory, assessment, and instructional practices* (pp. 215-248). Norwood, NJ: Ablex Publishing.

Perfetti, C.A. (1984). Reading acquisition and beyond: decoding includes cognition. *American Journal of Education, 33,* 40-61.

Rashotte, C.A., & Torgesen, J.K. (1985). Repeated reading and reading fluency in learning disabled children. *Reading Research Quarterly, 20,* 180-188.

Reitsma, P. (1988). Reading practice for beginners: Effects of guided reading, reading-while-listening, and independent reading with computer-based speech feedback. *Reading Research Quarterly, 23,* 219-226.

Rosegrant, T. (1985). Using the microcomputer as a tool for learning to read and write. *Journal of Learning Disabilities, 18,* 113-115.

Roth, S.F., & Beck, I.L. (1984). *Research and instructional issues related to the enhancement of children's decoding skills through a microcomputer program.* Paper presented at the annual meeting of the American Educational Research Association, New Orleans, LA.

Roth, S.F., & Beck, I.L. (1987). Theoretical and instructional implications of the assessment of two microcomputer word recognition programs. *Reading Research Quarterly, 22,* 197-218.

Selvey, A. & Torgesen, J.K. (1989). *A comparison of two variations of computer administered repeated reading with learning disabled children.* Unpublished manuscript, Florida State University, Tallahassee, FL.

Sindelar, P. (1987). Increasing reading fluency. *Teaching Exceptional Children, 19,* 59-60.

Stanovich, K.E. (1986a). Matthew effects in reading: Some consequences of individual differences in the acquisition of literacy. *Reading Research Quarterly, 21,* 360-406. ·

Stanovich, K.E. (1986b). Explaining the variance in reading ability in terms of psychological processes: What have we learned? *Annals of Dyslexia, 35,* 67-96.

Torgesen, J.K. (1986). Computer assisted instruction with learning disabled children. In J.K. Torgesen & B.Y.L. Wong (Eds.), *Psychological and educational perspectives on learning disabilities* (pp. 417-436). New York: Academic Press.

Torgesen, J.K. (1988). Thinking about the future by distinguishing between issues that have answers and those that do not. In S.T. Vaughn & C.S. Bos (Eds.), *Issues and future directions for research in learning disabilities* (pp. 55-67). San Diego: College Hill Press.

Torgesen, J.K., Greenstein, J., & Jones, K. (1987). *Computer guided reading practice with learning disabled children: Effects on decoding and comprehension skills.* Paper presented at National Reading Conference, St. Petersburg Beach, December.

Torgesen, J.K., & Torgesen, J.L. (1985). *WORDS* (computer program). Tallahassee, FL: Florida State University.

Torgesen, J.K., Waters, M.D., Cohen, A.L., & Torgesen, J.L. (1988). Improving sight word recognition skills in learning disabled children: An evaluation of three computer program variations. *Learning Disabilities Quarterly, 11,* 125-133.

Torgesen, J.K., & Wolf, M. (1986). Computers and reading instruction: lessons from the past, promise for the future. In G.T. Pavlidss & D. Fisher (Eds.),

*Dyslexia: Neuropsychology and Treatment* (pp. 279-296). Sussex, England: John Wiley & Sons.

Wagner, R.K., & Torgesen, J.K. (1987). The nature of phonological processing and its causal role in the acquisition of reading skills. *Psychological Bulletin, 101*, 192-212.

Warner, M.M., Schumaker, J.B., Alley, G.R., & Deshler, D.D. (1980). Learning disabled adolescents in the public schools: Are they different from other low achievers? *Exceptional Education Quarterly, 1*, 27-36.

Warren, B., & Rosebery, A.S. (1988). Theory and practice: Uses of the computer in reading. *Remedial and Special Education, 9*, 29-38.

Williams, J.P. (1980). Teaching decoding with an emphasis on phoneme analysis and phoneme blending. *Journal of Educational Psychology, 72*, 1-15.

Woodcock, R.W. (1973). *Woodcock Reading Mastery Tests*. Circle Press, MN: American Guidance Service.

Woodward, J.P., & Carnine, D.W. (1988). Antecedent knowledge and intelligent computer assisted instruction. *Journal of Learning Disabilities, 21*, 131-139.

# Social Interventions

# 8

# Social Interventions for Students with Learning Disabilities: Towards a Broader Perspective

## Sharon Vaughn, Ruth McIntosh, and Nina Zaragoza

Children who are rejected by their peers are at risk for school dropout, crime, delinquency, and psychological adjustment problems later in life (for review see, Parker & Asher, 1987). This empirically based finding supported by longitudinal data emphasizes the importance of early peer relationships in the social competence and adjustment of children throughout their lifetime. Thus, the work of Bryan (e.g., Bryan, 1974a,b, 1976), who initially identified the low peer acceptance and poor social relationships of many children with learning disabilities, has provided a catalyst for researchers to further examine the social competence of children with learning disabilities.

Repeated studies have consistently demonstrated that children with learning disabilities are more frequently rejected by their peers, less frequently identified as popular, infrequently selected as playmates, and not well liked by teachers (for reviews see, Pearl, 1987; Pearl, Donahue, & Bryan, 1986; Vaughn & LaGreca, 1988). Students with learning disabilities even prior to identification are significantly more rejected than their low-, average-, and high-achieving peers (Vaughn, Hogan, Kouzekanani, & Shapiro, 1990). Given the importance of early peer relations, what direction should research and practice take to meet the needs of those learning disabled students who are not well liked by their peers?

The most obvious answer to "what next?" is to develop, implement, and evaluate the efficacy of intervention approaches designed to facilitate the peer relations of children with learning disabilities. Another important step is to better understand why a disproportionate number of students with learning disabilities are rejected by their peers. Is the low peer acceptance of learning disabled students a consequence of skill deficits, e.g., inadequacies in social cognition, social skills, and interpersonal communication, or is their low acceptance related to other factors, e.g., low achievement, low participation in the regular classroom, and low teacher acceptance? A better understanding of these issues could yield direct guidelines for the nature of social skills interventions for students with learning disabilities.

This chapter provides a brief description of an ongoing prospective study designed to better understand why students with learning disabilities are not well accepted by their peers. Additionally, a description of several social skills interventions used with students who are learning disabled will be presented.

## Social and Behavioral Characteristics of Learning Disabled Students Prior to Identification

To more fully understand the social characteristics of high-risk children, e.g., students with learning disabilities, we (Vaughn, Haager, Hogan, & Kouzekanani, in press; Vaughn & Hogan, 1990; Vaughn, Hogan, Kouzekanani, & Shapiro, 1990) are conducting a prospective study aimed at assessing and describing the social competence of children early in their school career. In this study, social competence is conceptualized as a multidimensional construct which includes peer relations, self-acceptance, behavioral adjustment, and social skills.

Kindergartners, who were later identified as learning disabled, were matched with low-, average-, and high-achieving children. Variables were chosen to reflect the four components of social competence: peer relations (peer ratings of social acceptance and positive friendship nominations); self-acceptance (Pictorial Scale of Perceived Competence and Social Acceptance for Young Children; Harter & Pike, 1984); behavioral adjustment (Revised Behavior Problem Checklist; Quay & Peterson, 1987); and social skills (adapted version of the Social Skills Rating Scale for Teachers; Gresham & Elliott, 1986). These measures were administered in the fall and spring of the students' kindergarten year, and at least once a year during their first, second, and third grade years.

Results indicated there were significant differences among groups identified as learning disabled prior to identification (LDPI), low achieving (LA), average achieving (AA), and high achieving (HA) as early as eight weeks into their kindergarten year. The LDPI children's assessments indicated problems in all four factors of social competence: peer acceptance, self-perception, behavior problems, and social skills. On peer acceptance, LDPI students were more frequently rejected, less accepted, and received overall lower ratings of likability from their classmates. More specifically, 60% of the LDPI children were rejected and 0% were rated as popular. On self-perception, the LDPI children demonstrated distorted self-ratings of social acceptance. They perceived themselves as highly accepted by their peers despite significantly low peer acceptance scores. On behavior problems, the LDPI children demonstrated significantly higher attention problems than the AA and HA groups with their attention problem scores one standard deviation above age-appropriate norms. LDPI students were also significantly higher on psychotic behavior; however, their scores were within the normative mean. With respect to social skills, LDPI children's skills when compared with those of the LA, AA, and HA groups were less acceptable to their classroom teachers over time. The LA students scores were low on all four factors but not as significantly low as were those of LDPI students.

What emerges from these results is a portrait of LDPI children experiencing social and behavioral difficulties early in their kindergarten year. They have already been rejected by peers but their self perceptions of social acceptance do not reflect this rejection. In contrast they imagine themselves to be highly accepted. They are seen by teachers as children who are less socially and behaviorally acceptable in the classroom and who exhibit marked attention problems. In view of the stability of rejection status (Howes, 1988; Li, 1985), and the risk of future academic difficulties due to attention problems, early intervention appears necessary.

The results of this study suggest that the social difficulties characteristic of children identified as LD are not solely a function of the referral/identification process, e.g., teacher treatment, peer responses, less class participation. Since problematic social competence patterns occurred prior to identification and so early in the children's school career, hypotheses that contend social difficulties are a function of psychological processing and skill deficits need to be further investigated.

For example, if psychological processing and skill deficits affect social skills, perhaps academic tutoring to improve these areas would also positively influence peer acceptance. Recent work (see Coie & Krehbiel, 1984 for discussion) has shown that academic intervention has a positive effect on the social status of rejected children with low academic achievement. While the positive effects of academic tutoring on increasing peer acceptance of low achieving students is encouraging, these results need to be verified with children identified as learning disabled. Furthermore, knowledge about the social skills and friendship experiences of students outside of the school setting is needed. Since academic achievement and school behavior are highly related to peer acceptance, it is possible that the low peer and teacher ratings of LD students are influenced by their academic and school behavior. Perhaps their behavior outside of the school setting is less troublesome, and the perceptions of significant others from these setting is more positive.

## Social Skills Interventions

There have been several studies with learning disabled students that have attempted to enhance their social skills or increase their peer acceptance. Three interventions will be discussed in this section: a social skills program for adolescents, a contextualist intervention, and an intervention entitled Mutual Interest Discovery.

## A Social Skills Program for Adolescents (ASSET)

ASSET is a social skills program developed for adolescents and evaluated with adjudicated youth and LD adolescents (Hazel, Schumaker, Sherman, & Sheldon-Wildgen, 1981). There are eight foundation skills taught within the ASSET program that are considered fundamental for effective social interactions. These eight skills include giving positive feedback, giving negative feedback, accepting negative feedback, resisting peer pressure, problem solving, negotiation, following directions, and conversation. The assumption underlying the program is that many students with learning disabilities do not exhibit the critical behaviors essential to social functioning, not because they are unmotivated to do so, but because they do not have the skills or confidence to do so. The goal of the ASSET program is to provide systematic procedures for teaching students each of the eight foundation skills and to provide opportunities to practice and rehearse the skills until they are able to perform them outside of the social skills training setting.

The teaching procedures used in the program are based on success, successive approximations, mastery, and multiple exemplars. Teaching techniques includes providing a description of specific behaviors related to each of the eight skills, modeling the skills through videotapes, and rehearsal of the skills during group sessions.

Each of the eight foundation skills are taught to small groups of students by using nine basic steps. The nine step teaching procedure follows.

**Step One:** Review previously learned skills and check and discuss homework.

**Step Two:** Explain or describe the target skill for the lesson.

**Step Three:** Provide a rationale for why the skill should be learned.

**Step Four:** Discuss examples of when the skill could be used and how it might be helpful.

**Step Five:** Examine the skill sheet for the target skill and discuss each step from the skill sheet.

**Step Six:** Model the target skill by demonstrating, role playing, or using the videotape to illustrate the skill.

**Step Seven:** Use verbal rehearsal to practice and aid in memorizing the sequence of skill steps for the target skill.

**Step Eight:** Provide opportunities for each student to practice and demonstrate criterion performance on each of the skills on the skill sheet.

**Step Nine:** Assign and discuss homework to be completed for the next lesson.

In a study conducted by Hazel and colleagues (Hazel, Schumaker, Sherman, & Sheldon, 1982) eight students identified as learning disabled were taught six of the target skills: giving positive feedback, giving negative feedback, accepting negative feedback, resisting peer pressure, negotiation, and personal problem solving. Following training in the ASSET model on these skills, students were asked to perform behavioral role-plays to demonstrate the skills. When compared with two other groups, non–learning disabled (NLD) and court adjudicated youth, the LD students made only slight gains on cognitive problem solving. The ASSET model provides a specific social skills curriculum for LD adolescents that carefully delineates the subskills needed to meet criteria on each of the target social skills.

## A Contextualist Perspective for Social Intervention

Most programs developed to teach social skills to low-accepted students are based on a social skill deficit model (Hymel, 1986) that assumes changes in the child's behavior will affect the way the child is perceived. A previous literature review (McIntosh, Vaughn, & Zaragoza, in press) indicates that changes in behavior often do not result in increased peer acceptance.

We have attempted in the last few years to apply a contextualist perspective (Forman, 1987; Vaughn, McIntosh, & Hogan, 1990) for social skills intervention (Vaughn & Lancelotta, 1990; Vaughn, Lancelotta, & Minnis, 1988; Vaughn, McIntosh, & Spencer-Rowe, 1991). A contextualist perspective focuses on development as an interaction between the social, cultural, and historical effects of the system in which the child functions, and the intrinsic characteristics of the individual. A contextualist perspective does not suggest that the child is merely a product of how he/she is treated by others. The contextualist perspective assumes that development, in this case social development, is a product of a network of interactions and players. Vaughn et al. (1990) suggest that interventions designed to effectively alter both the social skills and status of students with learning disabilities must not only include social skills training for the child but involvement of significant others within the child's social system including peers, teachers, administrators, and staff.

As illustrated in Figure 8.1, the contextualist-based social intervention has three major components. The first component, *skills training*, teaches students social skills plus skills and techniques for working in small groups and leading group activities. Two to four target students from each class are selected to participate in the skills training and to be the official social skills trainers for their class. Participants include a low-accepted LD student and a high-accepted, same-sex peer who is not LD. Target students are taught social skills and problem-solving strategies for two to three days per week outside of the classroom. The social intervention includes modeling, role-playing, rehearsing skits, and practice with feedback.

Skills Training
Social Strategies
Academic Tutoring
Problem Solving/Small Group Instruction
Rehearsal for Large Group Activities

Informant Status
Social Skills Trainer Status
Selecting and Presenting Class Problems
Problem Solving Class Presentations

Significant Interactions
Peer Pairing
School Recognition
Parent Acknowledgment

Figure 8.1. Model for increasing peer acceptance of rejected students.

An example of a social skills strategy taught is the FAST strategy for interpersonal problem solving. The FAST strategy teaches skills associated with effective interpersonal problem solving: (a) developing, questioning, and monitoring skills, (b) generating a range of solutions to problems, (c) evaluating the consequences of the alternatives and selecting the best plan, and (d) implementing the plan, monitoring the outcome, and providing self-feedback.

**F  FREEZE**          Don't act too quickly. What is the problem?

**A  ALTERNATIVES**   What are all my possible solutions?

**S  SELECT ONE**     What is the best solution in the long run?

**T  TRY IT**          What do I need to implement the solution? And if it doesn't work, what else can I try?

A second component of the model is *informant status,* which emphasizes the role of the student as the giver rather than the recipient of information (Brown, Palincsar, & Armbruster, 1984). Students with learning disabilities often have low self-perceived competence in the role of informant and this is generally reinforced by the type of instruction they receive (Englert, Raphael, Anderson, Anthony, Fear, & Gregg, 1988). Children with academic difficulties who are not well accepted by their peers need opportunities to demonstrate they are capable and valued. Low-accepted students with learning disabilities are taught strategies, e.g., FAST, that other students in the class do not know, and are provided systematic opportunities to teach these strategies to their classmates. Examples

1.    Interpersonal Problem Solving (FAST)

    F    FREEZE.                 Don't act too quickly. What is the problem?
    A    ALTERNATIVES.           What are all my possible solutions?
    S    SELECT ONE.             What is the best solution in the long run?
    T    TRY IT.                 What do I need to implement the solution?  And if it
                                 doesn't work, what else can I try?


2.    Accepting Negative Feedback (SLAM)

    S    STOP      what you are doing and look at the person with an appropriate
                   expression.
    L    LISTEN    to what the person is saying until they are finished.
    A    ASK       a question about what you don't understand.
    M    MAKE      a response or answer their concerns.


3.    Making Friendship Overtures (PALS)

    P    PLAN      to look for someone in the room or group who seems friendly or
                   approachable.
    A    APPROACH  the person or group by walking over and saying hello.
    L    LISTEN    to what the person or group is talking about before you respond or
                   speak or ask a question.
    S    SAY       something related to what the person or group is discussing.


Figure 8.2. Social skills strategies.


of social strategies taught are provided in Figure 8.2. Target students are recognized by others in the class and in the school as the social skills trainers for their class/grade.

The third component of the model, *significant interactions*, provides opportunities for target students to work with classmates and other significant members of their school. These opportunities are provided in several ways including peer pairing, identification as a social skills trainer for class/school, school recognition through articles and newsletters, pictures and videotapes, and a certificate presented by the principal to target students as "Official Social Skills Trainer."

Research results based on this social intervention model have been more favorable for males than for females. While the initial case study resulted in significant gains in peer acceptance for a female, LD student with low peer acceptance (Vaughn, Lancelotta, & Minnis, 1988), these gains were not repeated for females in a later study. In the later study involving disabled, rejected students (7 males, 3 females), results yielded significant gains in peer acceptance for the males who participated in the study but not for the females (Vaughn, McIntosh, & Spencer-Rowe, 1991). The extent to which other factors such as ethnicity, attractiveness, and physical ability influence these results needs to be further examined.

## Mutual Interest Discovery

Mutual Interest Discovery (MID) was developed by Fox (1980) and evaluated with learning disabled students (Fox, 1989). The rationale is that the more we know about a person, how we are alike and different, the more likely we are to accept the person. Mutual Interest Discovery provides structured activities for NLD and LD students to find out more about each other.

Students who are well accepted by their classmates are paired with a same-sex LD student for approximately 40 minutes once each week for several weeks. Students interview each other on preassigned topics that relate to entertainment, hobbies, sports, and things they like and don't like. After the interview each of the students write three things they discovered they had in common about the assigned topic. Partners then present their findings to the entire group. Partners then complete a brief art activity that somehow represents the interview and what they learned about each other. At the bottom of the art activity each person writes two sentences they learned about their partner. All of the art exercises and written products are kept in a book that represents their interviews.

Partners who participated in the MID group have demonstrated higher ratings of their partners over time than partners in a control group (Fox, 1989). When MID was compared with an academic task group males responded about equally well to both groups, whereas, females responded better to MID. While the intervention is not designed to teach specific social skills, it demonstrates an approach to increasing peer acceptance through providing structured opportunities for students to get to know each other better.

## Suggestions for Social Skills Interventions

Teaching social skills is complex and requires extensive background in the area of social development. Understandably, teachers often inquire about what social skills training curricula are available for their students. Unfortunately, just as with other academic subject areas, teaching social skills without an understanding of the development of social behavior and friendship-making skills is inadequate (Vaughn, 1985). As with teaching reading, having a copy of a teacher's manual for reading instruction is insufficient without an understanding of the reading process. Teaching children appropriate social skills takes time. Meeting with students for a few hours over the course of a few weeks is unlikely to make long-lasting significant change.

Pointers that might assist teachers in developing and implementing social skills interventions in their classrooms follow.

1.  *Interact with all students in ways that communicate caring and acceptance.* Teachers' perceptions of students are subtly and not so subtly communicated. These perceptions are a powerful force in the classroom (Brophy, 1979, 1983), and influence peers' perceptions. Most students are aware of which classmates their teacher likes or doesn't like and these teacher attitudes influence peers' perceptions of their classmates. It is quite unlikely that any teacher truly feels equally positive about all of his or her students. It is possible, however, to interact with all students in ways that communicate caring and acceptance. It is difficult for most teachers to imagine that the expressions and tone of voice they use, along with the comments they make, have such a powerful influence on how children in the classroom feel about each other.

    Teachers can set a tone in the classroom that affirms the value of all students. Questions that may guide teachers in determining whether their classroom environment is one that promotes acceptance of all children follow:

    a.  Do I set up educational and social situations where each student feels successful and valued?
    b.  Do I subtly "put down" students?
    c.  Do I allow students to be "put down" by their classmates?
    d.  Do I develop learning activities that allow all students opportunities to interact with each of their classmates?
    e.  Do I know each of my student's areas of expertise?
    f.  Do I provide opportunities for my students to appreciate each other's talents?

2.  *Give all students the opportunity to be "knower."* Children who are learning disabled are provided with few opportunities to serve in the role of the "knower" or "informant." Self-perception and the perception of others is significantly influenced by the extent to which a person is perceived as having something important to say. Additionally, when the teacher places the student in the position of "knower," the teacher is communicating acceptance of that student. How can teachers place LD children, who by definition are low achievers, in the position of "knower"? There are multiple opportunities, many of which include a change in the type of questions teachers ask and activities they require. For example, the writing-process approach (Graves, 1983) emphasizes the student controlling the content area in their writing. This allows students to write about what they know. When children read their writing they are clearly in the position of "knower." Thus, classmates and the teacher can ask questions of the student that allow him/her to be an informant. Questions from the teacher and other students are

posed to emphasize the LD student's role as "knower." For example, "You wrote in your piece that when you go fishing with your dad you have to stop and buy bait. What kind of bait do you buy? Do you have to buy certain types of bait in order to catch certain types of fish?" These questions establish the author of the piece as the "knower."

Within the area of reading, Palincsar and Brown (1984) describe a reciprocal teaching process for increasing reading comprehension that provides opportunities for each child to be "knower." Within this model, children in reading groups are systematically taught to lead the groups and to ask reading comprehension questions of other children in the groups. Since group leadership is rotated among children in the group, all children are provided opportunities to serve in the role of the knower.

3.  *Involve high-status peers in the social skills training programs for low-social status students.* Many social skill's programs are effective in changing the social behavior of the target child, but are far less successful in altering the way peers perceive target children. Thus, despite positive changes in the social behavior of target students, they often retain their low peer ratings following social skills training. It is quite possible that classmates do not interact frequently or intensely enough with target students to observe behavioral changes when they occur.

One procedure for obtaining changes in peers' perceptions of target students is to involve peers in the training so they are aware of the changes and feel committed to maintaining and promoting these changes. Additionally, when target children are accepted by the most popular students in the class, the overall peer acceptance of the target student is likely to increase. Thus, social skills training may be more effective when it includes other students besides low-accepted youngsters.

4.  *Involve the school community in social skills training.* When possible, the entire school should develop a model for increasing the social skills and acceptance of all children. This includes a commitment from the principal, teachers, and other school personnel to design and implement curriculum and supplemental activities, e.g., lunch, recess, and transportation, that focus on increasing peer acceptance. Students involved in the social skills programs should be given positive and frequent recognition. Such recognition might include articles written about the social skills program in the student newspaper, flyers or notes sent home to parents, mention of the programs periodically in the school

announcements, and certificates given to students who successfully complete the social skills programs.

5.  *Teach social skills for transfer of learning and generalization.* Many social skills training programs effectively increase students' performance in social skills during training, but the skills do not generalize to other settings (Berler et al., 1982). Generalization often does not automatically occur, but needs to be systematically taught within the social skills training program. Procedures for teaching generalization have been developed (Vaughn, Bos, & Lund, 1986) and include such strategies as varying the setting, the trainer, the materials, the cues, and the task. Michaelson and Mannarino (1986) provide a summary of strategies for promoting generalization in social skills training: teach social behaviors the environment will support naturally; teach students alternative responses not just a "pat" phrase; teach students to adapt the training regimen so that it becomes their own; rehearse skills in a variety of settings using natural contingencies; involve peers in the intervention; and teach students to monitor their social skills.

6.  *Identify the social needs of the students and then develop an appropriate social skills intervention.* Because children with learning disabilities are extremely heterogeneous, their academic and social needs must be individually assessed and prescribed. For example, it is likely that children with language processing deficits may be in need of a very different type of social intervention strategy than students with visual-perceptual deficits. Also, many children with learning disabilities have attention problems that interfere with their acquisition and use of social skills strategies. A social skills intervention for these youngster would need to focus on controlling attention problems.

    Social skills intervention needs to include self-control and self-monitoring strategies as part of their training program. For example, a social skills intervention program with hyperactive children (Pelham & Bender, 1982) indicated that a combination of coaching (to improve social skills) and contingency management (to reduce noncompliant behavior) was necessary to reduce uncooperative peer interactions. Neither coaching nor reinforcement alone had positive effects.

7.  *Plan assignments and activities that allow all students to be successful and minimize attracting attention to student weaknesses.* Respect for individual differences is an important attitude to be modeled with all students. The attitude that all children are respected can be promoted through academic tasks. Some examples of ways to let all students be academically successful are giving students alternatives for both obtaining and reporting information, modifying assignments such as

dropping or adding steps, calling on students to answer questions within their capability, and cuing or giving hints and building correct responses from partial answers. These suggestions may not only improve social relationships and appropriate peer interactions, but are also likely to foster increased academic achievement.

8.    *Avoid teasing.* Many students take remarks literally. If it is your style to "kid around," he must be sure that all of his messages are encouraging. For example, it is all right to say "Simon, the world's greatest hall monitor" or "Juanita, our best office message taker" if it is sincere. Sarcasm toward students can diminish the teacher's stature as a trustworthy person. Also, if the teacher consistently teases students, he is serving as a model providing permission for students to tease each other. No student benefits from a class with a negative "got you" environment.

9.    *Promote peer interaction.* Children acquire social skills, not so much from training from adults or structured interventions, but from their interactions with one another. Children often discover through interactions with others which strategies work and which do not, and later reflect on what they have learned. The teacher should provide ways that all students can gain access to peer groups on an equal basis. Following are some suggestions for engaging students in peer groups.

*Specific Skill Training.* Identify specific social skills the student needs to learn and then provide specialized training involving highly skilled peers as role models.

*Hero Procedure.* Have students earn rewards for themselves, a friend, or a group of friends. Make failure impossible with time for earning the reward the only variable.

*Time to Shine.* Provide opportunities for students to demonstrate their expertise in areas other than academic tasks. For example, teach students to play chess, then become the school's chess sponsor. Sports and games are also good examples.

*Younger Peer Group.* It appears that younger children may be at a more compatible level for some LD students. For example, have students become "Big Brothers or Big Sisters" to a younger child's group to help in special activities.

*Buddy System.* Pair low-accepted students with high accepted peers. For example, have pairs decorate the school cafeteria for a special event, or pick up trash off the playground.

*School Aide.* Allow students to become office or guidance aides who take attendance, send for students, etc.

*Compliment Game.* Have students earn rewards by either paying or receiving compliments from each other.

*Peer Tutoring.* Provide opportunities for students with learning disabilities to serve as peer tutors for other students (younger students if necessary).

*Hesitation Skills.* Teach students acceptable and appropriate methods of viewing, evaluating, and then joining an ongoing activity.

*The Club.* Involve the class in a hobby, such as photography, school landscaping beautification, or rocket building and launching. Then begin a club for the school at large.

*Skits and Plays.* Encourage and promote students to become involved in extracurricular dramatic productions in the school. Membership in a presentation viewed by the student body increases peer acceptance (Oden & Asher, 1977).

## Summary

The peer acceptance of learning disabled students has been a much investigated and written about topic. The results of much of the research over the last fifteen years have identified and verified the low social acceptance of many learning disabled students. Learning disabled students are a heterogeneous group, many of whom are not well liked and are rejected by their peers, and some of whom are average or above average in popularity.

There have been several attempts to explain the low social acceptance of learning disabled students. Explanations include their low achievement, low teacher acceptance, language problems, difficulty with social cognition, and attention problems associated with learning disabilities. Recently, through a prospective study, the social competence of students later identified as learning disabled has been examined. Initial results indicate that students later identified as learning disabled, experience significant difficulties in peer relations, attention, and social skills as early as eight weeks into their kindergarten year.

As a result of the early and long-lasting peer difficulties of many learning disabled students there has been significant interest in developing interventions designed to increase their peer acceptance. This chapter described three interventions implemented with students with learning disabilities: a social skills program for adolescents, a contextualist-based intervention, and an intervention focused on developing mutual interests. Finally, this chapter provided pointers designed to assist teachers and other social-skills interventionists in developing and implementing social-skills interventions with learning disabled students.

# References

Berler, E.G., Gross, A.M., & Drabner, R.S. (1982). Social skills training with children: Proceed with caution. *Journal of Applied Behavior Analysis, 15,* 41-53.

Brophy, J. (1979). Teacher behavior and its effects. *Journal of Educational Psychology, 71,* 733-750.

Brophy, J. (1983). Research on the self-fulfilling prophecy and teacher expectations. *Journal of Educational Psychology, 75,* 631-661.

Brown, A.L., Palincsar, A.S., & Armbruster, B.B. (1984). Instructing comprehension-fostering activities in interactive learning situations. In H. Mondi, H.L. Stein, & T. Trabasso (Eds.), *Learning and comprehension of text* (pp. 255-286). Hillsdale, NJ: Erlbaum.

Bryan, T.H. (1974a). Peer popularity of learning disabled children. *Journal of Learning Disabilities, 7,* 621-625.

Bryan, T.H. (1974b). An observational analysis of classroom behaviors of children with learning disabilities. *Journal of Learning Disabilities, 7,* 26-34.

Bryan, T.H. (1976). Peer popularity of learning disabled children: A replication. *Journal of Learning Disabilities, 9,* 307-311.

Coie, J.D., & Krehbiel, G. (1984). Effects of academic tutoring on the social status of low-achieving, socially rejected children. *Child Development, 55,* 1465-1478.

Englert, C.S., Raphael, T.E., Anderson, L.M., Anthony, L.M., Fear, K.L., & Gregg, S.L. (1988). A case for writing intervention: Strategies for writing informational text. *Learning Disabilities Focus, 3,* 88-113.

Forman, E.A. (1987). Peer relationships of learning disabled children: A contextualist perspective. *Learning Disabilities Research, 2*(2), 80-89.

Fox, C.L. (1980). *Communication to make friends.* Rolling Hills Estates, CA: B.L. Winch & Associates.

Fox, C.L. (1989). Peer acceptance of learning disabled children in the regular classroom. *Exceptional Children, 56*(1), 50-57.

Graves, D. (1983). *Writing: Teachers and children at work.* Portsmouth, NH: Heinemann.

Gresham, F.M., & Elliott, S. (1986). *Social skills rating for teachers.* Baton Rouge: Louisiana State University.

Harter, S., & Pike, R. (1984). The Pictorial Scale of Perceived Competence and Social Acceptance for Young Children. *Child Development, 55,* 1969-1982.

Hazel, J.S., Schumaker, J.B., Sherman, J.A., & Sheldon, J. (1982). Application of a group training program in social skills and problem solving to learning disabled and non-learning disabled youth. *Learning Disability Quarterly, 5,* 398-408.

Hazel, J.S., Schumaker, J.B., Sherman, J.A., & Sheldon-Wildgen, J. (1981). *ASSET: A social skills program for adolescents.* Champaign, IL: Research Press.

Howes, S. (1988). Peer interaction of young children. *Monographs of the Society for Research in Child Development, 53*(217), 1-94.

Hymel, S. (1986). Interpretations of peer behavior: Affective bias in childhood and adolescence. *Child Development, 57,* 431-445.

Li, A.K.F. (1985). Early rejected status and later social adjustment: A 3-year follow-up. *Journal of Abnormal Child Psychology, 13,* 567-577.

McIntosh, R., Vaughn, S., & Zaragoza, N. (in press). A review of social interventions for students with learning disabilities. *Journal of Learning Disabilities.*

Michaelson, L., & Mannarino, A. (1986). Social skills training with children: Research and clinical application. In P.S. Strain, M.J. Guralnick, & H.M. Walder (Eds.), *Children's social behavior* (pp. 373-406). Orlando, FL: Academic Press.

Oden, S., & Asher, S.R. (1977). Coaching children in social skills for friendship making. *Child Development, 48,* 495-506.

Palincsar, A.S., & Brown, A.L. (1984). Reciprocal teaching of comprehension fostering and comprehension monitoring activities. *Cognition and Instruction, 1*(2), 117-175.

Parker, J.G., & Asher, S.R. (1987). Peer acceptance and later personal adjustment: Are low-accepted children "at risk"? *Psychological Bulletin, 102,* 357-389.

Pearl, R. (1987). Social-cognitive factors in learning disabilities. In S.J. Ceci (Ed.), *Handbook of cognitive, social, and neuropsychological aspects of learning disabilities* (pp. 273-294). Hillsdale, NJ: Erlbaum.

Pearl, R., Donahue, M., & Bryan, T. (1986). Social relationships of learning-disabled children. In J.K. Torgesen & B.Y.L. Wong (Eds.), *Psychological and educational perspectives on learning disabilities* (pp. 193-224). Orlando, FL: Academic Press.

Pelham, W.E., & Bender, M.E. (1982). Peer relationships in hyperactive: Description and treatment. In *Advances in learning and behavioral disabilities* (Vol. 1, pp. 365-436). Greenwich, CT: JAI Press.

Quay, H.C., & Peterson, D.R. (1987). *Manual for the Revised Behavior Problem Checklist.* Coral Gables, FL: University of Miami.

Vaughn, S. (1985). Why teach social skills to learning disabled students? *Journal of Learning Disabilities, 18*(10), 588-591.

Vaughn, S., Bos, C.S., & Lund, K.A. (1986). ...But they can do it in my room: Strategies for promoting generalization. *Teaching Exceptional Children, 18,* 176-180.

Vaughn, S., Haager, D., Hogan, A., & Kouzekanani, K. (in press). Self-concept and peer acceptance in students with learning disabilities: A four to five year prospective study. *Journal of Educational Psychology.*

Vaughn, S., & Hogan, A. (1990). Social competence and learning disabilities: A prospective study. In H.L. Swanson & B.K. Keogh (Eds.), *Learning disabilities: Theoretical and research issues* (pp. 175-191). Hillsdale, NJ: Erlbaum.

Vaughn, S., & Hogan, A., Kouzekanani, K., & Shapiro, S. (1990). Peer acceptance, self-perceptions, and social skills of LD students prior to identification. *Journal of Educational Psychology, 82*(1), 101-106.

Vaughn, S., & LaGreca, A.M. (1988). Social interventions for learning disabilities. In K.A. Kavale (Ed.), *Learning disabilities: state of the art and practice* (pp. 123-140). San Diego: College Hill Press.

Vaughn, S., & Lancelotta, G.X. (1990). Teaching interpersonal social skills to low accepted students: Peer-pairing versus no peer-pairing. *Journal of School Psychology, 28*(3), 181-188.

Vaughn, S.R., Lancelotta, G.X., & Minnis, S. (1988). Social strategy training and peer involvement: Increasing peer acceptance of a female LD student. *Learning Disabilities Focus, 4*(1), 32-37.

Vaughn, S., McIntosh, R., & Hogan, A. (1990). Why social skills training doesn't work: An alternative model. In T. Scruggs & B.Y.L. Wong (Eds.), *Intervention in learning disabilities* (pp. 279-303). New York: Springer-Verlag.

Vaughn, S., McIntosh, R., & Spencer-Rowe, J. (1991). Peer rejection is a stubborn thing: Increasing peer acceptance of rejected LD students. *Learning Disabilities Research and Practice, 6*(2), 83-88.

# 9
# The Gifted/Learning Disabled: An Oxymoron?

## Ruth B. Spodak

The complexities of the problems faced by the gifted/learning disabled individual are best expressed in a statement by clinician, Bobbie H. Jones (1986), "After twenty-three years in the pursuit of identification and remediation of the individual with learning problems, I can state with conviction that the gifted dyslexic is the most regularly misunderstood, poorly diagnosed, and ineffectively helped of any of those who ask us for assistance." Nevertheless, a significant portion of the population, both professionals as well as lay people, continue to hold the belief that, by definition, a gifted person cannot be learning disabled, and similarly, that a person who has been identified as learning disabled cannot also, be gifted.

As the knowledge base regarding giftedness and learning disabilities as separate entities has grown, there is an emerging body of data that documents and supports the classification of the gifted/learning disabled individual within the population of children and adults with special educational needs. In fact, as early as 1964, although there were significant methodological differences, Krippner and Herald (1964) performed a study investigating the prevalence of reading disabilities among the "academically talented." They recognized that academic talent, or superior intelligence, did not of itself exclude the possibility of reading difficulties.

The definition of learning disabilities is discussed elsewhere in this volume. It is, however, important to put forth a working definition of giftedness. The U.S. Office of Education definition (Marland, 1972) presents many characteristics relevant for the identification and programming for these children in academic environments:

> (T)hose identified by professionally qualified persons, who by virtue of outstanding abilities, are capable of high performance. These are children who require differentiated educational programs and services beyond those normally provided by the regular school program, in order to realize their contribution to self and society.

Children capable of high performance include those with demonstrated achievement and/or potential ability in any of the following areas: 1) general intellectual ability, 2) specific academic ability, 3) creative or productive thinking, 4) leadership ability, 5) visual and performing arts, and 6) psychomotor ability.

... Evidence of gifted and talented abilities may be determined by a multiplicity of ways. These procedures should include objective measures and professional evaluation measures which are essential components of giftedness.

This definition makes explicit the need for a multidimensional approach to assessment and identification, and a broader criterion for giftedness than simply the attainment of a particular score on an IQ test. It is also important to note that the definition accepts "potential ability" as well as "demonstrated achievement" as a sufficient criterion for giftedness. Although measurement of potential abilities can be problematic, its inclusion in this definition is significant for the population of learning disabled individuals who, because of their learning disabilities, are often not able to demonstrate achievement in the traditionally accepted manner.

Renzulli's definition (1978) of giftedness adds a component that becomes relevant in an educational setting as well as outside of the classroom. He defines giftedness as: "an interaction among three basic clusters of human traits ... above average general abilities, high levels of task commitment, and high levels of creativity." The addition of task commitment as a critical element is unique. Yet educators will verify that it is often this very characteristic that is lacking in the gifted/learning disabled individual and therefore the outstanding ability and creativity are not realized.

One of the few simple definitions focusing simultaneously on the characteristics of both the LD and the gifted populations offers that this person is an "individual who (is) highly intelligent, creative, or talented, but with one or more functions impeded" (Meisgeier, Meisgeier, and Werblo, 1978). These functions may be in the areas of expressive and/or receptive language, reading, writing, math, and difficulties in organization and social skills. The side-by-side existence of both giftedness and the learning disabilities can result in problems that are unique to this population. Their heightened abilities to see their own inadequacies, although unable to remedy them independently, often lead to secondary emotional problems. In addition, insensitive school placement usually groups these students with learning disabled of low to average intelligence, with the result that their own performance becomes limited and their giftedness is never developed.

All definitions and criteria demand the assessment of several different dimensions. How does one assess an individual's intelligence, creativity, and/or talent to determine if he is at an adequate level to qualify as gifted? Equally significantly, is there a particular score, or pattern of measurements, that is uniformly recognized as definitive of giftedness?

In an academic setting, primary emphasis is usually given to the intellectual component within the definition of giftedness. Intelligence is usually measured by a particular test or set of tests that define a gifted individual as one who obtains a score higher than "___." This number may vary from one investigator to another. It is then assumed in the school setting, that if the individual's intelligence score is sufficiently high, he will be successful in school. Conversely, it is assumed that if the student is successful in school, it is because he is highly intelligent.

Unfortunately, a parallel set of assumptions also exists. That is, if an individual's intelligence is described as low, it is expected that he will not be successful in school. A similar application of logic, however, leads to a not altogether logical conclusion; namely, if a student is not successful in school, it is because he does not have a very high level of intelligence. It is this latter reasoning that masks the giftedness of the learning disabled student, and in fact lends credence to the argument that there can be no such thing as a gifted learning disabled individual. For these students, performance on an IQ test is not an accurate predictor of success in school, nor is it even a valid measure of intelligence in a broad sense.

## Identification

To be valid, the identification of the gifted/learning disabled student must entail a multidimensional assessment, performed by a multidisciplinary team. No single measure or dimension can offer an accurate assessment. The specific combination of measures that produces the most valid diagnosis is still a matter of individual discretion among professionals, but as a minimum should include clinical interpretation of standardized test scores as well as a developmental history and a summary of interests and accomplishments.

The lack of precision and appropriateness in assessment tools, however, is only one obstacle to the accurate identification of gifted/learning disabled students. Their very intelligence acts as an obstacle in itself, in that the students use their abilities to develop compensatory mechanisms to disguise or partially compensate for their learning deficits. For example, some of the more ingenious develop a unique counting system to perform simple math operations since their memory deficits preclude mastery of math facts at an automatic level. Ultimately, such a strategy fails but not before the child has spent a considerable amount of time feeling frustrated and inadequate as a learner. During this time, he has also demonstrated sufficient academic adequacy to mislead most classroom teachers into believing that no special difficulties exist. Emotionally, this student withdraws or becomes the class clown rather than admit that he cannot do the work. This sense of failure and depression can become a lifelong disability of a much more serious nature than the originally undiagnosed learning disability.

Often, due to deficits related to the learning disabilities, the student's classroom performance is so marginal that teachers assume the student to be of average ability (Vaughn, 1989). The expectations therefore are considerably lowered for this very bright student, conforming to his depressed level of achievement. School staff thinks of him as a barely average student who is doing the best that he can. This message is then communicated to the student and to his parents who often accept the word of the professional educator as more valid than their own impressions. The result is that the child's potential is never explored. This is the student Daniels (1983a) refers to as the "gifted pseudoachiever," the student whose giftedness masks his disability so that grade-level performance is seen as appropriate and commensurate with a more limited potential.

Moreover, grades and assessments obtained in a school setting typically rely on students' performance on tests, which in most cases, are objective, and use formats of multiple-choice, short answers, or true/false. Tests with these formats leave no room for creative responses. Therefore, the very creativity and divergent aspects of the gifted student's thought processes cause him to test at a lower level. If one were to question the thought processes that led to the student's answers, it would be clear that the logic was valid but different from the norm, and "wrong" only in the sense that it was not the more frequently given answer. Nonetheless, the grading of a test rarely allows for divergent answers.

## Test Performance

Based on analyses of profiles of gifted/learning disabled students, Maker (1982) lists their strengths as being in the areas of logic, classification abilities, and a grasp of general trends, whereas weaknesses are reflected in the areas of memory, perception, and general information. Deficits in these particular areas impact significantly and result in lower scores on the most frequently used standardized measures of intelligence. The scores are depressed by the very learning disabilities known to be operating for these individuals, and yet not compensated for by cognitive strategies nor by the characteristics of the test.

Even though test scores alone cannot provide the basis for a clinician's diagnostic conclusions, there have been several investigations into characteristic test profiles of gifted LD individuals, that have reported somewhat consistent patterns of performance. Schiff, Kaufman, and Kaufman (1981) studied Wechsler Intelligence Scale for Children–Revised (WISC-R) profiles of thirty "uneven gifted" children, consisting of twenty-seven boys and three girls, to verify both the prevalence of subtest scatter characteristic of LD children's performance, and also the existence of particular patterns within the scatter. Results supported the finding of wide fluctuations among subtests, with a mean scaled score on the WISC-R subtests ranging from a low of 9.6 on Coding to a high of 16.2 on Similarities.

When scores were analyzed using Kaufman's factors (Kaufman, 1975), the variation was even more striking. This group of thirty students did best on the four Verbal Comprehension subtests of Information, Similarities, Vocabulary, and Comprehension, scoring at the 95th percentile; less well on the subtests comprising Perceptual Organization - Picture Completion, Picture Arrangement, Block Design, Object Assembly, and Mazes - scoring at the 80th percentile; and least well on those subtests measuring Freedom from Distractibility including Arithmetic, Digit Span, and Coding, where they scored at the 64th percentile.

Examination of the results using Bannatyne's structures (Bannatyne, 1974), presents another perspective. Weaknesses appeared in those tests comprising Sequencing Ability (including Digit Span, Arithmetic, and Coding) and parallel the weaknesses found with learning disabled students who are not gifted. However, the strengths shown by the students in the Kaufman et al. study are in marked contrast to those of other LD students who are not gifted. That is, the exceptional abilities in skills included in Bannatyne's Verbal Conceptualization (including Comprehension, Similarities, and Vocabulary) and Kaufman's Verbal Comprehension described above, are unique to this subgroup within the learning disabled population, and more closely parallel those of gifted non-LD individuals.

The other notable finding documented in this study is that the spread between verbal and performance scores is significantly greater when compared with the spread reported for other LD students, and/or for the population as a whole (Schiff, Kaufman, & Kaufman, 1981).

The significant conclusion to be reached from these studies is that there is a growing body of statistical data indicating a characteristic profile that can be used to identify the gifted LD population, differentiating it from both the gifted (non-LD) and the LD (non-gifted) students in ways that can be specified. The characteristic strengths in Verbal Conceptualization and Verbal Comprehension along with the wide verbal-performance disparity and the intertest scatter, are the typical indicators that have been cited as most pervasive.

## Behavioral Characteristics

In looking at other than objective test results, certain behaviors characteristic of the gifted LD population are frequently the antithesis of those of the purely gifted child who is not learning disabled. This further complicates the identification process. For example, the gifted child is extremely persistent and motivated, while the gifted LD is selectively distractible and frustrated; the gifted child has outstanding vocabulary and expressive language, while the gifted LD child may have word retrieval and processing difficulties that result in inadequate or disorganized verbal expression; the gifted child can and prefers to work independently, while the gifted LD child may need adult direction and support to initiate and/or complete a particular type of task successfully.

The disparities and inconsistencies between the traditional model of giftedness and that of the gifted LD continue to interfere with recognition, and in the extreme, even the acceptance, of the higher potential of these children. Data have shown that the most reliable source of information has been the parents. In speaking of the gifted population as a whole, Vail (1979) reports that "parents correctly identified 76% of a group of gifted children while their teachers identified only 22%." In all likelihood, this comparison would be even more extreme if one were to examine the identification of the gifted students who are also learning disabled, because parents are often the only ones who have the opportunity to observe the children in settings other than academic ones, and to see the range and diversity of their strengths and talents.

The essential ingredients of an identification program must therefore, include (a) parental information regarding history and early development, (b) interests and outside activities pursued by the child, (c) observational data from teachers and other adults, and (d) a knowledgeable interpretation of the results of objective testings. Frequently, information from activities and sources outside of the school setting can provide the most valuable information for understanding this population. Hobbies, independent projects, and observations of experiential learning highlight the student's giftedness without its being masked by the deficits of a learning disability as in a classroom setting. Questionnaires and interviews with parents, teachers, and other adults can be used to gain this additional information.

The involvement of adult professionals in the area of special talents, e.g., theater people, artists, choreographers, composers, and cabinetmakers, ensures an accurate assessment of the student's talents by people knowledgeable in the relevant areas. In this way, one can begin to broaden the interpretation of intelligence, as does Gardner (1985), to include not only what he calls the linguistic and logical-mathematical intelligences assessed in conventional IQ tests, but also musical, spatial, bodily-kinesthetic, intrapersonal, and inter-personal intelligences. This allows recognition of a very different combination of talents and capabilities, and would indeed compensate for the inadequacies of standardized testing and school-based assessment tools that are frequently the only ones recognized as valid.

In spite of the talents and capabilities shown by the gifted LD student, and perhaps because of these very same traits, another consistent pattern emerging from the research is that the gifted LD population as a group can be expected to have certain very specific emotional vulnerabilities. Daniels (1983a) indicates that by second grade, if placed in a conventional classroom, the gifted LD student is already experiencing emotional difficulties. The very characteristics that define gifted individuals–their heightened sensitivities to others and keener perception of the world around them–provide dramatic information to them of their own inadequacies. The resulting frustration, anxiety, depression, and lower self-concept become debilitating, and frequently become sources of serious emotional difficulty.

Senf (1983) makes an even stronger statement, emphasizing the importance of the emotional concomitant of a learning disability, especially with the gifted LD child. He maintains that it is "rather personality and behavioral disturbances which characterize those with 'true' disabilities... (T)he same disability which affects a school skill also affects information processing in the social and emotional realm. This general disruption is not the result of the school-skill problem but an integral part of the total symptomatology."

As research has progressed, behavioral and personality characteristics of the gifted LD child have begun to be identified in a more explicit fashion. It is no longer acceptable to deny the existence of this group of individuals simply because no single test profile prevails. At fault is the design of the objective instruments used for evaluation, and the criteria for their administration and scoring, which obscure the strengths as well as the deficits of the gifted/learning disabled individual. For example, the difficulties in sequencing, memory, or visual-motor integration, interfere with optimal performance on all objective tests traditionally used in school's assessments. Therefore, the lack of consistent data should not be taken as an argument for the nonexistence of the gifted learning disabled population, but rather as an indication of the need for differential and/or supplementary methods and parameters for diagnosis.

## Intervention

The gifted LD population shares characteristics with each of its component populations, i.e., gifted and learning disabled, to some extent. Specifically, heightened abilities in the areas of verbal comprehension and verbal conceptualization are similar to the qualities found in gifted individuals, whether or not they are learning disabled. On the other hand, according to the analyses of test results, distractibility, deficits in sequencing, and visual-motor integration are common to the learning disabled, whether or not they are gifted. Educational programming must therefore address both areas of exceptionality.

There is an additional set of characteristics that are reflected in the needs of both learning disabled and gifted individuals, and in fact, may come from either or both areas of exceptionality. These include uneven development, need for increased mobility and flexible pacing, difficulties with social relationships, and problems with self-concept. The gifted LD individuals may show these traits to an even greater extent since each area contributes in its own way. These needs also can and must be recognized in formulating effective intervention strategies for this population.

### Varying Levels of Performance

Uneven development is characteristic of individuals with learning disabilities and also of gifted individuals. The learning disabled child, in fact, diagnostically is often said to have a developmental delay in one or more areas. He may be more advanced in areas of math and logic and significantly less proficient in reading and writing. Similarly, the gifted student demonstrates giftedness in one or more areas, but rarely in all areas equally. From an observational point of view, there are similarities in the profiles presented.

Due to this unevenness, appropriate intervention must take into account the varying levels of performance, depending on the tasks presented. There must also be an appreciation for this unevenness as it affects social and maturational aspects. If, for example, a twelve-year-old LD student has second grade math skills, he cannot be treated like a second grader in other ways. The content and sophistication of the materials used, and the social interactions of the group setting must take into account his chronological age to be appropriate and effective.

In a related aspect, a gifted ten-year-old child may have mathematical talent that allows him to successfully complete algebra and beyond. This does not make him a high school student. The approach for him must also taken into account the disparity between his developmental level and his intellectual prowess in a given area. It may, for example, be inappropriate to give him the same amount of homework each night as older students, or to expect him to pursue studies in an independent manner regardless of his mathematical precocity. An inability to allow for these variations is frequently cited as justification for excluding a gifted student from a more advanced class when, in fact, each issue can be addressed separately. Consideration should first be given to the student's intellectual ability to understand the content, and secondarily, to the modifications necessitated by his age, maturity level, and other learning characteristics.

## Need for Flexible Pacing

Within the classroom setting, the pacing of work and the energy/activity levels of the gifted/learning disabled students must be taken into account. The learning disability may contribute to a student's heightened activity level and impaired sense of timing. He may need frequent breaks or a longer time to complete a given task. Transition times may have to be built into his daily schedule. Similarly, an individual's giftedness frequently causes him to operate at a different pace than others and to have little or no tolerance for modifying that pace to conform to a classroom routine. An academic setting, therefore, must be designed to allow self-pacing or flexible pacing based on individual needs and not put students into a lockstep schedule. This allows the student a more rapid pace applicable in areas of giftedness, while at the same time removing the pressure of time limits in areas of deficit.

## Social Needs

Areas that are outside of the narrow scope of classroom content and yet have impact on the student as an individual must also be taken into account.

Symptomatic of some children with a learning disability is difficulty in social relations stemming from the student's inability to accurately recognize and interpret social cues, facial expressions, tone of voice, and related nonverbal body language signs. This can result in his being rejected or made a scapegoat in social situations. By the same token, the giftedness of this individual whose interests and way of expressing himself set him apart from his peers, is equally likely to cause social isolation and rejection. Both situations indicate a need for social skills to be developed. Frequently, this becomes the responsibility of a counselor or social worker. It can also be accomplished or at least reinforced by a trained teacher in the classroom setting.

## Issues of Self-Esteem

All of the issues presented have impact on an individual's self-concept. With whatever gifts and talents he possesses, the gifted LD student also has the liabilities and vulnerabilities of the LD student, and perhaps to a greater degree. LD students as a group have lower self-esteem in comparison to their non-LD counterparts (Senf, 1983). Giftedness, on the other hand, although not necessarily leading to a lower self-concept, can result in a confused sense of oneself. Gifted LD students are advanced and exceptional in a given area or areas, and yet are very average in other ways. They are placed with older individuals and expected to assume a more mature posture, when socially and emotionally they may not be comfortable doing so. Frequently the intervention of a counselor or therapist is needed to help the student understand the source of these difficulties and deal with them constructively. Again, the needs produced by learning disabilities and giftedness overlap and require similar programming and intervention.

In addition to these more global parameters, there are some very specific issues to be examined and addressed in defining the methods for effective intervention. Classroom placement, instructional modification, and curriculum modification are the major categories to be examined in the school setting.

## Classroom Placement

It is an opinion shared by most educators (Whitmore, 1986) that intervention must assume within its goals the following four factors: the right of every child to an appropriate education, individual instruction based on individual needs, early identification for intervention purposes, and the education and involvement of parents. To the extent that classroom placement, and instructional and curricular modifications can satisfy these conditions, they are effective and desirable.

As indicated by many authors (Daniels, 1983a; Suter & Wolf, 1987; Wolf & Gygi, 1981), the class placement for the gifted/learning disabled student is critical in terms of both academic progress and social/emotional concerns.

Although there are several options, each is a compromise and presents a combination of advantages and disadvantages.

## Self-Contained Class

A self-contained class for LD students has the advantage of offering remedial services and does not put the student in a frustrating or failure environment. Difficulties, however, are also present; there is rarely if ever the availability of peers at a comparable intellectual level for stimulation and meaningful social interactions. In fact, often students in the self-contained classes have additional behavioral problems that complicate the situation even further. Second, of necessity for the other students, the classroom emphasis is on weaknesses and skill deficits, allowing no opportunity for development of areas of strength and giftedness.

## Resource Room

A second option is to assign students to resource room settings a given number of periods a day for remediation of deficit area skills. Although this placement allows them to be in the regular classroom where the level of stimulation may be more appropriate, two disadvantages ensue. First, going to the resource room entails being pulled out of the regular class and missing what is occurring there. Often students are then not informed about what had transpired when they were elsewhere, and they miss instructions or critical work assignments. Furthermore, it is often the case that the specific time during which they are in the resource room is the time when an area of potential strength and success is being addressed within the regular class schedule. Further, although the resource room offers systematic help with homework and classroom assignments, it does not offer consistent teaching of skills or effective remediation.

The other potential disadvantage is that when the student is in the regular classroom, care must be taken that materials and assignments, although appropriate intellectually, are also appropriate in terms of the student's skill limitations. These modifications are often overlooked.

## Gifted Class

The third alternative, which is a class or program exclusively for gifted students, can offer the most appropriate environment intellectually and socially. However, teachers of gifted children typically expect a higher level of reading on the part of the students, the ability to work independently for a prolonged period of time, and/or proficiency in written expression so that an assignment of a lengthy written report is not unusual. None of these expectations are easily met by the student with learning disabilities, regardless of his giftedness, and it is the rare class for gifted students that allows sufficient modifications for the gifted/learning disabled student to succeed.

## LD Gifted Class

The seemingly ideal setting would be a class of only gifted/learning disabled students, combining the availability of equally bright students for mutual stimulation and interaction with the necessity for modifications for all students since they are all also learning disabled. The small percentage of students who qualify for such a placement, however, makes it an impractical arrangement within many school settings and requires at least a multiage grouping or a single class servicing several school districts. This option then would require the combination of children of different ages, a point that some educators feel is undesirable. It could also require students to attend schools other than their neighborhood school to be serviced appropriately.

There is no single ideal placement of the gifted/learning disabled student within the traditional settings of the American school system. Each of these options has its own set of advantages and disadvantages. The most desirable setting for each student must be considered in light of his individual needs. Depending on the student's age, his emotional resiliency, and the availability of other resources in his life outside of school, apparent disadvantages of a particular setting may not be as significant for him at a given point in his academic career. At another point, the priorities may dictate a different choice. For example, the importance of peers of an appropriate intellectual level may increase, and the disadvantage of not being at a neighborhood school may decrease as a student gets older. Options, therefore, should always be examined in the context of the individual student's needs and re-examined as he matures and needs and priorities change.

## Instructional Modifications

Although classroom placements may vary, to the extent that each option speaks only partially to the student's needs instructional modifications will have to be made within that classroom for the gifted/learning disabled student.

In providing appropriate instruction for these children, French (1982) suggests, we must:

> Provide rules and categories by means of which the students can generate relationships between past information and new information or provide examples which they can use to formulate their own rules and categories.

Use materials which are meaningful, interesting, intellectually appropriate and motivating.

Plan activities which demand an active response by the students requiring that they attend to the task, use relevant schematic and generate relationships.

Provisions of these strategies would ensure that the student would not be bored by the repetitious drill and worksheet routine often part of a remedial program. Moreover, the student would be engaged in the process and forced to interact so that learning becomes an active, not a passive, process. The use of material in areas of interest to the student specifically addresses the gifted student's needs and allows an opportunity for emphasis on strength, while also addressing skill needs.

Flexibility and options for both input and output of information are areas that also require considerable attention for this population. Sophisticated and in-depth content is essential for continued intellectual growth and stimulation. Nevertheless, the sources of this advanced content are typically books written at an advanced reading level, and therefore not accessible or comprehensible to the majority of learning disabled children who have trouble reading independently. Therefore the books must either be read to them, or materials may be presented on audiotapes. Alternatively, discussions with others or experiential learning through museum displays or internships provide additional depth of content. Any or all of these options can offer accommodation for the needs of the LD gifted student whose reading skills do not allow the traditional means of exposure to more sophisticated content.

A parallel set of options must necessarily exist for output requirements in a classroom setting. Some gifted/learning disabled students can express themselves very well orally and have difficulty only when the product must be written. For these students, options can include opportunities for pictorial, graphic, three-dimensional, musical, or other nonverbal demonstrations of their acquired information.

Modern technology has added immeasurably to the options that can be used creatively. Not only are computers with word processor and spell-check facilities available in most schools, but the more artistically talented students can create multimedia presentations including film, sound, and special effects, all coordinated via computer, in ways not previously feasible.

These alternatives provide more than motivation. The students gain a significant amount of information without dependence on reading; they can communicate and share their information without being handicapped by their disabilities. Furthermore, they become valued members of the group and are respected for their knowledge and their creativity, which in turn enhances the self-esteem and social relationships that are sometimes lacking.

The further benefit to be recognized from these modifications is that the student becomes an ally in the educational process. He sees himself as valuable, and he sees his teacher(s) as respecting his abilities and willing to provide options for him. In this environment, the student feels safe enough to take risks and approach the remediation of his learning disabilities in a willing and participatory manner.

## Curriculum Modification

The gifted/learning disabled student comes to the classroom with two sets of needs. An effective curriculum must simultaneously, and in an integrated way, meet both of these requirements. The ingredients for success, as summarized by Udall and Maker (1983), derive from three premises: special methods are necessary, emphasis must be on the strengths of the population, and students must be active participants in the learning process.

In speaking of gifted students without learning disabilities, Maker (1982) further specifies that appropriate environmental considerations include opportunities for student-centered rather than teacher-centered programming, for development of independence rather than dependence, for open rather than closed situations, for an accepting attitude and not a judgmental one, and for the encouragement of a high level of mobility. Many of these are equally necessary for the gifted student who is also learning disabled.

To be most effective, the curriculum should be based on the student's interests to both encourage his involvement and also to further develop his area(s) of strength. Even when, or maybe especially when, remediation is to be addressed, inclusion of material that coincides with the student's interests is of primary importance. Not only does student participation increase in this situation, but the most successful mode of performance for most of these students, namely oral discussion, can also be stimulated.

The desire for independence within the academic setting provides a serious dilemma for the LD gifted student. He has the intelligence, the knowledge, and frequently the personality to desire and deserve the increased independence. However, the lack of adequate academic skills and strategies often interferes with this desire. For example, he cannot prepare a report independently if he cannot use the library efficiently, or read or write at a level commensurate with his intelligence and interests. The conflict between the desire for independence and the need for dependence is a frequent source of serious difficulty for this student. A sensitive teacher or parent can provide sufficient modifications or subtle assistance to enable the student to maintain his dignity and sense of self-worth, while allowing him to experience a sense of independent accomplishment.

The availability of an open environment versus a closed one can simultaneously offer solutions to obstacles, and yet present sources of frustration, for the gifted/learning disabled student. An openness that allows alternate means of acquiring information—tapes, interviews, films—as well as a variety of methods for sharing information once acquired—oral or taped reports, artistic representations, projects—provides the ideal classroom setting in which giftedness can be encouraged and developed. Care must be taken however, not to equate openness with lack of structure. Along with the provision of options, the learning disabled student requires the provision of structure, consistency, and clarity of expectations. The very carefully planned aspects of the LD classroom must carry over into this environment also, for the gifted LD student to succeed.

Not only must one's attitude communicate a level of acceptance and support rather than a judgmental posture, but the classroom requirements and routine must reflect the same values. Assessment procedures within a classroom must offer a variety of accommodations. The student may need more time to complete a test. He may need to be graded separately for content and information versus mechanics of writing and spelling. Alternate means of assessing one's knowledge in addition to written tests or reports are to be encouraged. Selection of students for special responsibilities or honors must communicate equal respect, regardless of the student's learning needs. These features have impact not only on academic performance but also on social relationships and the student's self-concept, because they reflect on the acceptance and valuing of students' talents regardless of other needs.

Mobility, both in the school setting and within outside environments to increase the resources for the student, enhances the learning opportunities for the gifted LD student. The need for activity and frequent breaks is a commonly cited characteristic of learning disabled students; it is also a requirement for many gifted students. These needs can be met in many ways. Allowing students access to resources and programs outside of the classroom not only accomplishes these ends, but also provides the very interaction and experiential learning that affords this student his optimal learning environment. These "outings" further provide an immediate and pragmatic arena in which to teach and reinforce the development of appropriate social skills, an area of need for many gifted and learning disabled students.

A recent article by Waldron (1991), reported the effectiveness of the use of computers for the LD gifted population, especially for remediation of skills. The combination of the higher cognitive abilities and the graphics capacity of the computer seem particularly suited to the needs of many within this population.

In summary, there is no single set of textbooks or curriculum guides to satisfy the needs of gifted/learning disabled students. The more important point is that the program and setting contain those ingredients, both academic and psychological, that are necessary due to the dual nature of the exceptionality, and that they provide those features on a consistent basis.

## Outside Supports

Different school settings and different teachers are able to meet the needs of the gifted/learning disabled student to a greater or lesser degree. None are able to speak to all his needs. For this reason, other sources of support are necessary and valuable.

Parents are the first source of stimulation for the child, and depending on that child's circumstances, may continue to be the ones who can provide the most appropriate ongoing stimulation and support for him as he develops. Their own daily conversations and interactions with him, exposure to other activities and opportunities, and the provision of emotional support are each significant for the child's total development.

It is frequently the case, however, that parents do not have the training, the understanding, or the ability to provide these additional resources without additional support themselves. This is especially true when both parents are also strongly involved in pursuing their own careers, a common occurrence within families of gifted abilities. A mental health professional with an understanding of children with special needs can provide the instruction and insights that will facilitate the development of a positive relation between parents and children. Support groups exist and new ones are being formed frequently to provide additional information about resources, as well as offering guidance and support. Teachers and other school staff knowledgeable about these resources perform an important service by sharing that information with parents.

Professionals are of greatest value to parents when they communicate in a direct, consistent, and supportive manner. In a survey reported by Dembinski and Mauser (1977), parents of students with learning disabilities indicated they wanted very specific services from professionals, including physicians, psychologists, and educators. These included information without professional jargon, attendance of both parents at meetings, recommendation of reading and resource materials, provision of written copies of reports, coordinated interdisciplinary communication, immediate and pragmatic advice, and attention to social as well as academic behaviors. Parents have the need and the responsibility to obtain as complete information as possible about their children. Professionals have the responsibility to provide that information in as meaningful and helpful a way as possible.

# Conclusion

As the research evidence and empirical reports demonstrate, there are gifted/ learning disabled individuals. The means of identifying these individuals and determining their needs are only beginning to be developed. Lack of sufficient data points to the need for additional resources and energy being devoted to this endeavor. It does not allow us to ignore the existence or the needs of this population until such time as data are conclusive.

Definitive figures regarding incidence of the gifted/learning disabled population are largely unavailable given the lack of uniformity of criteria and the limitations of current assessment instruments. In a study of over five thousand children in learning disability classes, using a criterion of IQ over 120, Mauser (1979) found 2.3% of the students in those classes falling into this category. Daniels (1983b) indicated that of a large group of children with reading and learning problems, approximately 4% could be identified as gifted on verbal or performance measures of intelligence. The disparity between these two statistics may be due to different criteria for inclusion in the gifted category.

Neither of these statistics should be seen as accurate estimates, given the limitations of the testing, and the frequency with which the gifted/learning disabled student is not even included in the population being tested, because the very dual exceptionality being investigated often masks the outward signs of difficulty.

A current trend that is becoming more popular is the creation of "enrichment" programs for which the criteria for acceptance are not as rigid as they are for "gifted" programs. These programs are often only marginally stimulating, and often preclude a truly gifted child from entering a more appropriate program. Although this flexibility may afford the gifted/learning disabled child an opportunity for participation in a program that can offer diversity of programming and stimulation without the explicit IQ scores of a certain magnitude, this is not a substitute for a program designed for gifted students.

Until the technology allows for more accurate diagnosis, it is the sensitive teacher, the involved parent, or the other adults in this child's world, who will confirm his unique set of needs and allow appropriate intervention. Unlike the tools for identification, the tools for that intervention are available. Creative integration of these tools into the academic world of the gifted/learning disabled student will ensure that the exceptional gifts and talents that he possesses can become a contribution not only to his own development but to that of society as a whole.

# References

Bannatyne, A. (1974). Diagnosis: A note on recategorization of the WISC scaled scores. *Journal of Learning Disabilities*, 7, 272-274.

Daniels, P.R. (1983a). *Teaching the gifted/learning disabled child*. Rockville, MD: Aspen Systems Publications.

Daniels, P.R. (1983b). Teaching the learning-disabled/gifted child. In L. H. Fox, L. Brody, & D. Tobin (Eds.),   *Learning-disabled/ gifted children: Identification and programming*. Austin, TX: PRO-Ed.

Dembinski, R.J., & Mauser, A.J. (1977). What parents of the learning disabled really want from professionals. *Journal of Learning Disabilities*, 10, 49-55.

Fox, L. (1981). Identification of the academically gifted. *American Psychologist*, 36, 1103-1111.

Fox, L.H., Brody, L., & Tobin, D. (Eds.). (1983). *Learning disabled/gifted children: Identification and programming*. Austin, TX: PRO-Ed.

French, J.N. (1982). The gifted learning disabled child: A challenge and some suggestions. *Roeper Review*, 4, 19-21.

Gardner, H. (1985). *Frames of mind: The theory of multiple intelligences*. New York: Basic Books.

Hokansen, D.T., & Jospe, M. (1976). *The search for cognitive giftedness in exceptional children*. New Haven, CT: Project SEARCH.

Jones, B.H. (1986). The gifted dyslexic. *Annals of Dyslexia, 36*, 301-317.

Kaufman, A.S. (1975). Factor analysis of the WISC-R at eleven age levels between 6½ and 16½ years. *Journal of Consulting and Clinical Psychology, 43*, 135-147.

Krippner, S., & Herald, C. (1964). Reading disabilities among the academically talented. *The Gifted Child Quarterly*, Spring, 12-20.

Maker, J. (1982). *Curriculum development for the gifted*. Rockville, MD: Aspen Systems Publication.

Marland, S.P. (1972). *Education of the gifted and talented* (Vol. 1). Report to the Congress of the United States by the U.S. Commissioner of Education. Washington, DC: U.S. Government Printing Office.

Mauser, A.J. (1979). *Prevalence of gifted children with special learning disabilities* (unpublished report). DeKalb, IL: Northern Illinois University.

Meisgeier, C., Meisgeier, C., & Werblo, D. (1978). Factors compounding the handicapping of some gifted children. *The Gifted Child Quarterly, 22,* 325-331.

Renzulli, J.S. (1978). What makes giftedness? Re-examining a definition. *Phi Delta Kappan, 60*, 180-184.

Schiff, M., Kaufman, A.S., & Kaufman, N.L. (1981). Scatter analysis of WISC-R profiles for learning disabled children with superior intelligence. *Journal of Learning Disabilities, 14*, 400-404.

Senf, G.M. (1983). The nature of identification of learning disabilities and their relationship to the gifted child. In L. H. Fox, L. Brody, & D. Tobin (Eds.), *Learning disabled/gifted children: Identification and programming*. Austin, TX: PRO-Ed.

Suter, D.P., & Wolf, J.S. (1987). Issues in the identification and programming of the gifted/learning disabled child. *Journal for the Education of the Gifted, 10*, 227-237.

Udall, A.J., & Maker, C.J. (1983). A pilot program for elementary-age learning-disabled/gifted students. In L.H. Fox, L. Brody, & D. Tobin (Eds.), *Learning disabled/gifted children: Identification and programming*. Austin, TX: PRO-Ed.

Vail, P. (1979). *The world of the gifted child*. New York: Walker Publishing Company.

Vaughn, S. (1989). Gifted learning disabilities. Is it such a bright idea? *Learning Disabilities Focus, 4*(2), 123-126.

Waldron, K.A. (1991). Teaching techniques for the learning-disabled/gifted student. *Learning Disabilities Research & Practice, 6*(1), 40-43.

Whitmore, J. (1986). Conceptualizing the issue of underserved populations of gifted students. *Journal for the Education of the Gifted, 10*, 141-153.

Wolf, J., & Gygi, J. (1981). Learning disabled and gifted: Success or failure? *Journal for the Education of the Gifted, 4*, 199-206.

# Author Index

# Subject Index